Hands-On Object-Oriented Programming with Kotlin

Build robust software with reusable code using OOP principles and design patterns in Kotlin

Abid Khan
Igor Kucherenko

BIRMINGHAM - MUMBAI

Hands-On Object-Oriented Programming with Kotlin

Copyright © 2018 Packt Publishing

Commissioning Editor: Richa Tripathi
Acquisition Editor: Sandeep Mishra
Content Development Editor: Manjusha Mantri
Technical Editor: Abhishek Sharma
Copy Editor: Safis Editing
Project Coordinator: Prajakta Naik
Proofreader: Safis Editing
Indexer: Mariammal Chettiyar
Graphics: Jisha Chirayil
Production Coordinator: Deepika Naik

First published: October 2018

Production reference: 1311018

Published by Packt Publishing Ltd.
Livery Place
35 Livery Street
Birmingham
B3 2PB, UK.

ISBN 978-1-78961-772-6

www.pack.com

To everyone who's been a part of my journey as well as to you, the readers.

– Abid Khan

`mapt.io`

Mapt is an online digital library that gives you full access to over 5,000 books and videos, as well as industry leading tools to help you plan your personal development and advance your career. For more information, please visit our website.

Why subscribe?

- Spend less time learning and more time coding with practical eBooks and videos from over 4,000 industry professionals

- Improve your learning with skill plans designed especially for you

- Get a free eBook or video every month

- Mapt is fully searchable

- Copy and paste, print, and bookmark content

Packt.com

Did you know that Packt offers eBook versions of every book published, with PDF and ePub files available? You can upgrade to the eBook version at `www.packt.com` and, as a print book customer, you are entitled to a discount on the eBook copy. Get in touch with us at `customercare@packtpub.com` for more details.

At `www.packt.com`, you can also read a collection of free technical articles, sign up for a range of free newsletters, and receive exclusive discounts and offers on Packt books and eBooks.

Contributors

About the authors

Abid Khan is an application developer and test engineer with over 10 years of experience. He has worked with different programming languages, including C/C++ and Java, and he now works with Kotlin as a primary language for Android development. Abid lives in Stockholm, Sweden. He spends his time to learn new technologies and then writes about it.

Igor Kucherenko is an Android developer at Techery, a software development company that uses Kotlin as the main language for Android development. Currently, he lives in Ukraine, where he is a speaker in the Kotlin Dnipro Community, which promotes Kotlin and shares knowledge with audiences at meetups. You can find his articles about Kotlin and Android development on Medium and a blog for Yalantis, where he worked previously.

I'd like to thank my colleague for imparting his knowledge, and Packt for the opportunity to write this book, as well as my wife for her patience while I was writing it.

About the reviewer

Hardik Trivedi is a self-taught computer programmer. He has been extensively working on Android and Java since 2010 and has also immersed himself in Kotlin and JavaScript. When he is not working on client projects, he loves contributing back to the development community by spending time on Stack Overflow and writing tech blogs. He has also coauthored two books on Kotlin, named *Kotlin Blueprints* and *Hands-On Serverless Applications with Kotlin*. Hardik also mentors college students, professionals, and companies who have a keen interest in mobile app development. He is also an active community speaker. Someday in the future, you may find him owning a restaurant and serving exquisite cuisines to his customers.

Packt is searching for authors like you

If you're interested in becoming an author for Packt, please visit `authors.packtpub.com` and apply today. We have worked with thousands of developers and tech professionals, just like you, to help them share their insight with the global tech community. You can make a general application, apply for a specific hot topic that we are recruiting an author for, or submit your own idea.

Table of Contents

Preface

Kotlin is a statically typed programming language that is designed to interoperate with Java code. Since the kotlinc compiler generates the same bytecode as javac, migrating to a new code base doesn't require a lot of effort. Kotlin is a modern language that contains many features from different paradigms that allow you to write concise and safe code. In light of all these points, Kotlin is growing in popularity and seeing an increase in the number of developers who use it.

Who this book is for

This book is intended for developers who would like to gain a deeper understanding of how Kotlin works under the hood. The material doesn't depend on a certain platform or framework, but it focuses on Java Virtual Machine. This book doesn't cover topics about Kotlin to JavaScript and Kotlin/Native features. It's a good choice for client-side developers because it contains examples involving user interfaces and multithreaded environments.

What this book covers

`Chapter 1`, *Getting Started with Kotlin*, provides a brief overview of the Kotlin programming language. This chapter also covers data types and how null safety and type casting works. It also provides an introduction to operators and flow controls. At the end of this chapter, we will look at loops and functions.

`Chapter 2`, *Introduction to Object-Oriented Programming*, discusses what object-oriented programming is and why it is different and better than procedural programming. This chapter explains classes and data classes in Kotlin, and how Kotlin makes them unique. It also discusses in detail constructors, types of constructors, and properties, and what is meant by properties as first class citizens.

Chapter 3, *The Four Pillars of Object-Oriented Programming*, provides a thorough description of four pillars of object-oriented programming. It also explains what encapsulation is and how inheritance works. We also look into topics such as why choose polymorphism and what the benefits of abstraction are. Finally, we will learn how to declare a parent class and how to utilize resources in child class. In addition to defining derived classes, this chapter discusses how variables and functions can be redefined in child class, explicit type casting, and implicit type conversion within class hierarchies.

Chapter 4, *Classes – Advanced Concepts*, describes the key concepts of programming that are provided exclusively by Kotlin. This chapter discusses the concepts of sealed classes, object and companion objects, and why they are different from traditional classes. It also explains properties and delegates in classes.

Chapter 5, *Data Collection, Iterators, and Filters*, describes the handling of data collection by using different data structures provided in Kotlin. We also learn how to define and use arrays and how to utilize different templates for the efficient management of object collections such as lists, sets, collections, and maps. Besides discussing different data collection techniques, this chapter explains the power of interfaces used in collection classes. You will learn what an iterator is, how iterators are used with different collections, and the issues you may encounter while using it. This chapter also explains what filters are, how filters work, and how to ignore irrelevant data. At the end, this chapter elaborates on how to write your own filters.

Chapter 6, *Object-Oriented Patterns in Kotlin*, deals with the advanced concepts of object-oriented programming referred to as design patterns. Design patterns are a general solution to a known problem in software design. Design patterns can speed up development processes and reduce the risk of design errors that may occur at a later stage. Different design patterns are used for different problems; this chapter discusses software design challenges and design patterns. Each design pattern is subdivided into different categories that will be discussed in further detail.

Chapter 7, *Coroutine – a Lightweight Thread?*, describes how Kotlin has introduced a new library called coroutine. Coroutines can be considered a lightweight thread that do not push CPU to its limits, even when thousands of requests are in progress. This chapter explains what a coroutine is, and why it is superior to traditional threads in Java.

`Chapter 8`, *Interoperability*, discusses the fact that Kotlin is a superset of Java that is designed with Java interoperability in mind. Interoperability means you can call Java functions in Kotlin, and vice versa, and you can have both Java and Kotlin files in the same application. This chapter discusses in detail the technology behind interoperability and how to write cross-platform code. Most importantly, it also explains how to handle nullable calls that may appear from Java.

`Chapter 9`, *Regular Expression and Serialization in Kotlin*, describes how regular expressions, also known as regex, are a combination of different characters that helps to find and locate the necessary information from a huge amount of text. This technique is also called pattern matching, where users provide a string (pattern) and get a list of exact or similar matches. All advanced text editors use regular expressions to find the variable in your code. In this chapter, you will see that Kotlin has provided complete support for regular expressions and how they support writing bug-free patterns. This chapter also discusses serialization and how Kotlin works with text formats such as JSON.

`Chapter 10`, *Exception Handling*, discusses exceptions and exception handling in detail. We also learn about what the different keywords are try, catch, throw finally, and more, the different types of exceptions, and how a user can create user-defined exceptions and handle them. This chapter also explains how to prepare test environments to be able to write some tests.

`Chapter 11`, *Testing in Object-Oriented Programming with Kotlin*, provides an insight into the importance of testing, why testing is required, and the repercussions if code is released without testing. This chapter also explains the testing techniques, the dedicated Kotlin library for testing, and how Kotlin can help to write clean and readable test cases.

To get the most out of this book

To run examples from this book, you will need a computer running Windows, Linux, or macOS. You will also need IntelliJ IDEA (the Ultimate edition version is preferable), and Android Studio. You will need a basic knowledge of GitHub and Git to clone a project with examples.

Since Kotlin is an official language of Android development, Android Studio supports this language out of the box. For IntelliJ IDEA, you need to install a plugin that is available for download from `https://plugins.jetbrains.com/plugin/6954-kotlin`.

Download the example code files

You can download the example code files for this book from your account at
www.packt.com. If you purchased this book elsewhere, you can visit
www.packt.com/support and register to have the files emailed directly to you.

You can download the code files by following these steps:

1. Log in or register at www.packt.com.
2. Select the **SUPPORT** tab.
3. Click on **Code Downloads & Errata**.
4. Enter the name of the book in the **Search** box and follow the onscreen instructions.

Once the file is downloaded, please make sure that you unzip or extract the folder using the latest version of:

- WinRAR/7-Zip for Windows
- Zipeg/iZip/UnRarX for Mac
- 7-Zip/PeaZip for Linux

The code bundle for the book is also hosted on GitHub at https://github.com/
PacktPublishing/Hands-On-Object-Oriented-Programming-with-Kotlin. In case there's an update to the code, it will be updated on the existing GitHub repository.

We also have other code bundles from our rich catalog of books and videos available at https://github.com/PacktPublishing/. Check them out!

Conventions used

There are a number of text conventions used throughout this book.

CodeInText: Indicates code words in text, database table names, folder names, filenames, file extensions, pathnames, dummy URLs, user input, and Twitter handles. Here is an example: "The Builder pattern assumes that we use the nested Builder class that obtains all arguments and creates a new instance."

A block of code is set as follows:

```
val range = 1..10
for (value in range){
    println(value)
}
```

Any command-line input or output is written as follows:

```
User(preferences=User Preference Node: /User, id=1, firstName=Igor,
lastName=Kucherenko)
```

Bold: Indicates a new term, an important word, or words that you see on screen. For example, words in menus or dialog boxes appear in the text like this. Here is an example: "In the IntelliJ IDEA menu, click on **Tools | Kotlin | Show Kotlin Byte code**, and press **Decompile**."

Warnings or important notes appear like this.

Tips and tricks appear like this.

Get in touch

Feedback from our readers is always welcome.

General feedback: If you have questions about any aspect of this book, mention the book title in the subject of your message and email us at customercare@packtpub.com.

Errata: Although we have taken every care to ensure the accuracy of our content, mistakes do happen. If you have found a mistake in this book, we would be grateful if you would report this to us. Please visit www.packt.com/submit-errata, selecting your book, clicking on the Errata Submission Form link, and entering the details.

Piracy: If you come across any illegal copies of our works in any form on the internet, we would be grateful if you would provide us with the location address or website name. Please contact us at copyright@packt.com with a link to the material.

If you are interested in becoming an author: If there is a topic that you have expertise in and you are interested in either writing or contributing to a book, please visit authors.packtpub.com.

Reviews

Please leave a review. Once you have read and used this book, why not leave a review on the site that you purchased it from? Potential readers can then see and use your unbiased opinion to make purchase decisions, we at Packt can understand what you think about our products, and our authors can see your feedback on their book. Thank you!

For more information about Packt, please visit packt.com.

Getting Started with Kotlin 1

Kotlin's popularity has skyrocketed in recent months due to the fact that it is a simple and concise language that is easy to learn and supports object-oriented and functional programming. Kotlin is a superset of Java that avoids all unwanted Java features, such as verbose, unsafe, and outdated syntax, and includes powerful features from different languages. These features include security, simplicity, and interoperability.

This chapter enables us to acquire knowledge about Kotlin and introduces its basic features and functionality, aiming to get us started as quickly as possible. Before reaching the end of this chapter, we will be familiar with Kotlin's syntax, simplicity, and security features, as well as Kotlin's underlying approach towards object-oriented programming.

The following topics will be covered in this chapter:

- Kotlin's history
- Data types and ease of declaration
- Kotlin's null safety and type casting
- Flow control and `if` statements as an expression
- Loops and labeled loops
- Functions, functions as an expression, and named parameters

Technical requirements

IntelliJ IDEA is used as a development environment, either Community or Ultimate Edition. This can be downloaded here: `www.jetbrains.com/idea/download`.

Make sure that the latest **Java Development Kit** (**JDK**) is installed and configured in our system. Download the JDK here: `www.oracle.com/technetwork/java/javase/downloads/index.html`.

The code for this chapter can be downloaded here: `https://github.com/PacktPublishing/` `Hands-On-Object-Oriented-Programming-with-Kotlin/tree/master/src/main/kotlin/` `Chapter01`.

Introduction to Kotlin

In 2010, Jet Brains started working on a project called Project Kotlin. This aimed to develop a language that is easy, concise, and expressive. This is also a language that can help to improve productivity without compromising on quality, including that of backward compatibility and interoperability with existing code bases. Other than freedom from semicolons, there are a number of reasons to use Kotlin.

For a start, a beginner programmer can feel as comfortable as an experienced developer when using it. It also compiles to Java-6 bytecode, which allows a developer to use advanced features such as lambda expressions with legacy code. Kotlin is 100% interoperable with Java, so it is possible to call Kotlin code in Java as well as calling Java code in Kotlin. Furthermore, it is concise and expressive, and it helps avoid the boilerplate code that is required in Java. Kotlin is safe, therefore most **Null Pointer Exceptions** (**NPEs**) can be avoided. By default, it is not allowed to assign null values to variables. If the type of the variable is verified at compile time, the language is considered to be statically typed. Kotlin is a statically typed language and the benefit of this is that all tricky and trivial bugs can be caught at an early stage. With dynamically typed languages, type checking is performed at runtime. Perl, Smalltalk, and Ruby belong to a dynamically typed language group. Kotlin has great tooling support because it is a product of Jet Brains, a company renowned for providing IDEs for development. In addition, Kotlin supports Android because it is officially supported by Google. Kotlin supports Kotlin/Native technology for compiling Kotlin code in native binaries which does not rely on virtual machine and Kotlin supports browsers because all modern languages should work with JavaScript. A number of big brands (including Pinterest, Uber, Gradle, and Evernote) have started using Kotlin as a main language, and they feel that it helps to improve their productivity and quality of code.

With the help of Kotlin, we will now create our first hello world application as follows:

1. Start IntelliJ IDE and click on **File**.
2. Click on the **New** option and then click on the **Project** in the **Menu**.
3. From the left pane in the newly opened window, select **Kotlin | Kotlin/JVM** and then press **Next**.
4. Assign a project name and location, making sure that the latest SDK is selected.

5. Click on **Finish**. IntelliJ IDE will open a new window with preconfigured files and folders. `src` is a source folder where all Kotlin files will be added.

6. Right-click on `src` and select **New**. Under this, click on **Kotlin File/Class**.

7. Assign a name, select a file from the **Kind** menu, and press **OK**.

8. Add the following code in the newly opened window:

```
fun main(args: Array<String>) {
    println("Hello world")
}
```

Data types in Kotlin

In the same way as any other modern language, Kotlin uses variables or data types, which are among the most important features in programming. These variables are created to handle different types of data, including numbers, letters, words, and so on. Variables are allocated locations in memory for storing all kinds of data.

The data types in Kotlin are as follows:

- Byte
- Short
- Integer
- Long
- Float
- Double
- Character
- Boolean

Declaring a variable in Kotlin

There are two keywords available in Kotlin—`var` and `val`. The `var` keyword declares a mutable data type and the `val` keyword declares an immutable or read-only variable.

The var keyword

The `var` keyword declares a mutable property or local variable. This means that the variable can be changed or updated as follows during the course of the entire program:

```
var age = 25
```

In the preceding code, `var` is a keyword, `age` is a variable name, and `25` is an assigned integer value. Let's see some other variable definitions to understand the declarations better:

- `var myChar = 'A'`: `myChar` is a single character variable
- `var name = "Bob"`: A `name` is a string type variable
- `var age = 10`: `age` is an integer type variable
- `var height = 5.10`: `height` is a double type variable

In Kotlin, a variable must have a value assigned. Without proper initialization, it does not allow variable declarations:

```
var age //In-Valid Declaration; compiler error
var age = 25
Valid Declaration
```

The value of the variable can be changed, but the variable type itself cannot be changed. If we try to re-assign an integer variable with double or string, the compiler will throw the mismatch error type:

```
var age = 10 // Data type integer - Valid declaration
age = 10.2 // Invalid assignment - not an integer compiler error
age = "hello" // Invalid assignment not an integer - compiler error
```

It is necessary that we declare different variables with the `var` keyword, as demonstrated here:

```
fun main(args: Array<String>) {
    var student = "Bob" // String variable
    var age = 25 // Integer variable
    var height = 5.6 // Double variable
    println("Name is $student age is $age and height is $height")
}
```

The val keyword

The `val` keyword is a read-only variable that is used to declare an immutable variable. Immutable means that once the variable is assigned, it will remain the same until the end of the application's life:

```
val age = 25
```

In the preceding code line, `val` is a keyword, `age` is a variable name, and `25` is an integer value assigned.

`val` is the same as `var`; the variable type is dependent on the value assigned to the variable.

 The read-only feature is actually one of the safety features provided by Kotlin.

Once the variable is declared, it is not possible to update it under any circumstances. This feature becomes more important when we are writing a complex application or a program of scientific calculations:

```
val pi = 3.14159
```

Knowing that the value of `pi` is constant, it would be a good practice to use `val` instead of `var` to make sure that the value remains constant and cannot be changed accidentally. Once declared as `val`, try to re-assign any other value to `pi` as follows:

```
pi = 123.345 // The result: Compiler will throw an error: "val cannot re-
assign".
```

It is necessary that we declare different variables with the `val` keyword:

```
fun main(args: Array<String>) {
    val name = "Herry" // String variable
    val PI = 3.1415   // Double variable
    val programmingLanguage = "Kotlin"
    programmingLanguage = "Java" // Error: val cannot be reassigned
    println("Name is $name and my favorite programming language is
$programmingLanguage")
}
```

Type inference

Type inference is a mechanism in which the Kotlin compiler plays its role to find out a variable type. Kotlin will determine the data type by understanding the value assigned. It intelligently infers the type by the value and then makes the variable of the data type respectively. This technique is called **type inference**. In all the previous code, whether a data type is declared with `val` or `var` are examples of type inference:

```
val age = 25
val name = "Bob"
```

In the preceding code, `age` is an integer and `name` is a string type variable. The type of these variables is inferred by the compiler.

Type annotation

In Kotlin, we can also declare a specific type of variable with `var variableName : nameOfDataType` type annotation:

```
var myInteger : Int
var myString : String
val myDouble : Double
```

Once the variables are declared, we can assign values to them:

```
myInteger = 10
myString = "Hello"
myDouble = 12.123
```

Having variable declarations with explicit data types and assigning a value at the same time is also possible:

```
val myInt : Int = 10
var myString : String = "Hello"
```

Variable declaration and initialization is explained in the following example:

```
fun main(args: Array<String>) {
    var myName: String // Variables can be initialized explicitly
    myName = "Jon" // Initialization
    // declaration and initialization in one line
    var myInt: Int = 10
    var myLong: Long = 11
    var myShort: Short = 11
    var myByte: Byte = -128
```

```
    var d1 = 5.10 // Declaration of Double and Float
    var d2: Double = 5.10
    var f1 = 5.10
    var f2: Float = 5.10f
}
```

Kotlin data types are divided into the following groups:

- Number data types
- Real data types
- Boolean data types
- Character data types

Now let's have a look at each category in the following sections.

Number data types

Number data types accept whole numbers and do not support fractions. Kotlin provides four different types of number variables—Integer, Long, Byte, and Short. These data types can be declared with and without type annotation. It can also be easily declared with the following syntax:

```
var myInt : Int =10   // For Integer variable
var myInt = 10
var myLong : Long = 11 // For Long Variable
var myShort : Short = 11 // For Short Variable
var myByte : Byte = -100 For byte variable
```

MAX_VALUE and MIN_VALUE can be used to find the capacity of each variable.

See the following example:

```
fun main(args: Array<String>) {
    println("max integer " + Integer.MAX_VALUE)
    println("min integer " + Integer.MIN_VALUE)
}
```

The following output shows the maximum and minimum value an integer can hold:

```
C:\Java\bin\java.exe ...
max integer 2147483647
min integer -2147483648

Process finished with exit code 0
```

Real data types

In this category, Kotlin provides two data types:

- Float
- Double

These data types can store values containing decimal places. Float and Double are the floating point data types that are used to store real number values. A Float can contain 4 bytes of information, while the Double data type can handle 8 bytes. Kotlin allows us to handle scientific notation with the Double data type as follows:

1. Create two Double types of variables as follows:

- Create d1 with an explicit declaration of the data type
- Create d2 with an implicit declaration:

```
fun main(args: Array<String>) {
    var d1 : Double = 7.20E15 // Scientific calculation
    var d2 = 7.20e-15
```

2. Assign scientific values to both variables and print:

```
println("Value of d1 = " + d1 + " and Value of d2 = " + d2)
}
```

The Value of d1 = 7.02E15 and Value of d2 = 7.02E-15 printed values are the same, except the value of d2 is capitalized.

Boolean data type

Boolean is a data type that contains one of two values—true or false. Because of its nature, the Boolean variable requires only one single bit for storing data. This bit can be on or off, true or false, 0 or 1. Let's declare some Boolean variables for further discussion:

```
var result : Boolean = true
var isEmpty : Boolean = false
```

In the same way as other variables, the Boolean variable can be declared without type inference:

```
var value = false
var result = true
```

Basically, this data type is used for comparing two values, getting results by setting a Boolean as a checkpoint to verify the results via comparison, and getting an answer by way of true or false. Let's see an example of how this can happen:

```
fun main(args: Array<String>) {

    var result : Boolean // Boolean variable
    var num1 = 20
    var num2 = 10

    result = num1 >= num2
    println("$num1 is greater than $num2 = $result")

    result = num1 < num2
    println("$num1 is greater than $num2 = $result")
}
```

In this example, we have two integer variables named num1 and num2, as well as a Boolean variable named result. If num1 is greater than or equal to num2, true will be assigned to result; otherwise, false will be assigned.

Character data type

The character data type is one of the data types available in Kotlin. This can contain 2 bytes of information and it can also store pretty much all the characters that you see on your keyboard. The syntax is the same as any other declaration—the word Char is used to declare a character variable and the value on the right-hand side must be enclosed by single quotes:

```
var mychar : Char = 'A'
```

Let's take a look at some examples. When character values are assigned to the `Char` data type, this can be displayed as follows:

```
var charA : Char = 'A'
var charZ : Char = 'Z'
var char1 = '1'
var char0 = '0'
```

Each character has a unique Unicode for its representation, and the character data type can be stored in Unicode values. Let's display `A`, `Z`, `1`, and `0` by using a Unicode character. The syntax for storing the Unicode is pretty much the same, except `\u` is required at the beginning of the code. This is demonstrated as follows:

```
var ucharA : Char = '\u0041'
var ucharZ : Char = '\u005A'
var uchar1 = '\u0031'
var uchar0 = '\u0030'
```

The following code shows how a character data type handles different characters:

```
fun main(args: Array<String>) {
    var charA : Char = 'A'
    var charZ : Char = 'Z'
    var char1 = '1'
    var char0 = '0'
    println("$charA $charZ $char1 $char0")

    // Unicode Character
    var ucharA : Char = '\u0041'
    var ucharZ : Char = '\u005A'
    var uchar1 = '\u0031'
    var uchar0 = '\u0030'
    println("$ucharA $ucharZ $uchar1 $uchar0")
}
```

Type checking with the is keyword

Type inference is one of the most powerful features in Kotlin, but sometimes it becomes hazardous when the type of variable is unknown. For example, we are asked to write a function that can take variable of the `Any` type. This can be float, string, or int:

```
fun func(x: Any) {
    // What is the type of x
}
```

To handle this tricky situation, Kotlin provides an `is` keyword to verify the variable type. The syntax for this is as follows:

```
x is Int
x is Char
```

This check will return `true` if x is an integer or character; otherwise, it will return `false`. Check the following examples:

```
fun func(x: Any) {
   if(x is Float){
      println("x is Float")
   } else if(x is String){
      println("x is String")
   }
}
```

`!is` can be used to verify whether or not a variable is a required type:

```
fun func(x: Any) {
   if(x !is Float){
      println("f is not Float")
   }
}
```

String variable

A string is a well-structured set of characters, words, sentences, and paragraphs. String is a widely used data type in Kotlin. Unlike other variables, such as Integer, Float, or Boolean, which contain one specific type of value, Strings can contain a collection of different values and can store pretty much everything and anything.

Like other Kotlin data types, String variables can be declared with or without type inference, and everything within double quotes will be considered as a string:

```
var variable_name : String = "value in double quotes"
var message : String = "Hello"
var question : String = "What is your name?"
```

A string variable, `message`, is initialized with `Hello`, and another string variable, `question`, is assigned with `What is your name?`. A string variable can be declared with the `var` or `val` keyword without stating the variable type, for example, `val name = "Bob"`:

```
fun main(args: Array<String>) {
    var message : String = "Hello"
```

```
    var question : String = "What is your name?"
    println(question)
    val name = "Bob"
    var address = "Stockholm, Sweden"
    println("My name is $name and i live in $address")
}
```

Null safety, type casting, Pair, and Triple

In this section, we will learn about one of the most important topic of Kotlin, which is null safety. We will learn how null safety works, why it is important, and how Kotlin helps to improve the code quality. Later in this section, we will learn about type casting and its implications and we will conclude this chapter by discussing to useful data structures Pair and Triple.

Null safety

Nullability is one of the reasons that most applications crash. Kotlin is very strict when it comes to safety. Every application user (especially mobile users) want a nice, simple, and smooth user experience. An application that crashes makes more than 90% of users frustrated, causing them to instantly uninstall the application.

See the following example of Java. Here, the variable name is assigned a `null` value, which is the correct syntax in Java:

```
String name = null; // OK in java
int length = name.length(); // application crashed
```

But when `name.length` will be executed, Java will throw `NullPointerException`. In Kotlin, it is very important to note that variables are non-nullable by default and we cannot assign null values to them. Let's take a look at an example and assign a `null` value to a variable as follows:

```
var notNull : String = null
```

If we try to assign a `null` value to a variable, the compiler will immediately throw an error:

Error: "Null cannot be a value of a non-null type String".

At the time of declaration, a value must be assigned to the variable as follows:

```
var notNull : String = "Hello"
```

It is now safe to use the `length` function. The `length` is a function provided by Kotlin that returns the length of a string:

```
var length = notNull.length
```

Kotlin is compatible with Java, and we can write both Kotlin and Java code in one application (see `Chapter 8`, *Interoperability*). Java is not a null-safe language, and because of this, Kotlin designers enable programmers to assign `null` values by defining a nullable variable:

```
var mayBeNull : String? = null
```

Adding a question mark to a command indicates to the compiler that a `null` value can be assigned to the variable:

```
fun main(args: Array<String>) {
    var notNull : String = "Hello"
    notNull = null // not allowed

    var len  = notNull.length
    println("Value is $notNull and length is ${notNull.length} ")
    var mayBeNull : String?
    mayBeNull = null // allowed
}
```

Safe call operators

Now we are able to declare a nullable type, but what if we try to get a length of a string that is nullable? See the following example:

```
var mayBeNull : String? = null
var length = mayBeNull.length
```

Kotlin null safety will trigger the following error:

**Only safe (?.) or non-null asserted (!!.) calls are allowed on a nullable
receiver of type String?**

In simple terms, a programmer will be notified that the declared variable (string in this case) can have a `null` value, and this must be verified before calling. It can be validated in different ways, but one way of doing this is by using an `if` statement:

```
var mayBeNull : String? = null
 if(mayBeNull != null && mayBeNull.length > 0){
    var length = mayBeNull.length
  }
```

Within the `if` condition, notice that Kotlin does not throw any errors. The `if` statement will be executed if the variable has a value, otherwise it will be skipped:

```
fun main(args: Array<String>) {
    var name : String?
    name = null // allowed
    var length = 0
    if(name != null && name.length > 0) {
        length = name.length
    }
}
```

In this example, we have declared a nullable string variable `name` and assigned a null to it. Later, we check if the `name` string variable is not `null` and length of the `name` variable is not zero. In this case, an `if` statement will skip the code block because `name` is assigned with `null`.

The ?. Safe call operator

An alternative way to verify the nullable variable is by using the safe call operator, which is a question mark followed by a full stop, `?.`:

```
var length = mayBeNull?.length
```

In this case, if the string variable is not null, the safe call operator will return the length of the variable. Otherwise, `null` will be assigned to the `length` variable. This means that when the `if` variable is `null`, everything after the `?.` operator will be ignored:

```
fun main(args: Array<String>) {
    var mayBeNull : String?
    mayBeNull = null // allowed
    var length = mayBeNull?.length // Safe Call
    println("value of length is " + length)
}
```

The output of this example is `"value of length is null"` because the safe call operator verified the `mayBeNull` variable and returned a `null` value.

The ?: Elvis operator

The safe call operator executes the called function if a variable contains a value. If not, it will return `null`. This is demonstrated as follows:

```
var mayBeNull : String? = null
  var length = mayBeNull?.length
```

If the `length` variable has a `null` value, we again need to verify whether the variable length is null or not. In this case, we may be stuck in an unnecessary verification loop. This problem can be solved by using the Elvis operator. The Elvis operator makes sure that one out of two values must be returned:

```
var length = mayBeNull?.length ? : 0
```

If `length` is not null, it will return the size of the variable; otherwise, it returns 0. See the following example:

```
fun main(args: Array<String>) {
    var message: String? = null
    var len = message?.length ?: 0
    println("value of length is $len")
    message = "Hello"
    len = message?.length ?: 0
    println("value of length is $len")
}
```

Create a nullable string variable called `message` and assign a null value to it. Use the Elvis operator, call the `length` function, and verify the value of the `len` variable, which should be 0. Now assign a value to `message` and verify the length.

The !! Sure operator

The not null assertion operator, also known as the **sure operator**, is used when it is sure that the provided variable always contains a value and is not null. Let's take a look at an example of how this works. Create a nullable string variable and assign a null value to it. Now try get the string's length with the null assertion operator:

```
fun main(args: Array<String>) {
    var sureNotNull : String? = null
    var length = sureNotNull!!.length // application will be crashed
    println("value of length is " + length)
}
```

Of course, the application will crash. In this case, the programmer takes responsibility for variable nullability. Let's elaborate on this further with the another example.

The string class provides the `lastOrNull` function. This function returns the last character of the string, or null if the string is empty. We must declare a nullable character for assigning a value from the `lastOrNull` function:

```
val ch : Char? = "abc".lastOrNull()
```

If we try to declare a normal variable instead of nullable, Kotlin will throw a compile time error. See the following example:

```
val ch : Char = "abc".lastOrNull()
// Type mismatch: inferred type is Char? but Char was expected
```

If we are confident that an object (the "abc" string, in this case) is not null and we don't want to create a nullable variable with the null safety operator, we can use the null assertion operator:

```
val ch : Char = "abc".lastOrNull()!!
```

See the following example to verify how variables can be declared with and without the null safety operator:

```
fun mayBeNull(s : String ) : Char? {
    val ch: Char? = s.lastOrNull()
    return ch
}

fun notNull(s : String ) : Char{
    val ch = s.lastOrNull()!!
    return ch
}

fun main(args: Array<String>) {
    var ch = notNull("abc")
    // var ch = notNull("") program will crash.
    println(ch)
}
```

The `myBeNull` function takes a string as a parameter and returns the last character of the string using the `lastOrNull` function. Notice that the function returns a nullable `Char` because function may receive an empty string as a parameter. On the other hand, the `notNull` function returns a normal character because this function uses the not null assertion operator to get the last character of the string, and we tell the compiler that this function will never receive an empty string.

Type casting

Converting data from one type to another is called **type casting**, for example, conversion from Float to Integer, or from Double to String. With Java or C++, type casting is a very straightforward process because these languages have primitive data types. Look at the following Java example:

```
double d = 10.50;
int i = (int) d;
```

In Kotlin, everything is an object and so it requires some extra steps to type cast from one type to another. However, Kotlin provides a rich library that helps perform these conversions. Let's explore this with the following example. Create a Byte variable and assign a value of 10 to it. Create an Integer variable and attempt to assign byteValue to intValue:

```
var byteValue : Byte = 10
var intValue : Int
intValue = byteValue
```

Since the data types are different, the preceding code block will throw a type mismatch error caused by the compiler. Using the following line will not help either:

```
intValue = (Int) byteValue
```

The preceding example shows that Kotlin does not support automatic type casting, so we will have to invoke it explicitly. Kotlin's library is packed with a number of useful functions, and each data type can use these functions for type conversion.

Converting from Byte to Float

Create a Byte variable and assign a value to it, then use the toFloat() function to convert this from Byte to Float as follows:

```
fun main (args: Array<String>) {
    var byteValue : Byte = 10
    var floatValue : Float
    floatValue = byteValue.toFloat()
    println("From Byte $byteValue to Float $floatValue")
}
```

Converting from Double to Integer

Similarly, we can convert a Double variable into an Integer. Use the `toInt()` function to convert from Double to Int as follows:

```
fun main (args: Array<String>) {
    var doubleValue : Double = 12.345
    var intValue = doubleValue.toInt()
    println("From Double $doubleValue to Int $intValue")
}
```

When converting from one type to another, we must take data loss into consideration. The following is the output of this example:

```
From Double 12.345 to Int 12
```

Double belongs to the real data type family. It can store values containing a decimal point. In contrast, Integer belongs to the number data type, which deals with whole numbers only. When the Double data type is converted to an Integer, the `intValue` variable simply ignores the `.345` fraction value.

Converting from String to Integer

It is also possible to cast from String to Integer or from String to Double. To do this, create a String variable and cast it by using the `toInt()` function. See this example:

```
fun main (args: Array<String>) {
    var stringValue: String = "125"
    var intValue = stringValue.toInt()
    println("From string to int $intValue")
}
```

Everything is fine if the String variable contains a valid integer value, but if the String variable contains anything other than integer, Kotlin will throw a `NumberCast` exception. Update the following `stringVariable` in the previous example and verify the exception like so:

```
var stringValue : String = "A125"
```

To avoid this situation, Kotlin provides the `toIntorNull` function. This function will return a null if the String variable has an invalid value, such as an alpha-numeric character, whereas it will cast a string to integer if the value is numeric. It is also important to mention here that the `toIntOrNull()` function can return a null value, and thus the integer variable must be nullable when declared as `Int?`. See the following example. Create a string variable and convert it into string by using `toIntOrNull` function:

```kotlin
fun main (args: Array<String>) {
    var stringValue : String = "125A"
    var intValue : Int? = stringValue.toIntOrNull()

    if(intValue is Int) {
        println("From string to int $intValue")
    }else{
        println("Not a valid String")
    }
}
```

If the string variable contains valid content, then conversion from String to Int will be successful otherwise false.

Smart cast

`Any` is a parent or a superclass of all classes in Kotlin. If our class is not derived from any class, then it has `Any` as a super class. All data types including Integer, Float, Double, and so on are derived from an `Any` class. (We will learn more about this in Chapter 3, *The Four Pillars of Object-Oriented Programming*). The following declarations are valid in Kotlin:

```kotlin
var any : Any? = null
any = 1234    // integer
any = "Hello" // String
any = 123.456 // Double
```

To understand the importance of smart casting, let's create a function with one parameter of the nullable `Any?` type:

```kotlin
fun mySmartCast(any :Any?)
{
    if(any is Int)
    {
        var i = any + 5
        println("Value is Int $i")
    }
    else if(any is String)
    {
```

```
        var s = "Hello " + any
        println("Value is String $s")
    }
    else if (any == null) {
        println("Object is null")
    }
}

fun main (args: Array<String>) {
    mySmartCast(8)
    mySmartCast("Kotlin")
}
```

In the first function call with the integer value, the `mySmartCast(8)` smart cast not only takes care of the null type but also recognizes which type of class object it contains. Type checking, null safety, and unwrapping the object is handled by using the `is operator`. In the first `if` statement, the `is` operator verifies the `null` value and performs type casting as well.

 `Any` is a superclass in Kotlin's class hierarchy.

Kotlin automatically converts `Any` into an integer to perform a mathematical operation on it, and we do not need to call `toInt()` function for type casting. Here is a smart cast example with the `when` expression:

```
fun mySmartCast(any :Any?){

    when(any) {
        is String -> println("String: $any")
        is Int -> println("Integer: $any")
        is Double -> println("Double: $any")
        else -> println("Alian...")
    }
}
```

Unsafe cast

The `as` operator is another method of type casting, but it is not considered a safe cast. Check out the following example of an unsafe cast:

```
fun myUnsafeCast(any : Any?) {
    val s : String = any as String
```

```
    println(s)
}

fun main (args: Array<String>) {
    myUnsafetCast("Hello")
}
```

This code will execute successfully because a string variable is passed to this function, but the following function calls will throw a `TypeCastException`:

```
myUnsafetCast(2)
myUnsafetCast(null)
```

It is very important to secure our code before it crashes, so try to avoid unsafe casting. However, if it is necessary, do the following:

- Declare a nullable variable with ? to store the value
- Add a safe call with the `as` operator as ?

If the type casting is successful, it will return the original value. If not, it will become null. Let's take a look at the correct way to use the `as` operator in the following example:

```
fun myUnsafeCast(any : Any?){
    val s : String? = any as? String
    println(s)
}
fun main (args: Array<String>) {
    myUnsafetCast(2)
}
```

This time, the program will execute normally without throwing any exceptions. Instead, it will display `null` on the screen.

Pair and Triple

`Pair` and `Triple` can store different values that are closely linked to each other, for example, a product name and price, x and y coordinates of a graph, or a phone book with a name, phone number, address, and so on. We can store these values by declaring a class and combining them in one object, but it is always good if a similar task can be performed by using pre-declared Kotlin classes. In this section, we will take a look at how to use `Pair` and `Triple` and how these data types help to organize different values in one place.

How to declare

Let's start by declaring `Pair` and `Triple`. Like other variables, `Pair` and `Triple` can be declared by using the `val` or `var` keyword:

```
val mobile = Pair("Google", 500)
val screenMirror = Pair("Chrome cast", 20.5)
val addressBook = Triple("Khan", 123456789, "Stockholm")
```

First, create a variable by directly assigning some values with `Pair` or `Triple`. As we can see, each `Pair` and `Triple` contains different data types—a `mobile` Pair contains a string and integer set, `screenMirror` contains a string and a double, and an `addressBook` Triple contains two strings and one integer. We can see that an explicit declaration of a data type is not required, as the Kotlin type inference automatically finds out the variable type.

How to retrieve values

There are plenty of ways to retrieve values from Pair and Triple, but let's start with simple one. The value of a Pair can be retrieved by assigning it to the following variables:

```
val (name , price) = mobile
```

The `name` variable is assigned with `Google` and `price` contains 500 Euros, which is the price of a Google mobile. We can verify this by printing these variables like so:

```
println("Mobile = $name , Prince = $price Euro")
```

A `Triple` can be deconstructed in a similar fashion:

```
val (name, phone, address) = addressBook
println("Name = $name , Phone = $phone , Address = $address")
```

There is another way to decompose the `Pair` and `Triple` classes. Each member of the `Pair` and `Triple` is assigned a name. The first element of the Pair can be accessed by using the property name `first`, the second with `second`, and in a `Triple`, the third element can be accessed with the property name `third`. For example, create a `Pair` and `Triple` of different types. Assign and retrieve the values as follows:

```
val mobile = Pair("Google", 500)
val (name , price) = mobile
println("Mobile = ${mobile.first} , Prince = ${mobile.second}")

val addressBook = Triple("Khan", 123456789, "Stockholm")
val (name, phone, address) = addressBook
```

```
println("Name = ${addressBook.first} , Phone = ${addressBook.second} ,
Address = ${addressBook.third}")
```

Kotlin also provides a default function for each element—component1() for the first element, component2() for the second element, and so on:

```
val (p_name, p_phone, p_address) = addressbook
println("Name = ${addressbook.component1()} , Phone =
${addressbook.component2()} , Address = ${addressbook.component3()}")
```

While retrieving these values, if any are not required, we can ignore them by using the underscore symbol. See the following example:

```
val coordinates = Triple(5 , 9 , 11)
val (x, y , _) = coordinates
```

The coordinates variable contains three values, but by using the underscore symbol, we have simply ignored the z coordinate.

Flow controls

Programming is the execution of different operations, and the **flow control** is an operation to control the execution of these operations. By using this, a programmer can decide how a program should behave or what section of code should be executed at a given time. Like other programming languages, Kotlin provides several structures that allow the control to be implemented.

We will now explore each of the flow controls in the following sections.

The if statement

The if statement can be perceived as a filter method that is designed to channel the relevant data, and further operate, drive, or act on that information.

As with most programming languages in common practice, there are code blocks that are dependent on certain parameters, variables, and conditions that may only execute when a certain situation is true or false. `if` statements are used when a decision needs to be made; this works with Boolean logic, which means that the conditions defined for an `if` can only have two outcomes, true and false:

```
if (a > b) {
    max = a
}
```

When an `if` statement is present and the condition is true, the primary code block is executed. If not, the code block is ignored, as we can see in the following example:

```
fun main(args: Array<String>) {
    val langName = "Kotlin"
    if ( langName == " Kotlin" ) {
        println ( "Hello"+ langName)
    }
}
```

The result would display as `Hello Kotlin`. When the value of the `langName` variable is anything other than Kotlin, the code block under the `if` statement would not be executed.

The if and else statements

The `if` and `else` statements have been around for a long time, and almost all languages are dependent on these types of conditional statements for filtering information. When the condition is satisfied, the primary code block will be executed. If the condition fails, the `else` statement comes into play.

Let's see an example of how this works:

```
fun main(args: Array<String>) {

    val langName = "Java"
    if ( langName == "Kotlin" ) {
        println ( "I love "+ langName )
    }
    else {
        println ("The name of the language is "+ langName )
    }
}
```

If the `langName` variable is assigned a `"Kotlin"` string, then the first code block of the `if` statement will be executed. If not, the `else` statement will be executed.

The if statement with a conditional operator

When we work in real time, more often than not the `if` statement is used to break down complex scenarios and define the flow without getting into the hassle of checking each individual condition separately. To reduce code complexity and encourage better implementation of program flow, we can use conditional operators to combine or group prerequisites into a single `if` condition to filter and execute the relevant code block.

The conditions can be combined or grouped in an `if` statement by using the `and` `(&&)`, or `(||)` and `not` `(!)` operators.

The if statement with the and (&&) operator

The `and` `(&&)` operator is used for absolute results. The `and` operator returns true if and only if all conditions grouped together are satisfied. In the event that either conditions fail to satisfy the grouped condition, the `if` statement will fail and the respective code block will be ignored until the grouped condition is satisfied as a whole.

An `if` statement with an `&&` operator can be written in ampersand form:

```
var studentMarks = 92
if (studentMarks >= 90 && value < 96) {
    println ("A")
  }
```

The `and` operator can also be written in word form:

```
if ((studentMarks >= 90) and (value < 96)) {
  println ("A")
}
```

The if statement with the or (||) operator

The or (||) operator is a fairly lenient operator which returns true when either of the two conditions in the group is true. The if statement fails when both conditions are not satisfied and skips the respective code block until one of the grouped conditions is satisfied. The if with || operator can be written in symbol form:

```
if ((b > a) || (b > c)) {
 println("b is a winner")
}
```

The or operator can be written in word form:

```
if (b > a or b > c) {
    println("b is a winner")
}
```

The if statement with the (!) Not operator

The Not operator, represented by an exclamation mark, !, is used when the condition with a NOT operator is true if the returning value is false. The Not operator also makes it possible to easily check if the condition is not true, in which case, the following result should be displayed:

```
if(a!=b) {
    println("a and b are different")
 }
```

if as an expression

Kotlin has introduced a new feature called if as an expression, which makes a programmer's life much easier. Instead of assigning a value in each if statement, Kotlin returns the value from a successful code block, which can be stored in a variable. Before writing an if statement, add a variable name with an assignment operator as follows:

```
grade = if (studentMarks >= 90) {
    "A"
}
```

See the following example with if as an expression, where `grade` will be assigned depending on `studentMarks`:

```
fun main(args: Array<String>) {
 val studentMarks = 95
 var grade = if (studentMarks >= 90) {
 "A"
 } else if (studentMarks >= 80) {
 "B"
 } else if (studentMarks >= 70) {
 "C"
 } else if (studentMarks >= 60) {
 "D"
 } else {
 "F"
 }
 println ( "Student achieved " + grade )
}
```

Notice that it is not required to write `grade` = "A" or `grade` = "D" in each else...if block, but while using `if` as an expression, there is one thing to remember—`if` as an expression cannot be used without an `else` statement:

```
val grade = if (studentMarks >= 90) {
    "A"
}
```

Kotlin will throw the following compile-time error:

'if' must have both main and 'else' branches if used as an expression

The When expression

Kotlin provides an alternative method to the `if` statement—the `When` expression. `When` can also be perceived as a filter method. This is similar in nature to the `Switch` statement in Java or C. `When` sequentially matches its arguments with all branches until a condition is satisfied for a branch.

The When expression works as follows:

- When can use arbitrary expressions and constants.
- It takes the variable in the expression and matches the value within the branches.
- If the condition for the variable is a match, the relevant code block of the branch will execute. If none of the other branch conditions are satisfied, the else branch is evaluated.

Writing the When statement:

- The When statement is followed by the expression defined within the parenthesis: when (expression).
- A branch is a condition followed by a code block. This is defined as {condition -> code block} and appears after the expression contained within the curly brackets.
- The else branch is mandatory with its own code block contained within the curly brackets.
- If there is no else branch in the when, all possible cases must be covered in the branches so that the compiler can validate all of the branches.

Write a program by using when as an expression to display the day on its corresponding number, 1 for Monday, 2 for Tuesday, and so on:

```kotlin
fun main(args: Array<String>) {
val day = 2
when (day) {
    1-> println("Monday")
    2-> println("Tuesday")
    3-> println("Wednesday")
    4-> println("Thursday")
    5-> println("Friday")
    6-> println("Saturday")
    7-> println("Sunday")
    else -> println("Invalid input")
  }
}
```

To verify and test various conditions, assign different values to the day variable. The program will display the respective day according to the value or error message if the input is out of range. We can rewrite the student grade program by using the when expression.

Combining cases

The When expression allows us to combine more than one cases in one line. In order to match with the expression, we concatenate more than one case in a comma-separated list:

```
fun main(args: Array<String>) {
    val grade = "b"
    when (grade) {
        "A","a" -> println("Excellent")
        "B","b" -> println("Very Good")
        "C","c" -> println("Nice work")
        "D","d" -> println("OK")
        "E","e" -> println("Hmmm")
        "F","f" -> println("Better luck next time")
         else -> println("Invalid input")
    }
}
```

In this example, a user can enter the student's grade without worrying about whether the keyboard caps lock is on or off. If input is "a" or "A", either way the output will be Excellent.

Ranges with When

It is also possible to match cases in range form. To make use of ranges, Kotlin provides the in operator. Using the in operator, we are asking for a value that is contained within a given range. This is specifically useful when more than one condition has the same result:

```
fun main(args: Array<String>) {
    val grade = "A"
    when (grade) {
        in "A".."E" -> println("You are promoted to the next level")
        "F" -> println("You need hard work.")
        else -> println("Invalid input")
    }
}
```

In this example, if the student grade is within the range of A to E then a You are promoted to the next level message will be displayed. If the grade is F, then You need hard work. will be displayed on the screen; otherwise, Invalid input is displayed.

When as an expression

Similarly to the if statement, when can also be used as an expression. To do this, create a variable and assign when as an expression as follows:

```kotlin
fun main(args: Array<String>) {
    val grade = "A"
    val remarks = when (grade) {
        "A","a" -> "Excellent"
        "B","b" -> "Very Good"
        "C","c" -> "Nice work"
        "D","d" -> "OK"
        "E","e" -> "Hmmm"
        "F","f" -> "Better luck next time"
        else -> "Invalid input"
    }
     println(remarks)
}
```

Introduction to loops

A loop is a cyclic code, routine, or statement that is defined once but may run several times, and can perform a set of instructions indefinitely or repeatedly (once for each of a collection of items, or until a condition is met). If we were asked to print numbers from 1 to 3 on the screen, this could have been done easily by writing the code using the three println statements. If we were to print hundreds or thousands of numbers, for example, we would need a better solution for performing one task repeatedly for as long as required. Loops are a great solution for these situations, and they are dependent on three parts:

- **Start**: Defining the beginning of the loop
- **Body**: Defining the code block to execute it on each iteration
- **Controller**: Defining when the loop should stop

In Kotlin there are two type of loops available:

- Condition-controlled loop:
    - While loop
    - Do while loop
- Count-controlled loop:
    - For loop

The while loop

A while loop is a statement or code that executes repeatedly based on a given condition. The while loop checks the condition before the block is executed. Similar to an if statement, the condition is assessed to see if the condition is true, and if so, the code within the block will execute, and the process will repeat until the condition becomes false. The while loop is useful when we want to perform one task as long as the condition remains true. Let's take a look at how to write a while loop in the following sections.

The while statement is followed by the condition defined within parentheses—(condition).

Defining the while loop

The construct of while is similar to an if statement. Both of these work with conditions before executing the code block within. See the following example. Here, an if statement was written with a simple print line statement:

```
if(i <= 3) {
    println("Print $i")
}

while(i <= 3) {
    println("Print $i")
}
```

Once you have replaced the if with the while statement, the while loop is ready to use. However, do not forget to increment the value of i, otherwise the while loop will execute forever:

```
fun main(args: Array<String>) {
    println("While loop")
    var i = 1
    while (i <= 3) {
        println("While $i")
        i++
    }
}
```

This loop will execute three times and it will increment the value of i by one on each iteration. On the fourth iteration, the value of i will be 4 and the controlling statement will become false.

The do while loop

A do while loop executes a block of code at least once, and then repeatedly executes the block (or not) depending on a given condition at the end of the block. This is a minor variation of the while loop. In do while, the body executes before the condition is verified, therefore executing the code block at least once:

```kotlin
fun main(args: Array<String>) {
    println("Do While loop")
    var j = 1
     do {
         println(j)
         j++
     } while( j < 5 )
}
```

In this example, variable j is initialized with value 1, the do block prints the value of j and increments it, while block verifies the condition. The loop will continues until the value of j is less than 5.

The for loop

A for loop is used to specify an iteration that allows code to be executed repeatedly. This is a famous loop because of its flexibility and convenience. The for loop works with lists, arrays, collections, or ranges; it can be a range of integers or a collection of objects. The for loop also requires a control variable with start and end values, iterates on a given range, and exits the loop automatically. In a nutshell, it takes care of most things that other loops are not able to take care of.

Defining the for loop

The following points are necessary to create a for loop:

- Declare a range with a start and end point. Ranges are defined with two dots, .., for example, var range = 1..3
- With a for loop, create a variable and assign a range with in operator.

- Define a code block that will execute a task:

```
fun main(args: Array<String>) {
    var range = 1..3
    for (i in range) {
        println("value of $i")
    }
}
```

On the first iteration, the `for` loop initializes the `i` variable with the first value of the `range`, and on each iteration the next value from the range will be assigned to `i`.

 Any object that has an iterator function implemented can be used inside a `for` loop, for example, range, list, array, and so on.

With each iteration, the `for` loop assigns the next member from the range, which can be utilized as a normal member variable. In this example, each value from the range is printed on the screen:

```
fun main(args: Array<String>) {
    val list = listOf(1,2,3,4)
    for (l in list){
        println("value of $l")
    }

    val message = "kotlin is awesome"
    for (m in message){
        println(m)
    }
}
```

The `for` loop with ranges and iterator will be discussed in `Chapter 5`, *Data Collection, Iterators, and Filters.*

The nested for loop

A `for` loop within a `for` loop is called a nested `for` loop. The outer `for` loop will assign a value from range to i, and the inner `for` loop will assign a value from range to j, and both values will be printed in the inner `for` loop:

```
for (i in 1..3) {
    for (j in 1..3) {
        println("$i , $j")
    }
}
```

Notice that on each iteration of the outer `for` loop, the inner `for` loop will be executed three times.

Break statements

Kotlin provides break statements, which are used to break the continuation of a loop. Break statements immediately terminate the iteration of a loop when the test condition is met. This is often used in `while`, `do while`, and `for` loops in order to end the current loop and exit where conditions may need to be defined inside the loop for specific reasons:

```
fun main(args: Array<String>) {
    for (i in 1..10) {
        println("For $i")
        if(i >= 5) {
            break;
        }
    }
}
```

Notice that the `break` statement terminates the program execution where it is placed. If the `break` statement is in an inner loop, the outer loop will perform its task normally. This is because only the inner loop will end and the outer loop will continue its iterations as defined until it fulfills its condition. Take an example of a nested loop and print the value of i and j but break the inner loop when both values are same:

```
for (i in 1..3) {
    for (j in 1..3) {
        println("$i , $j")
        if(i==j) {
            break;
        }
    }
}
```

The break statement with labeled for loop

Break statements always break the nearest or parent loop where the break is placed, as we saw in previous example. But what if we want to stop the loop iterations altogether whenever a certain condition is met in a nested inner loop? To address such conditions, Kotlin provides a concept called a labeled `for` loop. This means that an alias name is assigned to a `for` loop to break it by using the `break@nameOfTheLoop` statement. Assign a name to the `for` loop, as described here, and call the loop by using the `break` statement. When the variables i and j are equal to 2, by using `break@outLoop`, the `break` statement would know which `for` loop to terminate:

```kotlin
fun main(args: Array<String>) {

    println("Labled For Loop")
    outLoop@ for (i in 1..3) {
        for (j in 1..3) {
            if(i==2 && j==2) {
                break@outLoop
            }
            println("$i , $j")
        }
    }
}
```

So, the outer `for` loop would run once and the inner `for` loop would execute its body three times. On the second iteration of the outer loop, when both i and j would equal 2, the `break` statement would call the outer loop to terminate. So, if the outer loop terminates, this means that the inner loop terminates automatically.

What is a function?

As a program grows, complexity grows. If the code cannot handle this growth, it is easy to become bogged down in the complexity of application. The best way to manage our code is to break it down into small, self-contained portions and the complex problem can be solved by putting these portions together. Kotlin can help us to divide our code into small chunks, and we can then assign a meaningful name to our code. That block can perform one particular task for us. In different programming languages, this technique is called a method, subroutine, or procedure. In Kotlin, this technique is called a **function**.

There are several reasons for dividing code into functions:

- **Divide and conquer**: A programmer can solve a complex task by dividing it into small functions.
- **Reusability**: Pasting similar code in different places is not a good approach. In the future, if a program's logic changes, we must update the pasted code everywhere else. Functions help us to reuse code anywhere in our program, and if the function code changes, it will have an effect in all areas.
- **Debugging**: With big, complex problems, if the code does not work as expected, it is often difficult to find the hidden bug in spaghetti code. Without well-defined functions, it is a difficult, frustrating, and time-consuming task to fix the problem. If everything is divided into functions, a coder can test each function one by one in order to confirm its output.
- **Abstraction**: In order to use a function, it is enough to know its name and parameters. The programmer does not need to know how it is implemented and what logic is used by another programmer.

Function declaration

Kotlin is a fun programming language, and so the function name begins with the word **fun**. The `fun` statement is followed by the function name with parentheses ( ). The code block is defined after the parenthesis within the curly brackets as `{ code block }`. Once we have finished writing our code block, we can call this function from anywhere by using `nameOfTheFunction`. Writing `hello` function displays a greeting message on the screen. See the following example:

```
fun hello(){
    println("Hello from Kotlin")
}
fun main(args: Array<String>) {
    hello()
}
```

A simple `Hello from Kotlin` message will now display on the screen.

Functions with no parameter and no return type

This is the simplest form of a function. See the following example:

```
fun sayHello(){
    println("Hello from Kotlin")
}
```

If a function does not return a value, the Unit keyword can be declared right after the function name.

 Unit corresponds to the **void** type in Java.

The Unit keyword is optional. If no keyword is mentioned, Kotlin will consider Unit as a default value:

```
fun sayHello() : Unit{
    println("Hello from Kotlin")
}
```

Function with parameters

Functions can receive one or more parameters as arguments:

```
fun hello(message : String) : Unit {
    println("Hello from $message")
}

fun main(args: Array<String>) {
    hello("Kotlin")
}
```

The hello function takes a string variable as a parameter. When the hello function is called from main, a string value is passed to that function.

If the function takes more than one parameter, all parameters are separated with a comma (,). Here is another example of writing a function that takes two parameters:

```
fun add(a : Int, b : Int) {
    println("Result of $a + $b is ${a+b}")
}
```

```
fun main (args: Array<String>){
    add(4,5)
}
```

In a function declaration, variables cannot be declared with the `val` or `var` keywords, and the data type must be specified explicitly.

Functions with parameters and return types

Functions can receive parameters and return values as a result. See the following example, which takes a value as a parameter and returns the result:

```
fun myFun(message : String) : String {
    return "Hello from $message"
}

fun main (args: Array<String>){
    val result = myFun("Author")
    println(result)
}
```

This function takes a string as a parameter and *returns* a string value. Like other programming languages, Kotlin also uses the `return` keyword to return a value from a function. The return value must be the same as the return type defined in the function signature:

```
fun add(i: Int, j: Int): Int
```

If a return type of the function is integer, the `return` statement must be an integer, otherwise the compiler will throw an error. Here is an example of a function called `addValues`. This takes two integer parameters, adds them, and returns an integer as a result:

```
fun addValues(i: Int, j: Int): Int{
    val k = i + j
    return  k
}

fun main (args: Array<String>) {
    val result = addValues(5,6)
    println(result)
}
```

Function as an expression

In Kotlin, a function can behave as an expression. Let's take the example of the `add` function from the previous section and convert it into an expression:

```
fun addValues(i: Int, j: Int): Int {
    return i + j
}
```

This function takes two parameters, adds them, and returns an integer value. When the function contains only one line of code, it can be written as an expression.

Create a new function as an expression:

```
fun addValuesEx(a : Int, b : Int) : Int = a + b
```

The explicit declaration of the function return type can be removed as follows:

```
fun addValuesEx(a : Int, b : Int) = a + b
```

Now add an equals operator, remove the curly brackets, and remove the explicit type declaration of the return type along with the `return` keyword from the function body. The compiler will figure out the return type by itself. Next, call `addValues` and `addValuesEx` in our main. Verify the output of each function:

```
fun addValues(i: Int, j: Int): Int{
    return  i + j
}

fun addValuesEx(a : Int, b : Int) = a + b

fun main (args: Array<String>) {
    var result = addValues(5,6)
    println(result)

    result = addValuesEx(5,6)
    println(result)
}
```

Take another example. Write a function that takes two integer variables and returns the highest one. Return any value if both values are same:

```
fun getMaxEx(x: Int, y: Int) =
        if(x >= y){
            x
        } else {
            y
```

```
        }
fun main (args: Array<String>) {
    var val1 = 8
    var val2 = 6

    max = getMaxEx(val1,val2)
    println("$val1 , $val2 : Max value is $max")
}
```

Writing a function as an expression always helps to remove unwanted code, but sometimes this convenience can be problematic. Add minor changes in the following function by adding a string value in `if` and `else` statements and executing it:

```
fun getMaxExx(x: Int, y: Int) =
        if(x >= y){
            x
            "Scary"
        } else {
            y
            "Yes it is"
        }

fun main (args: Array<String>) {
    var val1 = 8
    var val2 = 6
    var maxEx = getMaxExx(val1,val2)
    println("$val1 , $val2 : Max value is $maxEx")
}
```

This function returns `Scary` as output. When a function is written as an expression and no return type is defined in the function signature, the type inference comes into action, which means that Kotlin always returns the last line of code and the compiler evaluates the return type at runtime. If the line is an integer or a string, it will be decided accordingly. In this example, the expected output is an integer, but a string is returned. This tricky situation can be overcome by declaring the function return type:

```
fun getMaxEx(x: Int, y: Int) : Int =
        if(x >= y){
            x
            "Scary"
        } else {
            y
            "Yes it is"
        }
```

If the return value is anything other than declared type, the compiler will throw the following error:

```
Type mismatch: inferred type is String but Int was expected
```

Functions with default arguments

Kotlin makes it possible to assign a value to a parameter in the function declaration. If the function is invoked without passing a value, then the compiler automatically assigns a default value to it. The `hello` function prints `Hello Kotlin` if no value is passed to the function:

```kotlin
fun hello(message : String = "Kotlin") : Unit{
    println("Hello $message")
}

fun main (args: Array<String>) {    hello()
    hello("World")
}
```

The default argument is a very helpful feature in many situations. For example, consider a situation in which we are writing a currency exchange function that converts dollars into another currency and applies service charges on the conversion:

```kotlin
fun currencyExchange(dollar: Double, currencyRate: Double, charges:
Double): Double {
    var total = dollar * currencyRate
    var fees = total * charges / 100
    total = total - fees
    return total
 }
```

Let's assume that we want to convert 100 US dollars to Swedish krona. 1 dollar is equal to 10 Swedish krona, and our company charges 5% on the total amount:

```kotlin
fun main (args: Array<String>) {
    var total = currencyExchange(100.0,10.0, 5.0)
    println(total)
}
```

This function works fine; it multiplies the dollar by the target currency, calculates the charges, and returns the total amount after deductions. In the currency market, currency prices move quite rapidly, so it is a good idea to check the currency rate before conversion. However, its highly likely that conversion charges (5% in this example) will remain the same for a long period of time. If this is true, then the default value can be assigned to the `charges` variable, as follows:

```kotlin
fun currencyExchange(dollar: Double, currencyRate: Double, charges: Double
= 5.0): Double {
    var total = dollar * currencyRate
    var fees = total * charges / 100
    total = total - fees
    return total
}
```

By setting the default value, the function can be invoked without a third parameter:

```kotlin
fun main (args: Array<String>) {
    var total = currencyExchange(100.0,10.0)
    println(total)
    var total = currencyExchange(100.0,10.0, 3.0)
    println(total)
}
```

Functions with named parameters

Kotlin makes it possible to specify the argument's name in a function call. This approach makes the function call more readable and reduces the chance to pass the wrong value to the variable, especially when all variables have the same data type. To understand the importance of this feature, let's take the previous example of currency conversion:

```kotlin
fun currencyExchange(dollar: Double, currencyRate: Double, charges: Double
= 5.0): Double {
    var total = dollar * currencyRate
    var fees = total * charges / 100
    total = total - fees
    return total
}
```

The `currencyExchange` function takes three parameters of the Double type—dollar, target currency, and conversion charges:

```
fun main (args: Array<String>) {
    var total = currencyExchange(100.0, 6.0, 10.0)
    println(total)
}
```

The `currencyExchange` function will perform the currency conversion and return the result. If the function contains a long list of variables as a parameter, then there is a high chance that values can be passed in the wrong order. In this example, the currency rate is swapped with conversion charges:

```
var total = currencyExchange(100.0, 6.0, 10.0)
 println(total)
 Output is 540 instead of 940 Swedish crown.
```

The program will execute without any errors because arguments passed to the function are the correct types but are in the wrong order. To solve this problem, Kotlin provides a feature called **named parameters**. Named parameters make it possible to pass different values to the function by explicitly defining a parameter's name. Using the argument's name helps to pass the correct value to each argument and makes the code clean and readable:

```
total = currencyExchange(dollar = 100.0, currencyRate = 10.0, charges =
6.0)
 println(total)
```

By mentioning the name of each argument, function arguments can pass in any order:

```
fun main (args: Array<String>) {
    var total = currencyExchange(dollar = 100.0, currencyRate = 10.0,
charges = 6.0)
    println(total)
    total = currencyExchange(currencyRate = 10.0, charges = 6.0, dollar =
100.0)
    println(total)
}
```

Functions and vararg

Kotlin allows programmers to pass arguments separated by commas to the function. These arguments are automatically converted into an array. This is called a `vararg`, a variable argument. Declare a `vararg` along with its type in the function declaration:

```
fun varargString(vararg list : String){
    for (item in list){
        println(item)
    }
}

fun main (args: Array<String>) {
    varargString("ett","tva","tre")
    varargString("Sat","Sun","Mon")
}
```

As another example, write a function that takes an integer `vararg` as a parameter, adds it, and displays the total on the screen:

```
fun addVararg(vararg list: Int){
  var total = 0
  for (item in list){
    total += item
  }
  println("Total $total")
}

fun main (args: Array<String>) {
  addVararg(1,2,3,4,5,6,7,8,9,10)
}
```

`vararg` makes a programmer's life easier, especially when he or she is not sure about how many parameters may be required for one function:

```
fun add(a: Int, b: Int , c: Int , d: Int, e: Int)
fun add(vararg list : Int)
```

The first `add` function is restricted to the limited amount of variables declared in the function signature, but the `add` function with `vararg` can operate on all comma-separated values that we will pass to it.

vararg with other arguments

There is a possibility that we will be asked to create a function with an integer `vararg` along with two integer variables. See the following example:

```
fun trickyVararg(vararg list: Int, a : Int, b: Int){
    var total = 0
    for (item in list){
        total += item
    }

    println("Total $total")
    println("a = $a , b = $b")
}

  fun main (args: Array<String>) {
     trickyVararg(1,2,3,4,5)
  }
```

The first three values (1,2,3) are for `vararg list`; parameter a is assigned with value 4 and parameter b is assigned with value 5. However, the compiler will throw the following errors:

```
Kotlin: No value passed for parameter 'a'
Kotlin: No value passed for parameter 'b'
```

`vararg list` is declared first in the function signature, and the compiler considers the all input for `vararg list`. This problem can be solved by declaring `vararg` as the last function argument:

```
fun trickyVararg(a : Int, b: Int, vararg list: Int){

    var total = 0
    for (item in list){
        total += item
    }
    println("Total $total")
    println("a = $a , b = $b")
  }
  fun main (args: Array<String>) {
     trickyVararg(4,5,1,2,3)
  }
```

The compiler will now assign the first two values to the a and b variables, and the rest will be assigned to vararg list. Declaring vararg at the end of the function signature is good practice, but it is not necessary. It can be declared at the beginning, but we must ensure that we call the rest of the variables by name:

```kotlin
fun trickyVararg02(vararg list: Int, a : Int, b: Int){
    var total = 0
     for (item in list){
         total += item
     }
     println("Total $total")
     println("a = $a , b = $b")
}

fun main (args: Array<String>) {
     trickyVararg02(1,2,3,a=4, b=5)
}
```

Notice that by declaring the parameters' names in the function call, the compiler does not complain about missing values.

Package-level functions

Programmers with a Java background are familiar with static methods. Static methods are declared within a class and can be accessed directly by using class names as a reference. Kotlin does not have a static method, but it does provide a package-level function instead. To create a package-level function, do the following:

1. Create a package.
2. Create a file in the package.
3. Create a function in the file.
4. In the project explorer, select a folder where we want to add a package and then right-click **New** followed by **Package**.
5. In the newly opened window, add a package name, for example, the Util package.
6. Once the Util package (folder) is created, right-click on package and add the Kotlin file. Call this file MyUtil. Our Kotlin file is now ready to have package-level functions added to it.

Now open the `MyUtil.kt` file. We should see the following line here:

```
package Util
```

A directory or folder is called a **package**, which is where the Kotlin file resides. The package name is used as a reference to access the function. Let's create a function with a greeting message as follows:

```
package Util
fun hello() = println("Hello from Package Util")
```

The package-level function `hello()` has now been created and can be accessed by using the package name as follows:

```
PackageName.FunctionName()
```

Let's create the `MyUtil` package and add the `MyTestUtil.kt` file:

1. Now open the `MyTestUtil.kt` file, add a `main` function, and call a package-level function, `hello`, to the file. A package-level function is always called using the package name as a reference:

   ```
   fun main(args: Array<String>) {
       Util.hello()
    }
   ```

2. Execute the program and verify the output, `Hello from Package Util`. Add different functions under the `Util` package as follows:

   ```
   fun hello() = println("Hello from Package Util")

   val PI = 3.1415926535 // Package level variable

   // Calculate power of given number
    fun myPow(base : Double, exp: Double) : Double {
        var result = 1.0
        var counter = exp
        while (counter > 0) {
            result*= base
            counter--
        }
        return result
    }

   // Calculate area of a circle
    fun areaOfCircle(radius : Double) : Double{
        return PI * 2 * radius
   ```

```
        }

        // Generate random number within given range
        fun myRandom(range: IntRange) : Int{
            return range.shuffled().last()
        }
```

3. Call these functions in the `main` function and verify the result as follows:

```
        fun main(args: Array<String>) {

            Util.hello()

            println("Power Function")
            println(Util.myPow(5.0,3.0))

            println("Random number generator")
            var range = 1..50
            for (i in 1..5) {
                println(Util.myRandom(range))
            }

            println("value of PI is ${Util.PI}" )
            println("Area of circle " + Util.areaOfCircle(4.0))
        }
```

How to access a function

There are a couple of ways to access a package-level function. One way to do this is by using a package name with each function. This method has already been used in the previous example:

```
Util.hello()
```

The second way to access a package-level function is to import each function explicitly by using the `import` keyword:

```
import Util.hello
fun main(args: Array<String>) {
    hello()
    println("Power Function")
    println(Util.myPow(5.0,3.0))
}
```

Notice that by adding import Util.hello, Kotlin allows us to use the hello function without using a package name with it. The third and most common way to import a package is with the wildcard:

```kotlin
import Util.*
fun main(args: Array<String>) {
    hello()
    println("Power Function")
    println(myPow(5.0,3.0))
    println("Random number generator")
    var range = 5..50
    for (i in 1..5) {
        println(myRandom(range))
    }
    println("value of PI is ${PI}" )
    println("Area of circle " + areaOfCircle(4.0))
}
```

This is the most convenient method. By using this approach, functions can be accessed by using a package name.

Summary

In this chapter, we have learned about the different types of variables and their declarations. We also discussed type inference and how Kotlin helps to improve productivity by allowing a programmer to ignore explicit type declarations. This chapter has explained null safety and how Kotlin helps us to write safe and concise code. We have also discussed if statements, else as an expression, loops, labeled for loops, continue, and break statements in detail. This chapter concluded by discussing functions and their important features, including functions as an expression, named parameters, and package-level functions.

Questions

1. Why is Kotlin's popularity growing?
2. What is type inference in variable declaration?
3. What is null safety and why is it important?
4. What are named parameters and why they are important in function calls?
5. What is a package-level function?
6. What is a labeled for loop?

Further reading

Programming Kotlin by Stephen Samuel and Stefan Bocutiu published by
Packt: `https://www.packtpub.com/application-development/programming-kotlin`.

Introduction to Object-Oriented Programming

2

Object-oriented programming is one of the most famous and practical software-development techniques. Traditional procedural programming is tedious and prone to error, especially when it comes to the development of large and complex applications. In this chapter, we will provide a quick introduction to object-oriented programming and its benefits. We will also try to understand why the object-oriented approach is easy to grasp and how it is similar to human nature. We will learn about classes, objects, and constructor declarations. By the end of this chapter, we will be familiar with properties, behaviors, function overloading, the concept of data classes, and how data classes can help to improve application development.

The following topics will be covered in this chapter:

- Object-oriented programming
- Syntax of class declaration
- The difference between classes and objects
- Properties and why they are special in Kotlin
- Constructors and their types
- Function declaration and function overloading

Technical requirements

Other than IntelliJ IDEA, this chapter does not require any specific installations.

The code for this chapter can be downloaded from the following GitHub repository: `https://github.com/PacktPublishing/Hands-On-Object-Oriented-Programming-with-Kotlin/tree/master/src/main/kotlin/Chapter02`.

Object-oriented programming?

In our day-to-day life, we deal with a number of different objects. Some of these objects talk to us, some move on the road, and some fly in the sky. We naturally observe everything about the characteristics and behaviors of these objects. As an example, let's think about an object with the following properties: it has a couple of doors, four wheels, one steering wheel, brakes, gears, and an engine, it moves on the road, stops when the brakes are applied, and turns left or right when the steering wheel moves. Based on these attributes and behaviors, we can carry out a *classification* of this object – it belongs to a class called `Car`. In programming, the technique to design and build an application by focusing on objects that interact with each other is known as object-oriented programming. In the object-oriented paradigm, class and object are two terms that are used quite often and it is very important for programmers to understand the difference between them.

Classes and objects

A class is a blueprint, a description about something. It represents a well-defined idea that explains the existence of an entity. It can be thought of as a template that contains lists of two things: attributes and behaviors. An attribute is the state of a class, while the behavior refers to what a class can perform. Let's take a look at some examples:

A `car` class can have the following attributes and behaviors:

- Its attributes include `color`, `doors`, `license number plate`, and `steering wheel`
- Its behaviors include the fact that it runs on the road and that it turns left or right when the steering wheel moves

A `person` class can have following attributes and behaviors:

- Its attributes include `name`, `age`, `height`, and `weight`
- Its behaviors include the fact that a person communicates by talking, sleeps when tired, and can move around

Cars, people, fruit, and tables, we interact with these objects and more on a daily basis. All these entities are tangible; things that can be touched physically. In the world of technology, however, there are many entities that are part of our daily life but cannot be touched physically. An example of this would be a bank account. Each bank account has attributes, which include a unique ID, an account type, and a current balance. The behaviors that a bank account can carry out include allowing a customer to deposit or withdraw money.

These are all different examples of classes. If the class is a description or a blueprint, what is the object? The object is an instance of a class. An object is an entity that contains the attributes and behaviors that a class describes. A `car` class, for example, defines the color, model, or license number plate, but the car object provides a value of these properties. Multiple objects can be created from one class. For example, a bank can open many accounts for different customers, knowing that all accounts share similar attributes. Similarly, car manufacturers can produce a number of cars using the same blueprint. In the real world, there are many objects of the same kind, which behave similarly, although they might have different statistics or characteristics. A car might be red or green, it might have two doors or four, but it will always reduce its speed when the brakes are applied, and it will always turn either left or right when the steering wheel moves. Similarly, a person varies in height and age, but person can behave by communicating with each other, moving from one place to another and much more.

Attributes and behaviors

Every class contains attributes and behaviors. Attributes are the characteristics of the class that help to distinguish it from other classes. Behaviors are the tasks that an object performs. A person's attributes, for example, include their age, name, and height, while their behaviors include the fact that a person can speak, run, walk, and eat. In Kotlin, attributes are called **properties** and behaviors are called **functions**. Properties are presented with different data types, and behaviors are described using functions. When we map a `Person` class in Kotlin, it may look as shown in the following class diagram:

Person
+ name: String
+ age: Integer
+ height: Double
+ speak()
+ eat()

The properties of a class can be presented with different data types. For example, `name` might be presented as a `String`, `age` might be presented as an Integer, and `height` might be presented as a Double. Similarly, a Person class can have functions with different implementations.

Before moving on, let's try to grasp these concepts one more time:

- **Class**: A blueprint that defines the properties and functions of an object
- **Object**: A noun, such as a car or a person, that assigns a value to properties
- **Property**: Characteristics of an object that help to differentiate it from other objects
- **Function**: An action performed by object

Benefits of object-oriented programming

Old programming languages, such as Assembly or FORTRAN, are not object-oriented languages. Instead, these are procedural programming languages, languages in which a program is written in one long procedure. The data and the logic are coupled together in one place and a program contains a list of routines or subroutines to instruct the computer step by step. This approach is also known as a top-down approach, because instructions are executed one after the other. Procedural programming comes with a number of drawbacks:

- There is no information-hiding mechanism; data is exposed to the whole system
- Data and functions are stored in separate memory locations
- It is difficult to map real-world objects
- The code cannot be reused; each module or instruction set requires its own tightly coupled routine
- The code cannot be extended; it is difficult to create a new data type using an existing module
- A change in one function may affect the rest of the application

Procedural programming does, however, have the following benefits:

- It is relatively simple and easy to implement functions and procedures
- It is easy to keep track of the program flow
- The application contains less complex logic

In object-oriented programming, the procedural code is divided into self-contained modules, called objects. In this form of programming, the focus is not on structures, but on modeling the objects. Each object represents a different part of the application and each object contains its own properties and functions in one place. An object is a complete entity and it does not rely on other objects. We will learn more about object-oriented programming and its implementations throughout this chapter, but first, let's have a look at some of its benefits:

- Data is completely hidden and protected from other parts of the application. This is known as encapsulation.
- Data can be exposed on request.
- The code can be reused and extended, which means you can create new data types. This is known as inheritance.
- Objects can behave differently in different situations. This is known as polymorphism.
- Data and functions are stored in one memory location.
- Object-oriented programming allows us to map different objects with which we are already familiar, such as person, bank account, car, and employee.
- Design patterns are based on object-oriented programming techniques.

Object-oriented programming has the following disadvantages:

- It has complex logic, so it requires more work to design well-structured architecture
- The complexity of the programming makes it difficult to find bugs
- It requires more memory space
- It is slower than procedural programming

Object-oriented programming is the best approach out of the available programming paradigms. Throughout this book, we will learn about classes, polymorphism, inheritance, and other concepts that are directly related to object-oriented programming techniques and design patterns.

Classes in Kotlin

In Kotlin, a class can be defined with the `class` keyword. Let's take a look at how to declare a class and how to add attributes to it. In Kotlin, a class can be declared as follows:

```
class Person
```

Compared to other programming languages, creating a class in Kotlin is very easy. All we need to do is open our IDE and create a person class with three attributes—name, age, and height. The name is a variable of the String type, age is a variable of the Integer type, and height is a variable of the Double type:

```
class Person {
    var name: String
    var age : Int
    var height : Double
}
```

We have now declared a `Person` class with three attributes enclosed in brackets. After writing this code, we will notice that compiler has immediately thrown a `Property not initialized` error, because we haven't decided that how these properties will be initialized. Let's take a look at how to initialize these properties:

```
class Person {
    var name: String = "Abid"
    var age : Int = 40
    var height : Double = 6.0
}
```

As we know, Kotlin is very strict when it comes to initializing variables. All properties of the class must be initialized before the object is ready to use. Once the properties are initialized, it's time to create an instance of the class. Creating a class object is similar to creating an instance of a String or Integer variable. The syntax of the object declaration is as follows:

```
val person = Person()
```

Use the `val` or `var` keywords for a variable and assign a `Person` object to it. The two small brackets ask Kotlin to instantiate a new object. Once the object is created, all properties can be accessed using the . (dot) operator.

Let's take a look at a complete example of the `Person` class, in which all the properties are initialized with the initial values. The main function creates a `Person` class object and prints all properties on the screen:

```
class Person {
    var name: String = "Abid"
    var age : Int = 40
    var height : Double = 6.0
}

fun main(args: Array<String>) {
    val person = Person()
```

```
    println("Name ${person.name}, Age ${person.age} Height
${person.height}")
}
```

When the instance of the class is created, Kotlin creates the properties and the constructor as well.

Properties – first-class citizens

Each class contains different attributes. The Person class, for example, contains the name, age, and height attributes. When a Person class is declared in Java or another programming language, these attributes are called fields of the class. When these fields are accessed by their corresponding getter and setter methods, they are called properties. To understand this concept in detail, create a Person class in Java, as follows:

```java
public class Person {

    String name;
    int age;
    double height;

    Person(String n, int a, double h){
        name = n;
        age = a;
        height = h;
    }

    public double getHeight() {
        return height;
    }

    public void setHeight(double height) {
        this.height = height;
    }

    public int getAge() {
        return age;
    }

    public void setAge(int age) {
        this.age = age;
    }

    public String getName() {
        return name;
```

```
    }

    public void setName(String name) {
        this.name = name;
    }
}
```

In this example, all attributes contain `get` and `set` methods. The `name` attribute is a field that will be turned into a property when the `getName` and `setName` methods are assigned to it for reading and writing purposes. A class may contain several different fields, and each field must have one or two corresponding methods to turn it into property. This approach not only adds unwanted boilerplate code, it also makes it harder to maintain the code. In Kotlin, classes don't contain fields; *by default each attribute is a property of a class.* Instead of interacting with fields by getter or setter methods, we can directly access the class properties. Kotlin provides all accessor functions under the hood. See the following example:

```
class Person (val name: String, var age: Int, var height : Double)
fun main(args: Array<String>) {
    val person = Person("Abid", 40, 5.10)
    val value = person.name
    person.height = 6.0
    println("name ${person.name}, age ${person.age}, height
{person.height}")
}
```

In IntelliJ IDE, go to **Tools | Kotlin | Show Bytecode,** press the **Decompile** button, and verify the Kotlin-generated Java code. We can see the automatically generated functions for each property: `getName` for the name property, `getAge` and `setAge` for the age property, and `getHeight` and `setHeight` for the height property.

 Kotlin will generate a getter function if the property is declared with the `val` keyword, meaning it is immutable. If the property is declared with the `var` keyword, however, meaning it is mutable, Kotlin will generate both getter and setter functions.

Each member variable of the class is a property by default and the *properties of the class are first-class citizens.* If we compare Java and Kotlin code side by side, we can appreciate the power of Kotlin. Over 30 lines of code in Java is turned into a single line in Kotlin.

Constructing a class with a constructor

When an object is created, all class members have to have an initial value. We can either initialize a property directly or the initial values can be provided by a constructor. A constructor is a special type of function that is used to initialize the properties of the class.

A constructor is invoked when the object is created, or, more specifically, when the space is allocated in the memory. This special function has two important characteristics:

- Constructors can be declared with the `constructor` keyword
- Constructors don't contain any return types, not even Units

In this section, we will learn about all of the different kinds of constructors that are provided by Kotlin. Let's start with the default constructor.

Default constructor

The following class declaration is an example of a default constructor, when all properties of the class are directly initialized in the class body:

```
class Person {
    var name: String = "Abid"
    var age : Int = 40
    var height : Double = 6.0
 }
val person = Person()
```

If you don't create a constructor for your class, Kotlin creates a default constructor automatically. The default constructor is a zero-argument constructor, in which all properties of the `Person` class contain some fixed initial values. The default constructor is not a good approach for object-creation. The object may have different values during its lifetime, but it will always have the same initial value at the time of creation.

In the following example, a `Person` class contains fixed initial values of each attribute:

```
class Person {
    var name: String = "Abid"
    var age : Int = 40
    var height : Double = 6.0
}

fun main(args: Array<String>) {

    val p1 = Person()
```

```
    println("Name ${p1.name}, Age ${p1.age} Height ${p1.height}")

    val p2 = Person()
    println("Name ${p2.name}, Age ${p2.age} Height ${p2.height}")

    p2.name = "Khan"
    p2.age = 31

    println("Name ${p2.name}, Age ${p2.age} Height ${p2.height}")
}
```

All objects created by this method contain similar values:

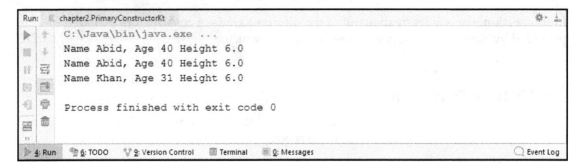

As we can see in this output, there are two instances of the `Person` class, p1 and p2, and both instances contain similar values. To assign different values to different objects, we can use a primary constructor.

Primary constructor

The best approach is to use a constructor that accepts initial values at the time of object-creation. This constructor is called a primary constructor of a class. The following class declaration is an example of a primary constructor that has three properties. This single line not only declares the class, it also declares the primary constructor of the class:

```
class Person (val name: String, var age: Int, var height : Double)
```

We can write primary constructors using the `constructor` keyword, as shown here:

```
class Person constructor(val name: String, var age: Int, var height :
Double)
```

This is not mandatory, however; constructors can be declared without the `constructor` keyword as well.

 Each class variable must be declared with either the `var` or `val` keyword. Variables without `val` or `var` will be considered a normal variable, not a property of the class.

Let's have a look at a complete example:

```
class Person constructor(val name: String, var age: Int, var height :
Double)

fun main(args: Array<String>) {
    val p1 = Person("Abid", 40, 6.0)
    println("Name ${p1.name}, Age ${p1.age} Height ${p1.height}")
    val p2 = Person("Igor", 35, 6.0)
    println("Name ${p2.name}, Age ${p2.age} Height ${p2.height}")
}
```

By using a primary constructor, each object is assigned different values and each object has its own unique identity:

```
Run:    chapter2.PrimaryConstructorKt

    C:\Java\bin\java.exe ...
    Name Abid, Age 40 Height 6.0
    Name Igor, Age 35 Height 6.0

    Process finished with exit code 0

4: Run    6: TODO    9: Version Control    Terminal    0: Messages                Event Log
```

As you may notice, the class declaration with the primary constructor is more convenient than the default constructor. A single line not only declares the class, but also the class properties. When creating the instance of the class, it is necessary to provide the initial value to each class property:

```
val p1 = Person("Abid", 40, 6.0)
val p2 = Person("Igor", 35, 6.0)
```

Class properties can be declared inside the class body and can be initialized using constructor parameters. This approach is the combination of the previous two approaches. We can declare the `name`, `age`, and `height` properties within the class body and initialize them using the `pName`, `pAge`, and `pHeight` constructor parameters:

```
class Person (pName: String, pAge: Int, pHeight: Double) {
    val name: String = pName
    var age: Int = pAge
    var height : Double = pHeight
}

fun main(args: Array<String>) {
    val abid = Person("Abid", 40, 6.0)
    println("Name ${abid.name}, Age ${abid.age} Height ${abid.height}")
}
```

Here, we have created an object of the `Person` class and passed the required values to the constructor parameters. These parameters assign their values to the class properties. Using a primary constructor is a good way to initialize properties, but Kotlin provides an even better method to do this.

Primary constructor with the init block

Having code directly in the class body is not a clean approach. Instead, Kotlin provides a very useful `init` block to initialize the class properties. We will describe the syntax of the `init` block here.

Create a block with the `init` keyword and initialize all properties within the block with class parameters:

```
class Person(pName: String, pAge: Int, pHeight : Double ) {
    var name : String
    var age : Int
    var height : Double
    init {
       name = pName
       age = pAge
       height = pHeight
    }
}
```

The primary constructor and the `init` function are linked together. The `init` function will only be executed when the class is created using a primary constructor:

```kotlin
class Person(pName: String, pAge: Int, pHeight : Double ) {
    var name : String
    var age : Int
    var height : Double

    init {
        name = pName
        age  = pAge
        height = pHeight
    }
}

fun main(args: Array<String>) {
    val abid = Person("Abid", 40, 6.0)
    println("Name ${abid.name}, Age ${abid.age} Height ${abid.height}")
}
```

The `init` function is not only a property initializer, it can also help to validate properties before initialization. In the `Person` class, for example, it can verify that the provided age and height are not negative and the person's name is not empty. Kotlin's `require` function can help to achieve this validation. You can mention the minimum requirement in the `require` function, as follows:

```kotlin
require(age > 0 ) {"Age is not correct"}
```

The `require` function verifies whether the provided `age` is greater than or equal to 0, or whether it is negative:

```kotlin
class Person(pName: String, pAge: Int, pHeight : Double ) {
    var name : String
    var age : Int
    var height : Double

    init {
        name = pName
        age  = pAge
        height = pHeight

        require(name.trim().isNotEmpty()) {"Name should not empty"}
        require(age > 0 ) {"Age is not correct"}
        require(height > 0) {"Height is not correct"}
    }
}
```

```
fun main(args: Array<String>) {
    val abid = Person("Abid", 0, 0.0)
    println("Name ${abid.name}, Age ${abid.age} Height ${abid.height}")
}
```

Kotlin throws `IllegalArgumentException` along with a message provided in
the `require` function:

Pass some invalid arguments to the `Person` class and verify the `init` function. The
following functions can also be used for validation:

- `require`
- `requireNotNull`
- `check`
- `checkNotNull`

Before moving to the secondary constructor, it is necessary to discuss an important topic:
the `this` keyword.

The this keyword

The `this` keyword is used to refer to the object that we are currently talking about. In our
current `Person` example, the `this` keyword refers to the `Person` object. Take a `Person`
class example and append the `this` keyword with each property:

```
class Person(pName: String, pAge: Int, pHeight : Double ) {
    var name : String
    var age : Int
    var height : Double
    init {
        this.name = pName
        this.age = pAge
        this.height = pHeight
    }
```

```
    }
```

The `this` keyword refers to the `name`, `age`, and `height` properties of the current object. The `this` keyword is optional and the main reason to use it is to remove the ambiguity between the class property and the local parameter.

Create a simple form of the `Person` class with one property name and pass a constructor parameter with a similar name:

```
class Person(name: String) {
    var name : String
    init{
        name = name
    }
}
```

This situation would be confusing for the Kotlin compiler and it would throw two errors:

- `Property name must be initialized`: This is the error regarding the class property
- `val cannot be reassigned`: This error is within the `init` block

The Kotlin compiler cannot distinguish between the class property and the constructor parameter, so the `this` keyword plays a vital role in this situation because it refers to the current object. Adding `this.name` tells the compiler that *the name is a class property*. You must use the `this` keyword inside the `init` method to avoid the ambiguity and improve code readability:

```
class Person(name: String, age: Int, height : Double ) {
    var name : String
    var age : Int
    var height : Double

    init {
        this.name = name
        this.age  = age
        this.height = height
    }
}

fun main(args: Array<String>) {
    val abid = Person("Abid", 40, 6.0)
    println("Name ${abid.name}, Age ${abid.age} Height ${abid.height}")
}
```

The this keyword is also used when a class contains more than one constructor, and it is required to call one constructor from within another constructor:

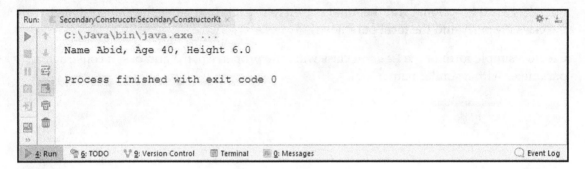

The output of the program doesn't change, but the this keyword increases the readability of the code.

Secondary constructor

In Kotlin, like other programming languages, a class can have more than one constructor. A secondary constructor is prefixed with the constructor keyword and it is created inside the class.

Let's take a look at the following example. The Person class contains a primary constructor with the init block and the secondary constructor with the constructor keyword:

```
class Person(name: String, age: Int) {
    var name : String
    var age : Int
    var height : Double
    init {
        this.name = name
        this.age = age
        this.height = 0.0
    }
    constructor(name: String, age: Int, height: Double) : this(name, age) {
        this.height = height
    }
}
```

Creating a secondary constructor becomes necessary when you need to initialize a class in different ways. In this example, the `Person` class contains two constructors: a primary constructor that takes two parameters, and a secondary constructor that takes three parameters. The `Person` class can be initialized with the secondary constructor if the person's name, age, and height is available, but if the height is missing, the primary constructor can create the instance by assigning a default value to height:

```
class Person(name: String, age: Int) {
    var name : String
    var age : Int
    var height : Double
    init {
        this.name = name
        this.age  = age
        this.height = 0.0
    }
    constructor(name: String, age: Int, height: Double) : this(name, age) {
        this.height = height
    }
}

fun main(args: Array<String>) {
    val abid = Person("Abid", 40)
    println("Name ${abid.name}, Age ${abid.age}")

    val igor = Person("Igor", 35, 6.0)
    println("Name ${igor.name}, Age ${igor.age} Height ${igor.height}")
}
```

Let's have a look at how things works under the hood:

```
Run:    SecondaryConstrucotr.SecondaryConstructorKt
        C:\Java\bin\java.exe ...
        Name Abid Khan, Age 40
        Name Igor, Age 35 Height 6.0

        Process finished with exit code 0

4: Run    6: TODO    9: Version Control    Terminal    0: Messages              Event Log
```

In this example, the `Person` class contains primary constructors with two parameters and a secondary constructor with three parameters:

```
val abid = Person("Abid", 40)
```

Creating an object with a primary constructor is straightforward. Kotlin initializes all the properties within the init block and assigns a default value of 0.0 to the height:

```
val igor = Person("Igor", 35, 6.0)
```

However, when the object is created using a secondary constructor, Kotlin calls the primary constructor using the this keyword to initialize the class properties:

```
constructor(name: String, age: Int, height: Double) : this(name, age) {
    this.height = height
}
```

Once the primary constructor is called, the secondary constructor initializes the rest of the properties.

 If a class contains more than one constructor, each constructor must have different parameters.

To understand the importance and the functionality of having multiple constructors in one class, let's have a look at constructor-overloading.

Constructor overloading

When a class contains multiple constructors and each constructor has different parameters, this is called constructor overloading. In Kotlin, each secondary constructor is prefixed with the constructor keyword and each constructor needs to call the primary constructor either directly or indirectly using the this keyword.

To understand this kind of constructor chaining, let's take a look at another example:

Write a Product class that contains name, category, price, and quantity. We can create an object of the Product class if we are provided with name and category. In total, there are three ways to create an object:

- Using the primary constructor with two variables
- Using the secondary constructor with three variables
- Using the final constructor with all provided information

The primary constructor contains the `name` and `category` parameters. The rest of the properties are initialized with the default values, as follows:

```
class Product(name: String, category: String)
    init {
        this.name = name
        this.category = category
        this.price = 0.0
        this.quantity = 0
    }
```

The secondary constructor contains `name`, `category`, and `price`. The `this` keyword calls the constructor with two parameters (the primary constructor) to initialize the properties:

```
constructor(name: String, category: String, price: Double) : this(name,
category){
        this.price = price
    }
```

The final constructor contains all the properties. The `this` keyword calls the constructor with three parameters, which eventually calls the primary constructor:

```
constructor(name: String, category: String, price: Double, quantity: Int) :
this(name, category, price){
        this.quantity = quantity
    }
```

The following is the class diagram of the `Product` class:

Product
+ name: String
+ category: String
+ price: Double
+ quantity: Int
+ constructor(name: String, category: String)
+ constructor(name: String, category: String, price: Double)
+ constructor(name: String, category: String, price: Double, quantity: Int)

This class diagram contains four properties and three constructors, as shown in the preceding diagram. Take a look at the following example of constructor-overloading:

```kotlin
class Product(name: String, category: String) {

  val name: String
  val category: String
  var price : Double
  var quantity : Int

  init {
  this.name = name
  this.category = category
  this.price = 0.0
  this.quantity = 0
  }

  constructor(name: String, category: String, price: Double) : this(name,
category){
  this.price = price
  }

  constructor(name: String, category: String, price: Double, quantity: Int)
: this(name, category, price){
  this.quantity = quantity
  }
}

fun main(args: Array<String>) {

 val audioPlayer = Product("MP3 Player","Electronics")
 println("Product name = ${audioPlayer.name}, Category =
${audioPlayer.category}, Price = ${audioPlayer.price}$ and Available
Quantity = ${audioPlayer.quantity}")

 val flashRam = Product("Flash Ram","Electronics", 35.0)
 println("Product name = ${flashRam.name}, Category = ${flashRam.category},
Price = ${flashRam.price}$ and Available Quantity =
${audioPlayer.quantity}")

 val toy = Product("Teddy Bear","Toy", 10.0, 54)
 println("Product name = ${toy.name}, Category = ${toy.category}, Price =
${toy.price}$ and Available Quantity = ${toy.quantity}")
 }
```

As we can see in following output, the `audioPlayer` object is initialized with two necessary values – the product name and the product category:

```
Run:    SecondaryConstrucotr.SecondaryConstructorKt
        C:\Java\bin\java.exe ...
        Product name = MP3 Player, Category = Electronics, Price = 0.0$ and Available Quantity = 0
        Product name = Flash Ram, Category = Electronics, Price = 35.0$ and Available Quantity = 0
        Product name = Teddy Bear, Category = Toy, Price = 10.0$ and Available Quantity = 54

        Process finished with exit code 0

  4: Run    6: TODO    9: Version Control    Terminal                                    Event Log
```

The rest of the class properties are initialized with default values. Similarly, the `flashRam` and `toy` objects are initialized with the secondary constructors.

Constructor with default parameters

Kotlin allows us to assign default values to constructor parameters. The compiler automatically assigns default values if the object is created without passing the relevant values to the parameters:

```
class Person(val name: String, var age: Int = 0, var height : Double = 0.0
)

fun main(args: Array<String>) {

    val jon = Person("Jon")
    println("name ${jon.name}, age ${jon.age}, height ${jon.height}")

    val abid = Person("Abid", 40)
    println("name ${abid.name}, age ${abid.age}, height ${abid.height}")

    val igor = Person("Igor", 35, 6.0)
    println("name ${igor.name}, age ${igor.age}, height ${igor.height}")
}
```

Take a look at the following output. The default parameter is a really powerful option provided by Kotlin that helps us to write clean and concise code:

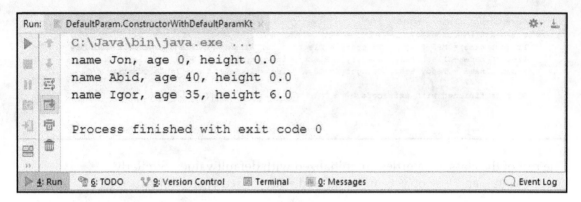

If we compare the power of default parameters with the primary and secondary constructors, we notice that a single line of a default parameter can achieve much more than the other approaches, in which we need to write hundreds of lines of code.

Constructor with named parameters

Kotlin allows us to specify the name of an argument when a class instance is created. This approach makes the object-creation more readable and it reduces the chance that we pass the wrong value to the parameters, especially when all of the parameters have the same data type.

To understand this concept, create a `Person` class and introduce a property, called `weight`, of the Double type:

```kotlin
class Person(val name: String, var age: Int = 0, var height : Double = 0.0,
var weight : Double = 0.0)

fun main(args: Array<String>) {
    val ali = Person(name = "Ali", age = 34, height = 6.1, weight = 78.5)
    println("name ${ali.name}, age ${ali.age}, height ${ali.height}, weight
${ali.weight}")
}
```

Create a `Person` class object by assigning the initial values. We can assign values to each property by using their name:

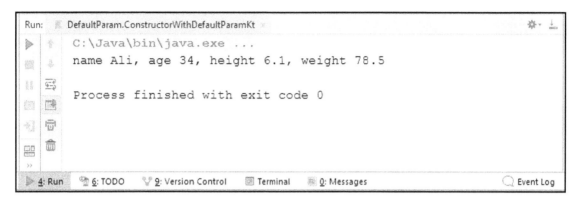

If the primary constructor contains a long list of parameters, the values may pass in the wrong order. If we observe the following example closely, the person's weight and height are swapped with each other but the program will still execute without any errors:

```
val ali = Person("Ali", 34, 78.5, 6.1)
```

By using a named parameter, the values can be passed in any order:

```kotlin
class Person(val name: String, var age: Int = 0, var height : Double = 0.0,
var weight : Double = 0.0)

fun main(args: Array<String>) {
    val ali = Person(name = "Ali", age = 34, height = 6.1, weight = 78.5)
    println("name ${ali.name}, age ${ali.age}, height ${ali.height}, weight
${ali.weight}")

    val bob = Person(weight = 73.5, age = 37, name = "Bob", height = 5.8)
    println("name ${bob.name}, age ${bob.age}, height ${bob.height}, weight
${bob.weight}")
}
```

As we can see, both the `bob` and `ali` objects are initialized by assigning values in different orders:

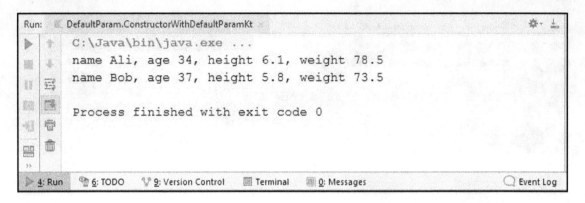

What are data classes?

During the application's development, classes are used quite often as a data-holder, not to carry out complex tasks. These classes only contain properties for reading and writing purposes. The person class is a simple example of a class used as a data-holder. If the sole responsibility of the class is to handle data, programmers may want the class to be able to carry out additional functionalities:

- The data should be in a well-presented format
- We should be able to compare object properties
- We should be able to clone existing objects

All these functionalities can be written by the programmer. Alternatively, an advanced IDE could generate this code automatically. Either way, the project would be filled with boilerplate code. Just as it automatically generates getters and setters, Kotlin assumes the responsibility for generating all of these functions using a data class. All you need to do is add the `data` keyword at the beginning of the class signature:

```
data class Person(var name : String, var age: Int, var height: Double )
```

By converting a normal class into a data class, Kotlin provides the following functions:

- `toString()`
- `equals()`
- `copy()`
- `hashCode()`

All these functions play a vital role in the application's development. To understand the importance of these functions, we will discuss them in detail in the following sections.

The toString() function

When the sole responsibility of the class is to hold some data, the data should be in presentable form. A data class provides the `toString()` function to display well-formatted class properties. Let's have a look at an example:

1. Create a `Person` data class:

   ```
   data class Person(var name : String, var age: Int, var height:
   Double)
   ```

2. Display all properties using string interpolation or concatenation:

   ```
   println("Name ${person.name}, Age ${person.age} Height
   ${person.height}")
   ```

3. Call the `toString()` function using the person object as a reference, `person.toString()`.

4. The `toString()` function converts the object into a string representation.

Check the following example:

```
ClassName (property=value)
fun main(args: Array<String>) {
    val person = Person("Abid", 40, 6.0)
    println("Name ${person.name}, Age ${person.age} Height
${person.height}")
    println(person.toString())
  }
```

Take a look at the output; the `toString()` function combines each property along with its value in string-representation format:

```
C:\Java\bin\java.exe ...
Name Abid, Age 40 Height 6.0
Person(name=Abid, age=40, height=6.0)

Process finished with exit code 0
```
4: Run   5: Debug   6: TODO   9: Version Control   Terminal   0: Messages   Event Log

The benefit of the `toString()` function is that Kotlin will automatically update the `toString` function if we add a new property or remove the existing one:

```
data class Person(var name :String, var age :Int, var country :String)
println(person.toString())
```

The `toString()` function can either be called explicitly, by using the `println(person.toString())` object, or it can be called automatically, by passing the object to the print function, `println(person)`.

The equals() function ==

The data class provides a useful function called `equals()`, which compares each property of the two classes. It comes back as true if all the properties of both classes are the same, otherwise it comes back as false. Let's take a look at an example:

1. Declare a normal class, `Person`, and create two objects with similar values. Compare them with `equal == operator`:

```
class Person(var name : String, var age : Int, var height : Double)
fun main(args: Array<String>) {
    val abid = Person("Abid", 40, 6.0)
    val khan = Person("Abid", 40, 6.0)
    if(abid == khan) {
        println("Both Persons are same")
    } else {
        println("Different persons")
    }
}
```

2. Run this code and verify the output. The output is `Different persons`, although the values of both objects are the same. There are two objects created in the memory, `abid` and `khan`, and Kotlin verifies both objects by doing reference comparisons. The equal operator compares both objects and returns `false` as a result because both objects are pointing to different memory locations:

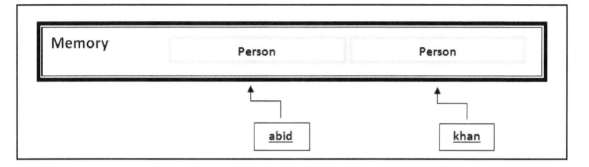

3. Add the `data` keyword in the class declaration and execute this code again. This time, the output is `Both persons are same` because Kotlin performs a properties comparison in data classes.

 The `equals()` function and the `==` operator are same. Behind the scenes, the `==` operator calls the equals function.

To understand this fully, carry out some more experiments by updating the property of an object and executing the following code:

```
if(abid.equals(khan)) {
    println("Both Persons are same")
} else {
    println("Different persons")
}
```

The copy function

The `copy` function helps to create an independent instance by copying the existing object. This function does not exist in the normal class, which makes it a bit inconvenient when we need a new object of an existing type. Let's create a normal class and try to create a copy of existing instance:

1. Create an object of `Person` and assign it to another person object:

```
class Person(var name : String, var age: Int, var height: Double)
val abid = Person("Abid", 40, 6.0)
val khan = abid
```

Ideally, both `abid` and `khan` should be two separate entities, but both objects are aliases of each other and point to the same memory location:

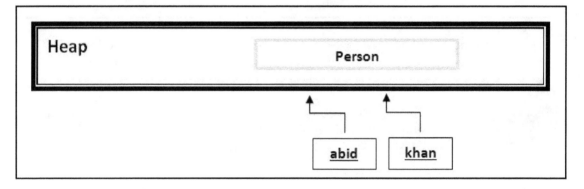

2. To verify that both variables are pointing to the same memory location, perform the following actions:

- Display the name of the first object
- Update the name of the second object
- Display the name of the first object

Let's implement this in the following code:

```
class Person(var name : String, var age: Int, var height: Double)
fun main(args: Array<String>) {

    val abid = Person("Abid", 40, 6.0)
    val khan = abid

    println(abid.name) //Print Abid name
```

```
khan.name = "Khan" // Update Khan name
println(abid.name) // Print Abid name
if(abid == khan) {
    println("Pointing to the same memory location")
}
}
```

When the `khan` object's name is updated, it will update the `abid` object's name and vice versa, because both instances are the same.

3. To get a new instance, the data class provides the `copy` function to clone the object. Create a data class, `Person`, and use the `copy` function to create a new object:

```
data class Person(var name : String, var age: Int, var height:
Double)
val abid = Person("Abid", 40, 6.0)
val khan = abid.copy()
```

The `abid` is an object of the `Person` type, and `khan` is another object of the `Person` type. Both have their own memory location. If the property of one object is updated, it won't affect the other:

```
println(abid) //Print Abid
khan.name = "Khan" // Update Khan name
println(abid) // Print Abid
```

The `copy` function does much more than object-cloning. When creating the object copy, we can change any attribute. For example, if we want to keep everything the same except for the user's name, we can pass the name attribute as a parameter to the `copy` function:

```
val jon = abid.copy("Jon")
println(jon)
```

4. Assign values to a new object using the named parameters:

```
val tom = abid.copy(name = "Tom", height = 5.11)
println(tom)
```

A complete code example is as follows:

```
data class Person(var name : String, var age: Int, var height:
Double)
fun main(args: Array<String>) {

    // Create new instance by using copy function
```

```
val abid = Person("Abid", 40, 6.0)
val khan = abid.copy()

println(abid) //Print Abid
khan.name = "Khan" // Update Khan name
println(abid) // Print Abid

println("Are objects pointing to the same memory locations =
${abid === khan}")

// Add new values into copied object.
val bob = abid.copy("Bob")
println(bob)

val jon = abid.copy(name = "Jon", height = 5.9)
println(jon)
}
```

If we verify the output of this code, we can see that the `copy` function helps to create a new object of `Person` in the memory:

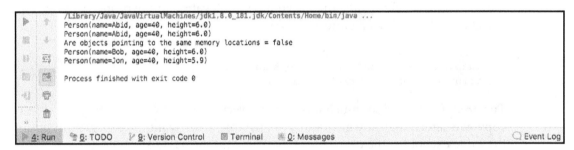

The hashCode() function

In mathematics, a **set** is a collection of unique values that does not allow duplicates. The `hashCode` is a function that generates a unique number for each input.

Let's take a look at the importance of the `hashCode` function:

1. Create three objects of a `Person` class, two with the same values and one with a different value:

```
class Person(var name : String, var age: Int, var height: Double)
val p1 = Person("Abid", 40, 6.0)
val p2 = Person("Abid", 40, 6.0)
val p3 = Person("Khan", 40, 6.0)
```

2. Create a hash set of the `Person` class and add all three objects in it:

```
val set = hashSetOf(p1,p2,p3)
```

3. Check the size of this collection. The set must remove the duplicates and keep only unique elements. In this case, the size of this set should be two.

Take a look at a complete code example and verify the output:

```
class Person(var name : String, var age: Int, var height: Double)
fun main(args: Array<String>) {

    val p1 = Person("Abid", 40, 6.0)
    val p2 = Person("Abid", 40, 6.0)
    val p3 = Person("Khan", 40, 6.0)

    val set = hashSetOf(p1,p2,p3)
    println("Set contains ${set.size} elements")

    val result = set.contains(Person("Abid",40,6.0))
    println("Search result = $result")
}
```

When we execute the code, the output window does not show the expected result:

```
C:\Java\bin\java.exe ...
Set contains 3 elements
Search result = false

Process finished with exit code 0
```

4: Run   5: Debug   6: TODO   9: Version Control   Terminal   0: Messages   Event Log

Although the first two instances are exactly the same, the output is `Set contains 3 elements`. This situation becomes more interesting when we see that `set.contains` couldn't find a person with the same properties. The reason behind this behavior is that the `Person` class has not implemented the `hashCode` function. The main responsibility of the `hashCode` function is to generate a distinct number for each object. If the properties of two objects contain the same values, the hash code of these objects is the same. The good news is that we do not need to implement this function, because the data class already implemented it for us. Turn the normal class into a data class and execute this code again:

```
data class Person(var name : String, var age: Int, var height: Double)
```

This time, the output is different; the set has 2 elements and the `set.contain` function successfully found the object of the specified values:

```
C:\Java\bin\java.exe ...
Set contains 2 elements
Search result = true

Process finished with exit code 0
```

Object decomposition

The data class also allows us to decompose an object into properties. Simply create a list of variables and assign an object to them:

```
val abid = Person("Abid", 40, 6.0)
val (name, age, height) = abid
```

This will assign each property to the distinct variable:

```
data class Person(var name : String, var age: Int, var height: Double)
fun main(args: Array<String>) {
    val abid = Person("Abid", 40, 6.0)
    val (name, age, height) = abid
    println("name=$name age=$age height=$height")
}
```

There is another way to access class properties by using the `component` function. The data class generates a component to correspond to each property. If a class contains two properties, there will be a `component1` and a `component2` function:

```
data class Person(var name : String, var age: Int, var height: Double)
fun main(args: Array<String>) {

    val abid = Person("Abid", 40, 6.0)
    println("name=${abid.component1()} " +
            "age=${abid.component2()} " +
            "height=${abid.component3()}")
}
```

Classes and functions

In this section, we will have a quick look at how behaviors and functions can be implemented. We will continue with our `Person` class, which has three behaviors—speak, eat, and walk.

As we know, class behaviors are represented by functions. We can declare a function within the class body:

1. Create a class with a primary constructor and add the `speak()` function by using `fun` keyword. When a function is declared in the class body, it becomes class behavior:

```
class Person (val name: String, var age : Int , var height :
Double) {
    fun speak() {
        println("My name is $name , i am $age years old and I am
$height feet tall")
    }
}

fun main(args: Array<String>) {
    val abid = Person("Abid", 40, 6.0)
    abid.speak()
}
```

2. Create an object of the `Person` class and call the `speak` function using the `.` operator. Execute this program and check that it has the following output:

```
C:\Java\bin\java.exe ...
My name is Abid , i am 40 years old and I am 6.0 feet tall

Process finished with exit code 0
```

3. Add some more behaviors (functions) in the `Person` class and call them in a similar fashion:

```
class Person (val name: String, var age : Int , var height :
Double){
```

```
    fun speak(){
        println("My name is $name , i am $age years old and I am
$height feet tall")
    }

    fun sleep(){
        println("Zzzzzzz....")
    }

    fun eat(){
        println("I am eating a delicious vegetarian dish")
    }
}

fun main(args: Array<String>) {
    val abid = Person("Abid", 40, 6.0)
    abid.speak()
    abid.eat()
    abid.sleep()
}
```

A function can also take a parameter as an argument and return some values. The `greet()` function takes a string variable as a parameter and displays a message on the screen, while the `info()` function returns a string variable with class properties:

```
class Person (val name: String, var age : Int , var height : Double){

    fun info() : String {
        return "My name is $name , i am $age years old and
        I am $height feet tall"
    }

    fun greet(message : String){
        println("Hi I am $name.... $message")
    }
}

fun main(args: Array<String>) {
    val abid = Person("Abid", 40, 6.0)
    abid.greet("Nice to meet you!!!")

    val text = abid.info()
    println(text)
}
```

A class contains different functions. Each function has its own name, but Kotlin allows us to write more than one function with the same name. This technique is called function-overloading.

Function overloading

Function-overloading is a feature where a class has more than one function with the same names. Each function is uniquely identified by its parameters. In the following example, a `Person` class contains two functions with the same name – `fun greet()`, which doesn't contain any parameters, and `fun greet(message : String)`, which contains one string parameter. Kotlin can determine the function call by the parameters provided:

```kotlin
class Person (val name: String, var age : Int , var height : Double){

    fun speak(){
        println("My name is $name , i am $age years old and
         I am $height feet tall")
    }
    fun greet(message : String){
        println("Hi I am $name.... $message")
    }

    fun greet(){
        println("Hi I am $name.... Nice to meet you!!!")
    }
}

fun main(args: Array<String>) {
    val abid = Person("Abid", 40, 6.0)
    abid.greet()
    abid.greet("How are you doing, it is a pleasure to have you here:")
}
```

As we can see, the Kotlin compiler automatically figures out which `greet` function to call:

```
/Library/Java/JavaVirtualMachines/jdk1.8.0_181.jdk/Contents/Home/bin/java ...
Hi I am Abid.... Nice to meet you!!!
Hi I am Abid.... How are you doing, it is a pleasure to have you here:

Process finished with exit code 0
```

Unexpected tokens (use ';' to separate expressions on the same line)   24:11 LF ÷ UTF-8 ÷ Git: dev ÷

Function overloading is a very powerful feature, especially where different activities of the same type that take different parameter types are performed. To understand the importance of function-overloading, declare a class called `Calculator`, which can perform different arithmetic operations, such as adding, multiplying, and subtracting. The following class contains four functions with the same name. The first `add` function takes two parameters of the `Integer` type, while the second `add` function takes two parameters of the `Double` type, and so on:

```kotlin
class Calculator{

    fun add(v1 : Int, v2 : Int) = v1 + v2
    fun add(v1 : Double, v2 : Double) = v1 + v2
    fun add(v1 : Float, v2 : Float) = v1 + v2
    fun add(v1 : Int, v2 : Int, v3 : Int) = v1 + v2 + v3

    fun max(v1 : Int, v2 : Int) = if (v1 >= v2) {
        v1
    } else {
        v2
    }

    fun max(v1 : Double, v2 : Double) = if (v1 >= v2) {
        v1
    } else {
        v2
    }
}

fun main(args: Array<String>) {
    val calc = Calculator()
    println(calc.add(2,2))
    println(calc.add(3.0,3.0))
    println(calc.add(4.0f,4.0f))
    println("MAX "+ calc.max(3,4))
}
```

Whenever a function is called, the Kotlin compiler compares the function name and the number of parameters along with the parameter type to invoke the correct function:

```
          /Library/Java/JavaVirtualMachines/jdk1.8.0_181.jdk/Contents/Home/bin/java ...
          4
          6.0
          8.0
          MAX 4

          Process finished with exit code 0
```

In our example, add(2,2) calls the add function with integer parameters, add(3.0,3.0) calls the add function with double parameters, and so on. The Kotlin compiler performs all the verification behind the scenes and the programmer doesn't need to do anything.

The overloaded function is being distinguished by its name and its parameters list, not by its return type. We cannot overload a function by changing its return type. The following code is not a valid example of function-overloading even they have different return types. The reason why this was unsuccessful is that when the add(2,2) function is called, the Kotlin compiler does not have enough information to choose which function to invoke:

```kotlin
fun add(v1 : Int, v2 : Int) : Int {
 return v1 + v2
}

fun add(v1 : Int, v2 : Int) : Double {
 return v1.toDouble() + v2.toDouble()
}
```

Summary

In this chapter, we learned about object-oriented programming and why it is better than procedural programming. We started the chapter by exploring classes and learning how to declare them. We also discussed the properties and behavior of classes, and why properties are known as first-class citizens. Then, we had a detailed discussion about data classes, constructors, and how parameterized constructors help us to write clean code. In the last section of this chapter, we covered functions and function overloading. In the next chapter, we will look at some more advanced topics and their implementations.

Questions

1. What is the difference between a class and an object?
2. What is an attribute and the behavior of the class?
3. What is a constructor and how many types of constructors are available?
4. What is function overloading?
5. What are data classes and why are they beneficial?

Further reading

Learning Object-Oriented Programming by Gastón C. Hillar published by Packt: `https://www.packtpub.com/application-development/learning-object-oriented-programming`.

3
The Four Pillars of Object-Oriented Programming

This chapter will continue on from `Chapter 2`, *Introduction to Object-Oriented Programming*, in which we discussed the basic concepts of object-oriented programming. In this chapter, we will discuss the four pillars of object-oriented programming, which are encapsulation, inheritance, abstraction, and polymorphism. We will try to understand what inheritance is and look at the different types of inheritance that are provided by Kotlin. We will also learn how inheritance can help us to write clean and reusable code. After that, we will discuss encapsulation, before moving on to taking a closer look at the polymorphism technique. Finally, we will take a look at some of the benefits of abstraction and how interface and abstract classes can help us to write bug-free applications.

The following topics will be covered in this chapter:

- Inheritance
- Overriding functions
- Encapsulation
- Polymorphism
- Abstraction
- Interfaces

Technical requirements

Other than IntelliJ IDEA, this chapter does not require any specific installations.

The code for this chapter can be downloaded from the following GitHub link: `https://github.com/PacktPublishing/Hands-On-Object-Oriented-Programming-with-Kotlin/tree/master/src/main/kotlin/Chapter03`.

Encapsulation

Procedural programming is a technique where a program is divided into small functions. Each module contains a number of variables to store different kinds of data and functions to operate on that data. While this approach is very simple, it can get much more complex as the application grows because we end up having functions all over the place. If one function changes, it requires the other functions to change. This strong interdependency between functions means that we end up with spaghetti code. This approach not only adds duplicate code in every part of the application, it also makes maintaining the code more difficult.

Take a look at the following example. Here, three variables are provided to the display function. By looking at variable names, we can gather that the function prints person-related information on the screen. There is no direct relation between the variables and the functions because they are decoupled. These variables may be declared in one file and the function in another:

```
char name[20] = "Bob";
int age = 10;
double height = 6.5;

void display( char name[], int age, double height)
{
    printf("Name is %d\n" , name);
    printf("Age is %s \n" , age);
    printf("Height value is %f \n", height);
}
```

The object-oriented paradigm helps to combine these related variables and functions in one capsule. As we have discussed, variables are called properties and functions are called behaviors. When the properties and behaviors are combined in one place, we call this encapsulation.

Let's create a `Person` class and compare it with the procedural programming approach:

```
class Person {
    var name: String = "Abid"
    var age : Int = 40
    var height : Double = 6.0

    fun display () {
        println("Name $name, Age $age Height $height")
    }
}
```

```
fun main(args: Array<String>) {
    val person = Person()
    person.display()
}
```

The `display` function of the procedural programming technique takes three parameters to display the content. The `display` function of the `Person` class, however, takes zero parameters, which is a much cleaner approach because the `Person` class contains tightly coupled parameters and functions that are gathered in one place.

Encapsulation is an object-oriented programming technique that involves binding the data and function into one unit, which is called a class. All examples in the previous sections are implementations of encapsulation, in which we have defined some properties that store the current state of the object and functions to perform some tasks. Encapsulation is useful not only to put different properties and functions in one class, but also to protect them from the outside world.

Information-hiding

Information-hiding is a term that is used very often with regard to encapsulation. The idea behind information-hiding is that the class or object should not expose any information to the outside world unless it is necessary for another part of system. Let's try to understand this with an example:

```
class Person(pName: String, pAge: Int, pHeight : Double ) {

    var name : String = pName
    var age : Int = pAge
    var height : Double = pHeight

    init {
        require(name.trim().isNotEmpty()) {"Name should not empty"}
        require(age > 0 ) {"Age is not correct"}
        require(height > 0) {"Height is not correct"}
    }
}

fun main(args: Array<String>) {
    val person = Person("bob",40,6.1)
    println("Name ${person.name}, Age ${person.age} Height
${person.height}"
}
```

This is a fully functional `Person` class from the previous chapter where the `init` function verifies all values before the object is created. If any of the values do not meet the requirements, such as if the name is empty or the age or height is a negative number or zero, Kotlin will throw an `IllegalArgumentException`. It is necessary to provide valid values when creating a `Person` object. However, if Kotlin is allowed to access the properties and change the current status of the object without verification, the following might happen:

```
person.age = -41
person.height = 0.0
```

The `person` properties are reassigned with the values that were prevented at the time of object-creation. The idea of information-hiding is to hide the class properties and prevent them from reaching the outer world. In Kotlin, properties are first-class citizens, which means they are directly accessible. This doesn't mean that these properties should be accessible all the time, however; we have to provide a getter function to read the properties and a setter function to update them. Before updating the properties, we can provide an additional layer of validation in the setter function to prevent objects with unwanted data.

Visibility modifier

The rule of thumb of encapsulation is to restrict the properties being accessible to the outside world and instead implement some functions to access class properties indirectly. Kotlin provides four visibility modifiers that hide the class members—`public`, `private`, `protected`, and `internal`. In this book, we will discuss `public`, `private`, and `protected`. Let's start by looking at the `public` and `private` modifiers.

The `public` is a default modifier that appears with each property and function if no other modifier is defined. The visibility modifier always appears before the declaration of a property or function:

```
public var name : String
```

The private modifier

The preferred `private` modifier is the most restrictive modifier. When the properties are declared with private access, they are not accessible from outside the class:

```
private var name : String
```

Let's take an example of the `Person` class and apply the `private` visibility modifier:

```
class Person(pName: String, pAge: Int, pHeight : Double ) {

    private var name : String = pName
    private var age : Int = pAge
    private var height : Double = pHeight

    init {
        require(name.trim().isNotEmpty()) {"Name should not empty"}
        require(age > 0 ) {"Age is not correct"}
        require(height > 0) {"Height is not correct"}
    }
}

  fun main(args: Array<String>) {
      val person = Person("bob",40,6.1)
      println("Name ${person.name}, Age ${person.age} Height
${person.height}"
  }
```

As soon as we implement the `private` modifier on each property of the `Person` class, the Kotlin compiler throws the following error in the `main` function:

```
Cannot access 'property name': it is private in 'Class name'
```

The only way to access the private properties is to add our own functions. Write the `getAge` function to read the `age` property and the `setAge` function to update it. In the previous section, we mentioned that one of the disadvantages of having direct access is that we cannot protect our properties from unwanted values:

```
person.age = -41
  person.height = 20.0
```

By assigning the private visibility modifier to the `age` or `height` properties, we are not permitted to access them directly. Let's add the `getAge` and `setAge` functions to read and write the `age` property:

```
class Person(pName: String, pAge: Int, pHeight : Double ) {

    private var name : String = pName
    private var age : Int = pAge
    private var height : Double = pHeight

    init {
        require(name.trim().isNotEmpty()) {"Name should not empty"}
        require(age > 0 ) {"Age is not correct"}
```

```
            require(height > 0) {"Height is not correct"}
        }

    fun getAge() : Int{
        return age;
    }

    fun setAge(age : Int) {
        require(age > 0 ) {"Age is not correct"}
        this.age = age
    }

    fun display(){
        println("Name ${name}, Age ${age} Height ${height}")
    }
}

fun main(args: Array<String>) {

    val person = Person("bob",40,6.1)
    person.display()
    person.setAge(42)
    person.display()
}
```

Now, if we need to update a property, we can verify it beforehand. The setAge function verifies the age before assigning it to the age property.

 If the class properties are declared private, the Kotlin-generated Java code would not contain getter or setter functions.

Similarly, we are required to add the display function within the class to print the class properties on the screen because all properties are declared as private and cannot access person.age or person.name in the main function.

The protected modifier

Kotlin provides another modifier, which is less restrictive as compared to the private modifier but very important when it comes to class hierarchy. This is called the protected modifier. Class properties and functions that are declared protected are accessible only in child classes. Take a look at the following example.

Create class A with two properties, i with protected visibility and j with public visibility. Create a child, class B, and inherit it with class A. Create a display function in class B and print all properties of class A in it:

```
class A {
    protected val i = 1
    public val j = 2
}

open class B : A() {
    fun display(){
        println("Protected i $i" )
        println("Public j $j")
    }
}

fun main(args: Array<String>) {
    val b = B()
    b.display()
}
```

All public and protected properties can be displayed without any problem. Let's create class C, create an instance of class A inside class C, and access all properties of class A in it:

```
class C {
  val obj = A()
  fun display(){
  // println("Protected i ${obj.i}" )
  println("Public j ${obj.j}")
  }
}
```

Only the j property with the public modifier is available, and if we will try to access the protected modifier, Kotlin will throw the following error because protected members are accessible only in subclasses, not outside the class hierarchy:

```
Kotlin: Cannot access 'i': it is protected in 'A'
```

Implementation-hiding

Another important concept to do with encapsulation is implementation-hiding. The idea behind implementation-hiding is to hide the inner workings of the function from the outside world. Let's take a look at an example to understand this concept.

In our everyday life, we meet and interact with many people. When we ask how someone is feeling or the name of their new pet, that person exhibits some behavior to provide the answers to our questions, such as saying *I am fine, thank you!* or *My cat's name is Catty*. The information about which language this information was stored in that person's brain and how they processed this information is hidden from the outside world.

Similarly, every smartphone contains an address book application that stores contact details and provides them when for us when we tap on the right place on the screen. How the mobile phone stores this information, whether it applies any encryption, and whether it loads the data in an array or in a list is hidden from us. Even if the inner implementation of the application completely changes, it wouldn't matter to us as long as the way in which we can access the information is the same.

A further example would be motor cars. All cars reduce their speed when the brake pedal is pressed. How does the brake system work—are they mechanical drum brakes, hydraulic brakes, or disk brakes? All these details are hidden from the outside world. We know that braking systems have evolved from simple to more complex mechanics, but we are unlikely to know any further information; everything is fine as long as the car reduces its speed when the brake pedal is pressed.

Let's create a bank account class. The simplest form of a bank account has two properties: the account ID and the current balance. It also has two behaviors—depositing money and withdrawing money:

```
class BankAcc(private val accID : Int, private var balance : Double){
    fun withdraw(remove : Double) {
        if(balance >= remove){
            balance -= remove
            println("$remove money has withdrawn from $accID account,
              current balance is $balance")
        } else {
            println("Not enough balance in $accID account,
              current balance is $balance")
        }
    }

    fun deposit(add : Double){
        if(add > 0){
            balance += add
```

```
        println("$add money has deposited in $accID account,
          current balance is $balance")
      } else {
          println("Cannot process....")
      }
    }
  }
}

fun main(args: Array<String>) {

    var account = BankAcc(123, 500.0)
    account.withdraw(600.0)
    account.withdraw(100.0)
    account.deposit(600.0)
}
```

In the `main` function, we create an object of the `BankAcc` class with two initial values: the account number and the amount of money in the account. Next, the `withdraw` function deducts the money from the current balance, verifying the action before deduction. The function displays an error message if the withdrawal request is more than the current balance. We then have a `deposit` function, which allows us to deposit money in our account. We also verify that the deposit should not be a negative value.

Encapsulation can help here in the following ways:

- All properties and functions are placed in one container
- All properties are declared as private
- Properties are restricted and cannot be accessed directly
- The deposit and withdraw implementation is hidden from the outside world and all private properties can be accessed after verification

What is inheritance?

Inheritance is one of the key concepts in object-oriented programming. It involves avoiding code-repetition, especially where different classes have common features and all the classes belong to the same type. Let's say we are writing software for an educational institute in which three different entities are involved—**Student**, **Professor**, and **Employee**:

Student	Professor	Employee
+ first name : string	+ first name : string	+ first name : string
+ last name : string	+ last name : string	+ last name : string
+ age : int	+ age : int	+ age : int
+ student id : string	+ professor id : string	+ employee id : string
+ speak() + greet() + aboutEducation() + attendLectures()	+ speak() + greet() + aboutSpecialization() + deliverLectures()	+ speak() + greet() + aboutDesignation() + attendMeetings()

All these entities have some properties in common, including **name**, **age**, and **id**. Each entity exhibits some behaviors, such as **speak** or **greet**. Let's convert the diagram of the `Professor` class into code:

```
class Professor(val fName: String, var lName: String, var pAge: Int, val
professorId : String ) {

    fun speak() {
        println("My name is $fName $lName age is $pAge and my
        ID is $professorId")
    }

    fun greet() {
        println("Hi there... Professor $fName ")
    }

    fun aboutSpecialization() {
        println("I have a done my Phd in Computer science")
    }

    fun deliverLecture() {
        println("I am teaching Introduction to Kotlin.")
```

```
        }
    }
    fun main(args: Array<String>) {
        val jon = Professor("Jon","Jack",40, "PR-101")

        jon.greet()
        jon.speak()
        jon.aboutSpecialization()
        jon.deliverLecture()
    }
```

This example works fine, but it is a poor way to solve our problem. If we look closely, we can see that each class contains similar lines of code because of their similar attributes and behaviors. If we decide to change how a particular function works, or if we add a new attribute, such as **address**, in each entity, we would need to implement new requirements for all three classes. The preceding implementation may be acceptable up until this point because of the low complexity of the program. As new requests are received, however, for new classes, such as **graduate student, visitor**, or **contractor**, the maintenance of the code will become a nightmare.

Inheritance is a technique that helps us remove code-duplication. Inheritance identifies all the common features of different classes and combines them into one class. All the classes with the same features can be inherited from a parent class. A student, an employee, and a professor all belong to a person class and each person has a name, an age, and an ID. Let's create a class called **Person** and combine all the common attributes and behaviors in it:

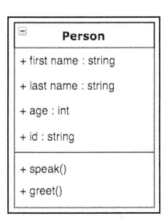

Once the **Person** class has been created, all other classes can extend this class. In inheritance, the main class is called a super or parent class. Classes that extend this class are called child classes. All child classes automatically include the functionality of the parent class. In Kotlin, the inheritance syntax is as follows:

```
class Child  :  Parent {
   ... ...
   }
```

Let's convert the diagram of the `Person` class into code:

```
class Person (val fName: String, var lName: String, var pAge: Int, val id :
String) {

    fun speak() {
        println("My name is $fName $lName, my id is $ID and age is $pAge")
    }

    fun greet() {
        println("Hi How are you...")
    }
}
```

Each child class can inherit the `Person` class and utilize all the properties and behaviors of the parent class. It can also have its own behaviors. As we can see, the `Person` class contains three important properties: first name, last name, and age. These are required for every person. When the child class inherits the parent class, it is necessary to pass the required variables to the parent class. We can now create a `Student` class and inherit the `Person` class as follows:

```
class Student(fName: String, lName: String, pAge: Int, ID: String ) :
Person(fName, lName, pAge, ID) {
   }
```

As soon as we inherit the `Parent` class, the compiler throws an error that states `this class is final and cannot be inherited from`. This is because each class is final by default and we must open them before extending them. A complete example of this code can be found on GitHub: `https://github.com/PacktPublishing/Hands-On-Object-Oriented-Programming-with-Kotlin/tree/master/src/main/kotlin/Chapter03`.

Using the open keyword

To open classes in Kotlin, we can add the open keyword at the beginning of the superclass signatures:

```
open class Person (val fName: String, var lName: String, var pAge: Int, val
ID : String) {

    fun speak() {
        println("My name is $fName $lName, my id is $ID and age is $pAge")
    }

    fun greet() {
        println("Hi How are you...")
    }
}

class Student(fName: String, lName: String, pAge: Int, ID: String ):
Person(fName,lName,pAge, ID) {
    fun aboutEducation(){
        println("I am a student of Computer Science.")
    }

    fun attendLectures() {
        println("I am studying Introduction to Kotlin lecture.")
    }
}
```

Now, the Student child class has access to all the functions of the Person class, and has its own properties and functions as well. We will add two functions in the Student class—aboutEducation and attendLecture:

```
fun main(args: Array<String>) {
    val bob = Student("Bob", "Peter", 25, "A-123")
    bob.speak()
    bob.greet()
    bob.attendLectures()
    bob.aboutEducation()
}
```

Once the object of the derived class is created, it can implicitly get access to all the functions and properties of its parent class:

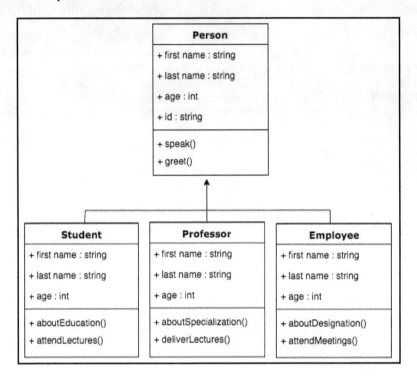

Just like **Student**, we can also extend the **Employee** and **Professor** classes from the **Person** class.

Using the super keyword

So far, all classes were inherited using a primary constructor. If the `Student` class doesn't have a primary constructor but a secondary constructor instead, the secondary constructor can be preceded by the `super` keyword:

```
class Student: Person {

    constructor(fName: String,lName: String, age: Int, id: String) :
super(fName,lName,age, id)

    fun aboutEducation(){
        println("I am a student of Computer Science.")
    }
```

```
        fun attendLectures() {
            println("I am studding Introduction to Kotlin lecture.")
        }
    }
```

The `super` keyword will call the constructor of the super or parent class to initialize the properties of the parent class.

Class-initialization hierarchy

In the previous section, we explored the functionalities of inheritance by extending the `Person` class with the student and professor classes. In this section, we will have a closer look at the constructor and class-initialization. Let's take a very simple example:

1. Create a super or parent class, A, with the init function.
2. Create a similar class, B, with the init function and extend it with the A class. Do the same with the C class.
3. Add a print message in each init function. The `init` function will be called just before the initialization of the constructor:

```
open class A {
    init {
        println("Class A is initialized")
    }
}

open class B : A() {
    init {
        println("Class B is initialized")
    }
}

class C : B() {
    init {
        println("Class C is initialized")
    }
}

fun main(args: Array<String>) {
    // val a = A()
    val c = C()
}
```

When a base or non-derived class is called, Kotlin creates a constructor of the class. When a derived class is initialized, however, things are not so straightforward:

```
/Library/Java/JavaVirtualMachines/jdk1.8.0_181.jdk/Contents/Home/bin/java ...
Class A is initialized
Class B is initialized
Class C is initialized

Process finished with exit code 0
```

```
4: Run    6: TODO    9: Version Control    Terminal    0: Messages                    Event Log
```

As we know, the derived class inherits all properties and behaviors from the base class and these properties must be initialized before we use them. Usually, all properties are initialized in either the primary or the secondary constructor. When the derived class is instantiated, the constructor of the derived class calls its superclass constructor as part of its initialization. This superclass checks whether it is derived from another class. If it has no parent class, it initializes all properties and sends the control back to the derived class to initialize its properties. In our case, class C is derived from class B, and class B is derived from class A. When the object of class C is initialized, it jumps to the class B constructor and class B jumps to class A. This means that the first print statement comes from class A, the second from class B, and the last from class C.

Abstraction

To understand the concept of the abstract class, let's discuss a few examples. When we draw a rectangle, we don't say that we have drawn a shape, we always use the name of that particular shape so that other people can understand what we mean. Similarly, if we are developing an application for an institute, we always create a student or teacher object. We don't need to create an object of the Person class, because *person* is a vague concept. Student, manager, or teacher, however, are concrete examples of a person. All concepts that are based on a general idea are known as abstract concepts. Classes that correspond to these abstract ideas are called abstract classes.

Abstract classes

An abstract class is a generic concept and it does not belong to a concrete idea. We do not create an instance of an abstract class; its only responsibility is to facilitate the creation of other classes. An abstract class is used to define which behaviors a class should have instead of how it should be implemented. Take a look at the following example from the previous section:

```
open class Person (val fName: String, var lName: String, var pAge: Int) {

    fun speak() {
        println("My name is $fName $lName age is $pAge")
    }
    fun greet() {
        println("Hi there...$fName ")
    }
}

class Student(fName: String, lName: String, pAge: Int , val studentId :
String) : Person(fName,lName,pAge) {
    ...
    ...
}
```

Notice that the `Person` class is a normal class and we can create an instance of it:

```
val person = Person("Bob","Peter",25)
```

In this case, however, we do not need to create an instance of the `Person` class, because *person* is an abstract idea. We want to prevent objects from being created from the `Person` class. This is what the abstract class is used for. Update the `Person` class, replace the open keyword with `abstract`, and the rest of the implementation will remain the same:

```
abstract class Person (val fName: String, var lName: String, var pAge: Int)
{
}
```

The program will execute without any errors unless we create an instance of the `Person` class in the main function. In this case, the Kotlin compiler will throw the following error:

Cannot create an instance of an abstract class

The abstract class can have both normal and abstract functions. We will look at abstract functions in the following section.

While creating an abstract class, it is not necessary to provide the open keyword because the abstract class is open by default.

Abstract functions

An abstract function is a function without a function body. To understand this concept, let's take the example of the Shape class:

```
abstract class Shape(val name: String) {
    init {
        println("Drawing $name")
    }
    open fun draw(){}
    open fun getArea() : Double{ return 0.0 }
}
```

The Shape abstract class contains two normal functions: draw and getArea. Both functions are open and available for inheritance. Having non-abstract functions in an abstract class, however, does have some drawbacks. If a function is a normal or non-abstract function, it must provide a function body even if it is empty. If a child class inherits a parent class, it won't know whether it is necessary to provide an implementation of the inherited functions.

Abstract functions are similar to abstract classes. They do not contain a function body. The biggest advantage of declaring an abstract function is that any class that inherits the parent class has no choice but to provide the implementation of this abstract function. By declaring an abstract function in the parent class, we can force the child classes to use similar signatures with their own implementation.

Shape is an abstract class because it is a generic idea. The draw and getArea functions must also be abstract, because we cannot draw a generic shape. Remove the open keyword from the function body and add the abstract keyword at the beginning of the function signature:

```
abstract class Shape(val name: String) {
    init {
        println("Drawing $name")
    }
    abstract fun draw()
    abstract fun getArea():Double
}
```

Now, each child class has to provide the implementation of all abstract functions of the parent class. In our shape example, all shapes are different to other shapes but each shape must implement two functions: `getArea()`, to calculate the area, and `draw()`, to draw the shape on the screen:

```
class Rectangle(_width : Double, _height : Double, name: String) : Shape(
name) {}
```

As soon as the child class extends the abstract class with the abstract function, the compiler will immediately trigger a compile-time error:

```
'Rectangle' is not abstract and does not implement abstract base class
member public abstract fun draw():
```

This is an indication that the child class has to provide the implementation of all abstract functions that are listed in the parent class.

There are a few key things to remember with regard to abstract classes:

- Abstract classes are like normal classes. They contain properties, functions, and constructors. Abstract classes, however, cannot be instantiated.
- Abstract classes are open by default.
- Only abstract classes can have abstract functions.
- Abstract functions are declared without a function body.
- Abstract functions cannot be declared privately.

Abstract functions must be implemented by child classes. This ensures that we conform to compile-time safety, which means that any class that extends the abstract class must provide an implementation to continue. If the child class does not provide the implementation, the function must be declared as an abstract function so that another child class can provide the implementation.

Interfaces

An interface is somewhat similar to an abstract class in that it provides a list of functions to implement. An interface is basically a contract between classes in which each class has to provide an implementation of the functions that are defined in the interface. An interface is declared with the `interface` keyword. Let's take a look at an example:

```
interface interface_name{
    fun func1()
    fun func2()
```

```
}
interface IPrintable {
    fun print()
}
```

Creating an interface is similar to creating a class. The names of the interfaces start with the letter I. This is not a syntax requirement, but a common practice to differentiate between classes and interfaces because their syntax is similar:

```
class Invoice : IPrintable {
    override fun print() {
        println("Invoice is printed")
    }
}
```

In this example, the `Invoice` class implements the `IPrintable` interface and provides an implementation of the `print` function. The interface is a contract that requires a class to implement certain functions. For example, the invoice class interface must have a function to print the invoice. While creating a button or checkbox class, we can implement the `IClickable` interface to enforce the button or checkbox class to implement the `click` function because a button without click functionality is just an image:

```
interface Clickable{
    fun click()
}

class Button : Clickable {
    override fun click() {
        println("Button is clicked")
    }
}
fun main(args: Array<String>) {

    var invoice = Invoice()
    invoice.print()

    var button = Button()
    button.click()
}
```

As we can see, the `Button` class implements the `click` function and the invoice class implements the `print` function. The interface acts as a contract that states that any class that implements it has to guarantee that the function signatures listed in the interface are implemented.

The abstract class can have both abstract and non-abstract functions. Each function mentioned in the interface, however, is necessarily public and abstract by default so there is no need to use the `abstract` keyword with the function signature.

Multiple interfaces

Kotlin does not allow multiple inheritance, but it does allow classes with more than one interface. To understand the concept of multiple interfaces, let's take the example of a `Calculator` class. There are few basic operations that every calculator performs—add, `subtract`, `multiply`, and `divide`. We can create an interface for each operation and let the class implement as many interfaces as it wants:

```kotlin
interface IAdd {
    fun add(a : Int, b : Int)
}

interface ISubtract {
    fun subtract(a : Int, b : Int)
}

interface IMultiply {
    fun multiply(a : Int, b : Int)
}

interface IDivide{
    fun divide(a : Int, b : Int)
}
```

Now, each class must follow the rules and define the same function name and parameters that are defined in the interface. This is one of the benefits of interfaces—classes are bound to follow the rules that are mentioned in the interface, instead of providing their own definitions. We can now create a `Calculator` class and implement more than one interface in our class. To do this, the name of the interfaces will be separated with a comma:

```kotlin
class Calculator() : IAdd, ISubtract {

    override fun subtract(a: Int, b: Int) {
        println("$a - $b = ${a-b}")
    }

    override fun add(a: Int, b: Int) {
        println("$a + $b = ${a+b}")
    }
}
```

```kotlin
fun main(args: Array<String>) {
    val calc = Calculator()
    calc.add(5, 4)
    calc.subtract(5, 4)
}
```

We can add as many interfaces as we want. An interface can also extend other interfaces and provide its own function definition. In the following example, the `InterfaceBasicCalculator` interface extends the other interfaces:

```kotlin
interface InterfaceBasicCalculator : IAdd, ISubtract, IMultiply, IDivide {
    fun displayMessage()
}
```

When a class implements this interface, it has to provide an implementation of all the functions that are defined in the extended interfaces:

```kotlin
class Calculator() : InterfaceBasicCalculator {
    override fun multiply(a: Int, b: Int) {
    }
    ::::
    override fun displayMessage() {
        println("All functions are implemented")
    }
    :::::
}
```

As well as function signatures, interfaces are also able to provide function implementations. Let's create an interface called `IDriveable`, which can be implemented by the `Car` class. This interface might have many function signatures, such as `MoveForward`, `tunLeft`, `turnRight`, or `engineStart`. For simplicity, we are going to define two functions—`engineStart` and `moveForward`. We will provide an implementation of each function within this interface. Let's implement the `startEngine` function first:

```kotlin
interface IDriveable {
    fun startEngine(){
        println("Engine is ready ...")
    }
    fun moveForward()
}
```

Create a `Car` class with a property name and implement the `IDriveable` interface. Notice that the Kotlin compiler only throws an error for the `moveForward()` function implementation because the `startEngine` function is already implemented in the `IDriveable` class:

```
class Car(val name : String) : IDriveable {

    override fun moveForward() {
        println("$name is driving on the road")
    }
}
```

We can override the function with our new implementation. We can also utilize functions that have already been implemented from the interface. The `super` keyword is used to call the function from the interface:

```
class Car(val name : String) : IDriveable {

    override fun moveForward() {
        println("$name is driving on the road")
    }

    override fun startEngine() {
        super.startEngine()
        println("Turbo technology is activated ...")
    }
}
```

We can also declare class properties within the interface but we cannot assign any value to them because the interface does not contain any state. Let's add an integer property called `numberOfDoors` and implement it in the `Car` class using the `override` keyword:

```
interface IDriveable {
    val numberOfDoors : Int
    fun startEngine()
    fun moveForward()
}

class Car(val name : String, override val numberOfDoors: Int) : IDriveable
{
    override fun moveForward() {
        println("$name is driving on the road")
    }
    override fun startEngine() {
        println("Turbo technology is activated ...")
    }
}
```

```
fun main(args: Array<String>) {
    val tesla = Car("Tesla" , 4)
    tesla.startEngine()
    tesla.moveForward()
}
```

In the following section, we will look at what happens if a class implements more than one interface and each interface contains functions with the same name.

Resolving conflicts between interfaces

As we know, a class can implement more than one interface. What happens if two interfaces have the same signatures; how can we choose one of these functions? To understand this concept, we need to create another interface called `IFlyable` with two functions—`fly` and `engineStart`. We can implement the `engineStart` function and define the fly function as follows:

```
interface IFlyable {
    fun startEngine(){
        println("Jet engine is ready ...")
    }
    fun fly()
}
```

Let the `Car` class implement the `IFlyable` interface to create an advanced vehicle that can drive and fly:

```
class Car(override var numberOfDoors: Int, val name : String) : IDriveable,
IFlyable {

    override fun startEngine() {

    }

    override fun fly() {
        println("$name is ready to fly...")
    }

    override fun moveForward() {
        println("$name is driving on the road")
    }
}
```

The `IFlyable` and `IDriveable` interfaces contain a function called `startEngine`. In the `Car` class, there is no conflict for the `startEngine` function, as long as we want to provide our own implementation. When we try to use a function from one of the interfaces, however, it will look as follows:

```
override fun startEngine() {
    super.startEngine()
}
```

Kotlin will throw the following error:

Many supertypes available, please specify the one you mean in angle brackets, e.g. 'super<Foo>'

We need to call the function by explicitly providing the interface name with the `super` keyword:

```
override fun startEngine() {
    super<IDriveable>.startEngine()
}
```

By using the `super` keyword and the diamond operator, Kotlin knows which function to call.

Interfaces and polymorphism

In our previous example, we can see that the car class implements two interfaces—`IDriveable` and `IFlyable`. The `tesla` class object can run on the road and fly in the sky.

We can restrict an object to a specific interface, even if a class has implemented more than one interface. Let's say we want to create an instance of a normal class that should not contain the functionalities of a flying object. To achieve this, we need to define the type of the interface that we want to expose. Create an object called `Toyota`, declare it with the `IDriveable` interface, and initialize it with `Car` along with the required parameters:

```
fun main(args: Array<String>) {
    val toyota : IDriveable = Car(4, "Toyota")
    toyota.startEngine()
    toyota.moveForward()
}
```

Because the `Car` class has implemented the `IDriveable` interface, it is possible to declare one of the interfaces by creating a `Car` object. This is a very powerful feature. Notice that by opening the `IDriveable` interface, the class instance can access only the functions that are implemented in the `IDriveable` interface. If we try to access the fly function from the `IFlyable` interface, Kotlin will throw a compile-time error.

Overriding

Inheritance is a method in which a child class can access all the functions and properties of its parent class. What if, however, the derived class wants its own specific implantation of the function that is already provided by the derived class? To understand this problem, let's take a simple example of a `Person` class with two properties, `name` and `age`, and a function, `displayInfo()`:

```
open class Person(pName: String, pAge: Int) {
    var name     = pName
    var age      = pAge

    fun displayInfo(){
        println("My name is $name, I am $age old. ")
    }
}
```

Create another class called `Student` with some extra properties (`id`, `education`, and `institute` name) and extend it with the `Person` class:

```
class Student(name: String, age: Int, id : Int, education : String,
institution : String) : Person(name , age ) {
    var studentID = id
    val institutionName = institution
    val education = education
}
```

All the properties and functions of the `Person` class are part of the `Student` class. Create an object of the `Person` and `Student` classes and call the `displayInfo()` function:

```
fun main(args: Array<String>) {

    val p = Person(pName = "Jon",pAge = 35)
    p.displayInfo()

    val bob = Student(name = "Bob Peter",
    age = 25, id = 100,
    education =   "Computer programming", institution = "Stockholm
```

```
University")
    bob.displayInfo()
}
```

The output of this code block is as follows:

My name is Jon, I am 35 old.
My name is Bob Peter, I am 25 old.

The output of the `Person` class looks fine, but the output of the `Student` class is not as expected. We don't have any information about their education, institution, or ID. When a parent class function does not fulfill the requirements of the child class, it is necessary to rewrite it.

What is overriding?

Redefining the inherited function in a child class is called overriding. The purpose of function-overriding is to allow the derived class to give its own implementation because the provided implementation is not sufficient. In Kotlin, there are few rules to override a function:

- The function in the parent class must be declared `open`
- The function in the child class must use the `override` keyword

Let's add the `displayInfo()` function in the `Student` class and include more information using the `print` function. This works as follows:

```
open class Person(pName: String, pAge: Int) {
    var name    = pName
    var age     = pAge

    open fun displayInfo(){
        println("My name is $name, I am $age years old.")
    }
}

class Student(name: String, age: Int, id : Int, education : String,
institution : String) : Person(name , age ) {
    var studentID = id
    val institutionName = institution
    val education = education

    override fun displayInfo() {
        println("My name is $name, I am $age old.\n" +
                "I am a student of $education in $institutionName and my ID
```

```
is $studentID")
    }
}
```

The `Student` class now contains its own `displayInfo()` function with all its properties included. This function overrides the function declared in the `Person` class. The `Person` class has to `open` the `displayInfo()` function and the `Student` class can then override it:

```kotlin
fun main(args: Array<String>) {

    val p = Person(pName = "Jon",pAge = 35)
    p.displayInfo()

    val bob = Student(name = "Bob Peter", age = 25,
    id = 100, education =  "Computer programming", institution = "Stockholm
University")
    bob.displayInfo()
}
```

The output shown here looks more like what we would expect. The `Person` object calls the `displayInfo()` function of the `Person` class, and the `Student` class object calls the function of its own class because the `displayInfo()` function is overridden:

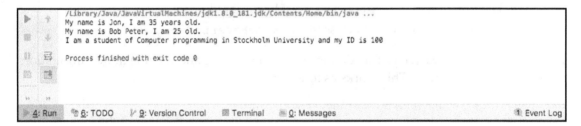

```
/Library/Java/JavaVirtualMachines/jdk1.8.0_181.jdk/Contents/Home/bin/java ...
My name is Jon, I am 35 years old.
My name is Bob Peter, I am 25 old.
I am a student of Computer programming in Stockholm University and my ID is 100

Process finished with exit code 0
```

In the new implementation, the overridden function contains additional information about the student's education and institute, but there is some code repetition. If we compare both the `displayInfo()` functions, we can see that the name and age information is displayed in both functions. This is not a good programming technique. When the overridden function does not require a completely different implementation, it is always a good idea to call the parent class function to the child class.

The super keyword

The `super` keyword is used to call the functions of the parent class. In the following example, we call the `displayInfo()` function from the `Student` class by using the `super` keyword:

```
override fun displayInfo() {
    super.displayInfo()
    println("I am a student of $education in $institutionName and
     my ID is $studentID")
}
```

Notice that by calling the parent class, the function in the child class displays the same output as before.

The final keyword

Let's create another child class, `Alien`, and extend it from the `Student` class. Override the `displayInfo` function and add a print message:

```
class Alien (name: String, age: Int, id : Int, education : String,
institution : String): Student(name, age, id, education, institution){
    override fun displayInfo() {
        super.displayInfo()
        println("I know everything")
    }
}
fun main(args: Array<String>) {

    val alien = Alien(name = "Alien eli", age = 225,
    id = 10101, education = "Computer Virus", institution = "Pluto")
    alien.displayInfo()
}
```

Don't forget to open the `Student` class so that the `Alien` class can extend it. However, we can see that we don't need to add the `open` keyword with the `displayInfo()` function in the `Student` class. Once the function in a parent class is open for overriding, it is available for the complete hierarchy, but we may want to restrict this function at a particular level. For example, if we want the `displayInfo()` function of the `Student` class to be a final implementation so that no child class can override it, we can do that by adding the `final` keyword in the function signature. Let's restrict the `displayInfo` function at the level of the `Student` class:

```
open class Student(name: String, age: Int, id : Int, education : String,
institution : String) : Person(name , age ) {
   override final fun displayInfo() {
        super.displayInfo()
        println("I am a student of $education in $institutionName and
        my ID is $studentID")
   }
}
```

As soon as `displayInfo` in the `Student` class is declared `final`, the Kotlin compiler will throw the following error in the `Alien` class:

```
Kotlin: 'displayInfo' in 'Student' is final and cannot be overridden.
```

We must remove the `displayInfo` function from the `Alien` class to compile the code.

 The `final` keyword restricts the child class from overriding the function, but the child class can still access the function of the parent class.

Rules for function-overriding

The main advantage of function-overriding is that each class can provide its own implementation to the inherited function *without modifying the superclass*. This is helpful when a class has more than one derived classes. If a child class wants to replace the parent's class function with its own implementation, it is free to do that as well as use the implementation of the parent class.

There are few rules of overriding:

- The function in the parent class must be declared `open`
- The function in the child class must use the `override` keyword
- The function in the child class must have the same name as in the parent class
- The function in the child class must have the same parameters as in the parent class
- To restrict the child class from overriding the function, the function in the parent class must be declared as `final`

Property-overriding

Kotlin also allows us to override class properties to provide new definitions. Overriding the property is similar to overriding the function: the property must be declared as `open` in the parent class and the `override` keyword must be used in the child class to make sure that the property is being overridden explicitly and not accidentally.

Property-overriding is possible in the following cases:

- Immutable properties can be overridden by immutable properties
- Immutable properties can be overridden by mutable properties
- Mutable properties can be overridden by mutable properties

We can override the `val` properties with either the `val` or `var` properties, and we can override the `var` properties with other `var` properties, but `var` properties cannot be overridden with `val` properties.

Let's take a look at the following example. The `Programming` class, which has one read property, `name`, and one function, `info()`, is derived by the `AdvancedProgramming` child class.

The child class overrides the `name` property and changes the property type from `val` to `var`:

```
open class Programming (open val name: String){
    open fun info(){
        println("Programming language $name")
    }
}

class AdvancedProgramming(override var name : String) : Programming(name){
    override fun info(){
        println("Advanced Programming language $name")
    }
}
```

In the main function, we will create an object of the `Programming` class with one parameter, `Java`. As we can see, the `name` property is declared as immutable and cannot be changed:

```
fun main(args: Array<String>) {

    var programming = Programming("Java")
    // name is read only
    // programming.name = "Kotlin"
    programming.info()

    var advancedProgramming = AdvancedProgramming("Kotlin")
    advancedProgramming.info()

    // name is read-write
    advancedProgramming.name = "Kotlin 2.0"
    advancedProgramming.info()
}
```

When we change the property type to mutable by overriding it in the `AdvancedProgramming` class, the property can be reassigned as many times as we need:

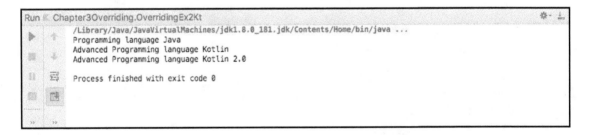

The object of the `Programming` class does not allow us to change the value of the `name` property. The value of `name` in the child class can be updated, however, because the property has been overridden from immutable to mutable.

Types of inheritance

Kotlin provides four types of inheritance:

- Single inheritance
- Multilevel inheritance
- Hierarchical inheritance
- Hierarchical multilevel inheritance

We will discuss each of these inheritance types in detail.

Single inheritance

Single inheritance is the simplest form of inheritance, whereby a derived class has only one parent class. In the following diagram, class **B** is derived from class **A**, and class **A** is a superclass of class **B**. The programming and advanced programming examples in the `property-overriding` section were examples of single inheritance:

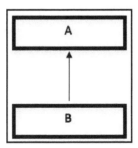

Multilevel inheritance

When a class is derived from a class that is already derived from another class, this inheritance is called multilevel inheritance. This refers to a situation where at least one class has more than one parent class. As we can see in the following diagram, **B** is derived from **A**, and **C** is derived from **B**. **C** not only contains the properties and behaviors of **B**, but also from class **A**, as well as its own. Let's create a superclass, `Person`, a derived class, `Employee`, and another derived class, `Programmer`:

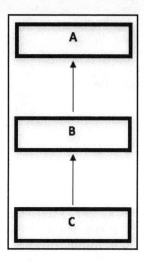

The `Person` class contains one property, `name`, and two behaviors, `sleep` and `speak`. The `Employee` class inherits everything from the `Person` class. It has one property, `company`, and one behavior, `work`. Finally, the `Programmer` child class contains all the behaviors and properties from its parent classes and has two functions, `code` and the overridden `sleep` function:

```
open class Person (val name : String){
    fun speak(){
        println("My name is $name")
    }

    open fun sleep(){
        println("I like to sleep 7 hours a day")
    }
}

open class Employee(name: String, val company : String) : Person(name) {
    fun work(){
        println("I work for $company")
```

```
    }
}

class Programmer(name: String, company: String) : Employee(name, company){
    fun code(){
        println("Coding is my passion")
    }

    override fun sleep(){
        println("I like to sleep when i get a chance.")
    }
}

fun main(args: Array<String>) {

    val coder = Programmer("Abid", "Kotlin Conf")
    coder.speak()
    coder.work()
    coder.code()
    coder.sleep()
}
```

Let's run this code and function call:

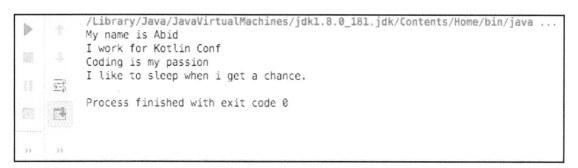

The `Person` class contains two functions, `speak` and `sleep`. The `Employee` class contains three functions, two from the `Person` class and `work`, which is its own. The `Programmer` class contains two of its own functions, `code` and `sleep`. `sleep` is an overridden function from its grandparent's `Person` class:

```
val coder = Programmer("Abid","Kotlin Conf")
```

It is very important to know which version of the function will be called:

- `coder.speak()`: The `coder` instance calls the `Person` class' `speak` function
- `coder.sleep()`: The `coder` instance calls the `Programmer` class' `sleep` function
- `coder.work()`: The `coder` instance calls the `Employee` class' `work` function
- `coder.code()`: The `coder` instance calls the `Programmer` class' `code` function

When a function is called, Kotlin searches from bottom to top. It looks in the lowest class in the hierarchy first and moves upward until it finds the function.

Hierarchical inheritance

A situation in which a parent class is inherited by many subclasses is called hierarchical inheritance. This is shown in the following diagram, where **A** is a parent class and **B**, **C**, and **D** are child classes. In this inheritance model, two or more classes are derived from the parent class:

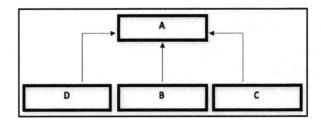

Create a superclass, `Person`, and two derived classes, `Student` and `Employee`:

```
open class Person (val fName: String, var lName: String, var pAge: Int, val
ID : String) {

    fun speak() {
        println("My name is $fName $lName, my id is $ID and age is $pAge")
    }

    fun greet() {
        println("Hi How are you...")
    }
}

class Student(fName: String, lName: String, pAge: Int, ID: String ):
Person(fName,lName,pAge, ID) {

    fun aboutEducation(){
```

```
        println("I am a student of Computer Science.")
    }

    fun attendLectures() {
        println("I am studying Introduction to Kotlin lecture.")
    }
}
fun main(args: Array<String>) {

    val bob = Student("Bob", "Peter", 25, "A-123")
    bob.speak()
    bob.greet()
    bob.attendLectures()
    bob.aboutEducation()
}
```

The `Person` class contain four properties—first name, last name, age, and ID. It also contains two functions. The student class inherits all properties and behaviors from the `Person` class and has its own functions. Both classes share properties from their parent class.

A complete example can be found on GitHub: `https://github.com/PacktPublishing/ Hands-On-Object-Oriented-Programming-with-Kotlin/tree/master/src/main/kotlin/ Chapter03`.

Hierarchical multilevel inheritance

Hierarchical multilevel inheritance is where a parent class is derived from more than one class and one of the child classes is derived from another class. Take a look at the following diagram, where **A** is a parent class of **D**, and **D** is a parent class of **E**:

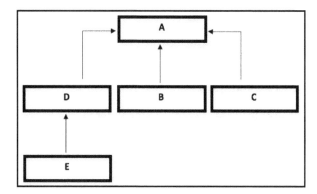

A classic example of this type of inheritance is the `Shape` class. Different shapes make up our everyday surroundings. All shapes are unique because of their structures. Some shapes, such as a circle and a cylinder, are quite similar, but other shapes, such as a square, an oval, and a triangle, are shapes that are completely different from each other. In this example, we are implementing the following shapes that are derived from the `Shape` class:

- Rectangle
- Triangle
- Circle
- Cylinder

The general characteristics of the `Shape` class are as follows:

- Each shape has a name
- Each shape can be drawn
- The area of the shape can be calculated

Let's create `Shape` class hierarchy:

1. Create a superclass, `Shape`, that has one property, `name`, and two functions, `draw` and `getArea`. Keep the function body empty because *shape* is very generic concept and we do not know which shape will be implemented. When the concept is generic, it is always a good idea to make the superclass abstract. This will be discussed in more detail in the *Abstract* classes section:

```
open class Shape(val sName: String) {
    init {
        println("$sName is drawn ")
    }
    open fun draw() {}
    open fun getArea() = 0.0
}
```

2. Create a class called `Rectangle` and extend it from the `Shape` class. The rectangle class has two properties, `height` and `width`, two overridden functions, `getArea` and `draw`, and one function, `getPerimeter`:

- **To get the area of rectangle**: *area = height * width*
- **To find the perimeter of the rectangle**: *perimeter = (height * 2) + (width * 2)*

The perimeter of a rectangle is the length of the distance around the edge of rectangle. Override the `getArea` function to calculate the area, implement the `getPerimeter` function to calculate the perimeter, and override the `draw` function to display the calculated area:

```
class Rectangle(_width : Double, _height : Double, _sName: String)
: Shape(_sName) {

    var width = _width
    var height = _height

    override fun getArea() = width * height

    private fun getPerimeter() = (width * 2) + (height * 2)

    override fun draw() {
        println("Area of $sName is ${getArea()} and perimeter is
${getPerimeter()}")
    }
}
```

3. Create another class called `Triangle` and extend it with the `Shape` superclass. The simplest form of the `Triangle` class contains two properties, `base` and `height`, and two overridden functions from the super class.

   To calculate the area of the triangle: *area = (base * height) / 2*:

```
class Triangle(_base : Double, _height: Double, _sName: String) :
Shape(_sName) {
    var base    = _base
    var height  = _height

    override fun getArea() = (base * height)/2
    override fun draw() {
        println("Area of the triangle is ${getArea()}.")
    }
}
```

4. Create a class called `Circle` and extend it from the `Shape` class. The `Circle` class contains two properties, `pi` and `radius`. To calculate the circumference of the circle, use the following formula:

   Area of circle = PI * radius * radius

The distance from the center of a circle to any point on its circumference is called its radius:

```
open class Circle (_radius : Double, _sName: String) :
Shape(_sName) {

    val PI = 3.1415
    var radius = _radius

    override fun getArea() = PI * radius * radius
    override fun draw() {
        println("Area of the circle is ${getArea()}.")
    }
}
```

Let's have a look at the class diagram:

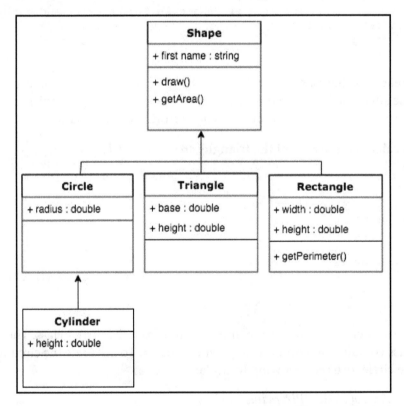

The **cylinder** class is the most powerful class in the hierarchy because it receives all properties and functions from its immediate parent class, **Circle**, and from its parent class, **Shape**, as well. The **cylinder** class has one property, height, and one overridden function, draw. We can carry out three different calculations on a cylinder:

- **To calculate the area of the circle of the cylinder**: *Circle = PI * radius * radius*
- **To calculate the volume of the cylinder**: *Volume = height * PI * radius * radius*
- **To calculate the area of the cylinder**: *area = (2 * PI * radius * radius) + (2 * PI * radius * height)*

The `getArea()` function of the `Circle` class provides the circumference of the circle. All other functions and properties are also derived from the circle class:

```
class Cylinder(_radius : Double, _height: Double,_sName: String) :
Circle(_radius, _sName) {

    var height = _height
    override fun draw() {

        var circle = getArea()
        println("Circle of cylinder is $circle")

        var volume = circle * height
        println("Volume of cylinder is $volume")

        var area =  (2 * circle) + (2 * PI * radius * height)
        println("Area of cylinder is $area")    }
}
```

We can now execute the complete program. The following code creates different types of shapes and each shape takes advantage of inheritance. The circle class, for example, reuses the code from the shape class, while the cylinder class makes use of the circle class:

```
fun main(args: Array<String>) {

    var rectangle = Rectangle(_width = 5.0, _height = 5.0, _sName =
"Rectangle")
    rectangle.draw()

    println()
    var triangle = Triangle(_base = 6.0, _height = 5.0,  _sName =
"Triangle")
    triangle.draw()

    println()
    var circle = Circle(_radius = 2.5,  _sName = "Circle")
```

```
    circle.draw()

    println()
    var cylinder = Cylinder(_radius = 2.5, _height = 4.0, _sName =
"Cylinder")
    cylinder.draw()
}
```

The is-a relationship

Before moving forward, it is very important to understand how to find a relationship between different classes. How do we know that a student can be inherited from `Person` or that `Circle` can be inherited from the `Shape` class? If the designed hierarchy is correct, the child class must be a type of the parent class and both classes must have an is-a relationship between them. Take a look at the following examples:

- Student is a person
- Circle is a shape
- Football player is a basketball player
- German shepherd is a dog
- Sofa is a bedroom

Most of these examples are correct but a few of them are completely false. *Student is a person* is correct because students have all the attributes and behaviors that a person has. Students also have some unique features as well. *Circle is a shape* is also correct, because every shape has a size and a color, so circle can be inherited from shape. *Sofa is a bedroom* does not make any sense, however, nor does *Football player is a basketball player*, because both games are completely different.

If the inheritance and the classes are well designed, every inherited class **is a** type of its parent class. If class *B* is inherited from *A*, then *B* is a type of *A*. As a circle is inherited from the `Shape` class, a circle is a type of shape. If class *C* is inherited from *B* and *B* is inherited from *A*, then *C* contains all features that both *A* and *B* have. A cylinder is inherited from a circle and a circle is inherited from a shape. A cylinder is therefore a type of shape as well as a circle.

An important thing to remember is that inheritance always works in one direction. A student is inherited from the `Person` class, which means that every student is a person. This is one-directional relationship; it won't work the other way around, because every person is not a student. Similarly, all dogs are animals, but not all animals are dogs. For this reason, a dog can be inherited from the animal class, but an animal cannot be extended from the dog class.

Polymorphism

In object-oriented programming, polymorphism is a concept where a function behaves differently, depending on the type of object that calls it. To understand the concept of polymorphism, we will continue with the `Shape` class example. Every shape has its own type and dimensions, but all shapes can be drawn on the screen. When the `Circle` class calls the `draw` function, it calculates the area and draws it. Similarly, if the `Triangle` class calls the `draw` function, it calculates the base and height and draws it. The same applies to the other classes. The idea behind polymorphism is that the `draw` function can display different shapes and the program can determine which shape of the function to call at the time of execution. There are different types of polymorphism used in Kotlin. In this section, we are discussing inheritance-based polymorphism. The idea behind this is that the base class can define a function and the derived class can override it by providing its own definition.

How polymorphism works

To understand polymorphism, let's create a normal instance of a class. Create a variable and assign a new rectangle object to it:

```
var rectangle : Rectangle = Rectangle(5.0 , 5.0, "Rectangle")
rectangle.draw()
```

The important point here is that the `rectangle` variable is a type of Rectangle and the created object is also a Rectangle. Both the reference and the object are same. We can reassign the `rectangle` variable to a new Rectangle object as many times as we want:

```
rectangle = Rectangle(10.0 ,  7.0, "Another Rectangle")
rectangle.draw()
```

However, we cannot assign a `Circle` class object to the `rectangle` variable. If we do, Kotlin will throw a type-mismatch error:

```
rectangle = Circle(2.5, "Circle")
Type mismatch: inferred type is Circle but Rectangle was expected
```

In polymorphism, however, the reference variable and the object can be of a different type. Polymorphism allows us to assign an object of a child class to a reference of a superclass:

```
var anyShape : Shape = Rectangle(5.0, 9.0, "Rectangle")
anyShape.draw()
```

When a reference of the parent class is declared, every object of a class that extends the reference type class can be assigned to that variable. In this example, `anyShape` is a reference of the `Shape` class and the `Rectangle` class inherits the `Shape` class, so the `Rectangle` class object can be assigned to `anyShape`.

Execute the following example and notice the convenience of polymorphism:

```
var anyShape : Shape = Rectangle(5.0, 5.0, "Rectangle")
anyShape.draw()
anyShape = Circle(2.5,"Circle")
anyShape.draw()
```

Assign a `Rectangle` object to a shape reference and call the `draw` function. The `draw` function from the `Rectangle` class will be called. Now, reassign a `Shape` class reference with a `Circle` class object. This time, the draw function of the `Circle` class will be executed automatically. The following example will make this clearer. Declare a list of the `Shape` type and initialize it with a list of different objects that inherit the `Shape` class:

```
val shapes : MutableList<Shape> = mutableListOf(triangle, circle,
rectangle, cylinder).
```

Loop through the list of shapes and call the `draw` function. Each shape will call its own `draw` function:

```
for (shape in shapes){
    shape.draw()
}
```

If we add new shapes, such as a line or an obtuse triangle, we can simply add them to the list and the polymorphism technique will handle the rest:

```
fun main(args: Array<String>) {

    var rectangle = Rectangle(_width = 5.0, _height = 5.0, _sName =
"Rectangle")
    var triangle = Triangle(_base = 6.0, _height = 5.0,  _sName =
"Triangle")
    var circle = Circle(_radius = 2.5,  _sName = "Circle")
    var cylinder = Cylinder(_radius = 2.5, _height = 4.0, _sName =
"Cylinder")

    val shapes : MutableList<Shape> = mutableListOf(triangle, circle)

    for (shape in shapes){
        shape.draw()
    }

    shapes.add(rectangle)
    shapes.add(cylinder)

    for (shape in shapes){
        shape.draw()
    }
}
```

Let's discuss polymorphism in more detail.

Dynamic binding

Runtime polymorphism, which is also known as *late or dynamic binding,* is used to determine which function to invoke at runtime. When a variable of a superclass is initialized with the object of a child class and the child class provides its own function definition by overriding it, a compiler cannot predict which object type it is and which function should be called. This is also difficult when a list of different shapes is assigned to the shapes list variable:

```
val shapes : MutableList<Shape> = mutableListOf(triangle,circle)
for (shape in shapes){
        shape.draw()
  }
```

When a compiler can't resolve the binding at compile time, this is decided later when the program executes. This technique is called late binding or dynamic binding. All calls to the overridden functions are dynamically bound and resolved at runtime. When a list of randomly inserted objects is passed to the list variable, the compiler can't recognize the shapes in the list so the decision of which function to call is made at runtime.

Summary

In this chapter, we have explored the four main pillars of object-oriented programming—inheritance, encapsulation, polymorphism, and abstraction. We started with inheritance and its benefits in software development. We then discussed the different types of inheritance and their implementations. We also discussed the concept of overriding and encapsulation, and we learned that functional programming is not suitable for advanced application development. Then, we had a detailed discussion about abstraction and its advantages, and we looked at the concept of interfaces. In the next chapter, we will discuss some advanced concepts to do with classes that make the Kotlin language unique.

Questions

1. What is inheritance?
2. Why does encapsulation help us to write clean code?
3. What are visibility modifiers?
4. How many types of inheritance are provided by Kotlin?
5. What is polymorphism and dynamic binding?
6. Why are abstract classes important?

Further reading

- *Learning Object-Oriented Programming* by Gastón C. Hillar Published by Packt: https://www.packtpub.com/application-development/learning-object-oriented-programming.
- *Hands-on Design Patterns with Kotlin* by Alexey Soshin Published by Packt: https://www.packtpub.com/application-development/hands-design-patterns-kotlin.

Classes - Advanced Concepts

4

This is the last chapter of the object-oriented programming series, in which we are going to learn about some more advanced concepts. Kotlin provides a neat, convenient, and concise way of implementing these concepts, unlike traditional programming languages, which require us to write lengthy and complex code.

In this chapter, we will discuss sealed classes and enumeration. We will also try to understand what a singleton is and how to use companion objects instead of static functions. After that, we will discuss the important topics of composition and aggregation, and we will end by exploring class properties and delegation to see how Kotlin helps to improve application development.

The following topics will be covered in this chapter:

- Sealed classes and enumeration
- Object and companion objects
- Composition and nested classes
- Properties
- Delegate properties
- Built-in delegates

Technical requirements

Other than IntelliJ IDEA, this chapter does not require any specific installations.

The code for this chapter can be downloaded from the following GitHub link: `https://github.com/PacktPublishing/Hands-On-Object-Oriented-Programming-with-Kotlin/tree/master/src/main/kotlin/Chapter04`.

Sealed classes and enumeration

So far in this book, we have learned about different types of classes, including normal and abstract classes. The main purpose of writing classes is to allow other classes to extend each other and to take full advantage of code reusability and maintainability. These classes can be called and used in any part of the application. For example, if class A is declared in the File1.kt file and class B is declared in the File2.kt file, then class B or any other class can extend class A. This is a normal practice and is referred to as inheritance. However, Kotlin provides another type of class that is restricted to limited classes and cannot be further inherited. These classes are called sealed classes.

Sealed classes

Every sealed class is tagged with the sealed keyword and is limited to a set of classes that can be declared inside the class body. Here is an example of a sealed class:

```kotlin
sealed class A(val number : Int) {
    class B(n: Int) : A(n) {
        fun display() { println("number = $number" ) }
    }

    class C(n: Int) : A(n){
        fun square() { println("Square = "+ number * number) }
    }
}
```

class A is a sealed class and class B and class C are the classes that are inherited from class A. Before Kotlin 1.1, declaring a child class inside a sealed class was the only method of declaration. Now, however, we can extend the sealed class from outside the class body, as shown in the preceding example, where class C extends class A. Remember that both the sealed and the child classes must be declared in the same file:

```kotlin
class D(n: Int) : A(n){
    fun cube(){ println("number = " + number * number * number ) }
}

fun main(args: Array<String>) {
    var b = A.B(1)
    b.display()
    var c = A.C(2)
    var d = D(3)
}
```

Declaring an object in a class that is declared within a sealed class body isn't as clean as declaring an object in a class that is declared outside of the sealed class:

```
var c = A.C(2)
var d = D(3)
```

Both approaches, however, work fine.

Sealed classes with the when block

The sealed class and its child classes are very convenient when we use the when block. To understand this concept, let's create a function, status, that takes the sealed class A as an argument:

```
fun status(a: A) {
    when (a) {
        is A.B -> a.display()
        is A.C -> a.square()
        is D -> a.cube()
    }
}
```

The status function takes one parameter of class A and contains a when block that switches based on the class type. When the status function is called, Kotlin verifies the object type and performs a smart cast. Notice that we do not use else at the end of the statement because the Kotlin compiler is able to work out that these are all of the cases that are covered by this sealed class.

If, for some reason, we do not supply all the cases, or we want to remove any of the options, we can then insert an else clause:

```
fun status(a: A) {
    when (a) {
        is A.B -> a.display()
        is A.C -> a.square()
        else -> {
            println("unknown")
        }
    }
}
```

Why do we need sealed classes?

Sealed classes are designed for situations in which a limited set of functionalities are required and no other class is allowed to be part of this set. For example, let's say we are writing an application for an order-delivery service in which a limited number of steps are involved:

1. The order is received at depot
2. The order is dispatched to the customer
3. The order is delivered to the customer

Let's create an `Order` class with the `item` property:

```
class Order(val item : String)
```

Create a sealed class, `OrderDelivery`, with one property, `Order`. We then need to create three child classes, each of which represents one of the steps:

```
sealed class OrderDelivery(val order : Order)

class ReceivedAtDepot(val depotName : String, order: Order) :
OrderDelivery(order)

class Dispatched(var truckId : String, var driverName : String, order:
Order) : OrderDelivery(order)

class Delivered(var destination : String, var isDelivered : Boolean, order:
Order) : OrderDelivery(order)
```

Let's create an `orderStatus` function with a `when` expression, using which we can see the current status of the order delivery:

```
fun orderStatus(delivery: OrderDelivery) {
    when (delivery) {
        is ReceivedAtDepot -> println("${delivery.order.item} is received
at ${delivery.depotName} depot.")
        is Dispatched -> println("${delivery.order.item} is dispatched,
Truck ID is ${delivery.truckId} and driver is ${delivery.driverName}")
        is Delivered -> println("${delivery.order.item} delivered at
${delivery.destination}.\n"+
            "Delivery to customer = ${delivery.isDelivered}.\n")
    }
}
```

In the `main` function, create an order and pass it to the `ReceivedAtDepot` class. Create a `Dispatched` class object with the vehicle and driver information and dispatch the order to the customer. When the order is delivered to the correct address, update the delivery status. By using polymorphism, we can create a list of the delivery statuses and pass them to the `orderStatus` function one by one:

```kotlin
fun main(args: Array<String>) {

    var book        = Order("OOP in Kotlin Book")
    var atDepot     = ReceivedAtDepot(depotName = "Stockholm City", order =
book)
    var dispatched  = Dispatched(truckId = "AXV-122", driverName = "Logan",
order = book)
    var delivered   = Delivered(destination = "älvsjö kommun", isDelivered =
true, order = book)

    var orderDeliverySteps = listOf(atDepot, dispatched, delivered)

    for (step in orderDeliverySteps) {
        orderStatus(step)
    }

    var knife       = Order("Kitchen knife set")
    atDepot         = ReceivedAtDepot(depotName = "Stockholm City", order =
knife)
    dispatched      = Dispatched(truckId = "JVY-354", driverName = "Peter
Parker", order = knife)
    delivered       = Delivered(destination = "Stockholm city", isDelivered =
true, order = knife)

    orderDeliverySteps = listOf(atDepot, dispatched, delivered)

    for (step in orderDeliverySteps) {
        orderStatus(step)
    }
}
```

The `main` function contains two orders, each of which represents an order status. We have a list of `OrderDeliverySteps` that contain instances of different classes. The `orderStatus` function takes the parent class as a parameter and displays the order-related information.

Enum classes

In Kotlin, enum classes are similar to sealed classes, except that all the values of the enum class are the same type. The enum class is useful when the expected outcome is within a small set, such as a small range of colours or the days of the week. Let's create a few examples of enum classes and see how they work:

```
enum class Color {
     RED,
     GREEN,
     BROWN,
     YELLOW
 }
```

The enum keyword is used to declare the enum class. Each value can be declared with a comma-separated list.

Each value of the enum class can be accessed by using the name of the enum class. As we can see in the preceding example, enum Color contains four colors. We can access the name and value of each color using the member name and the ordinal property:

```
fun main(args: Array<String>) {
    println(Color.RED)
    println(Color.RED.name)
    println(Color.RED.ordinal)
}
```

The output of this example is as follows:

```
RED
RED
0
```

Notice that the output of name is RED and ordinal is 0. This is because each member of the enum class contains a default value, which starts from 0. The default value of green is 1, while brown is 2, and yellow is 3.

We can create an enum type variable using the valueOf function along with the member name in string format. We can access the name and the value using the name and ordinal properties:

```
fun main(args: Array<String>) {
    val color = Color.valueOf("GREEN")
    println(color.name)
    println(color.ordinal)
}
```

It is very important to remember that Kotlin will throw an exception if the `valueOf` function could not find a name in the enum. In the next section, we will discuss the enum class and constructor.

The enum class with a constructor

Each member of the enum class contains an integer value that starts from 0, but Kotlin also allows us to assign a value of our own choice using a constructor:

```
enum class Week(val value: Int) {
    MONDAY(2 ), TUESDAY(4), WEDNESDAY(6), THURSDAY(8), FRIDAY(10),
SATURDAY(12), SUNDAY(14)
}
```

The `Week` enum class has a constructor with one integer property. Each member in the enum class is bound to provide an initial value:

```
fun main(args: Array<String>) {
    val week = Week.valueOf("TUESDAY")
    println("Item type: " + week)
    println("Name: " + week.name)
    println("Value: " + week.value)
}
```

Verify the output by assigning a different values of the `week` enum.

The output of the preceding example is as follows:

```
Item type: TUESDAY, Name: TUESDAY, Value: 4
```

The enum class and functions

Just as the enum class can have a property, it can also have a function. Let's create an application in which we can store the land area of different states:

```
enum class US (val totalArea : Double, val landArea : Double) {
    NEWYORK     (141_297.0,  122_057.0),
    VIRGINIA    (110_787.0, 102_279.0) ,
    HAWAII      (28_313.0,    16_635.0),
    NEWJERSEY   (22_591.0, 19_047.0) ;

    fun getWaterArea() = totalArea - landArea
}
```

Although we don't often use semicolons in Kotlin, we do need to place a semicolon at the end of a list when the enum class contains a constructor with more than one property. `enum class US` contains different states, each of which contain information about the land and total area. The enum class contains the `getWaterArea` function, which returns information about the water area of each state:

```kotlin
fun main(args: Array<String>) {

    println("Square kilometer")
    for (state in US.values()){
        println("$state state's total area is ${state.totalArea} and " +
                "Land area is ${state.landArea}" )
        println("Water area " + state.getWaterArea())
    }
}
```

Get a list of all the states using the `values()` function, iterate over it, and print the information on the screen:

```
Square kilometer
NEWYORK state's total area is 141297.0 and Land area is 122057.0
Water area 19240.0
VIRGINIA state's total area is 110787.0 and Land area is 102279.0
Water area 8508.0
HAWAII state's total area is 28313.0 and Land area is 16635.0
Water area 11678.0
NEWJERSEY state's total area is 22591.0 and Land area is 19047.0
Water area 3544.0

Process finished with exit code 0
```

Convert concatenation to template   21:1   LF÷ UTF-8÷ Git: dev÷

The enum class and interfaces

Just like normal classes, the enum class is also able to implement interfaces. In this case, each member in the enum class will be responsible for providing the function body of each function signature that is mentioned in the interface.

Let's create an interface, `printable`, with one function, `show()`. Create an enum class, `NEWS`, and implement the printable interface:

```kotlin
interface printable {
    fun show()
}

enum class NEWS : printable {

    NORTH {
        override fun show() {
```

```
            println("Can you explain to me what summer is")
        }
    }, EAST {
        override fun show() {
            println("Can you explain to me what cold is")
        }
    }, WEST {
        override fun show() {
            println("I know what winter and summer are")
        }
    }, SOUTH {
        override fun show() {
            println("Oh .. its humid here...")
        }
    }
}
```

As we can see, each enum member has implemented the `show` override function.

Call the enum class in the `main` function and see the output:

```
fun main(args: Array<String>) {

    var item = NEWS.valueOf("EAST")
    item.show()

    item = NEWS.valueOf("SOUTH")
    item.show()
}
```

Each item of the enum class displays the appropriate message, as we can see in the following output:

```
Can you explain to me what cold is
Oh .. its humid here...
```

Objects and companion objects

The term **singleton** refers to a class that contains only one instance during the application life cycle. This instance is globally available for all functions and classes. Compared to Java or other programming languages, Kotlin provides an easier way to create a singleton class using the `object` keyword:

```
object singletonClassName {
    properties
    fun function(){
```

```
        function body
    }
}
```

The singleton class is similar to other normal classes; it contains properties and functions and can implement interfaces. However, there are a few things that make this class unique:

- The `object` keyword is used for class declaration
- We cannot create an instance of this class
- We cannot declare a constructor with this class

Let's take an example of a `Button` class that has one property and one function:

```
object MyButton {
 var count = 0
 fun clickMe() {
    println("I have been clicked ${++count} times")
 }
}
```

The `object` keyword performs two important tasks for us. First, it creates the `MyButton` class, and then it creates a single instance of this class. This instance can be accessed using the class name:

```
fun main(args: Array<String>) {
    MyButton.clickMe()
    MyButton.clickMe()
}
```

The first call to the `clickMe()` function will increment the count and display the message. The second call to the `clickMe()` function will do the same, but this time it will display the count as = 2, because the instance of the class has already been created.

To make this clearer, let's create two different functions and call the `clickMe()` function from them:

```
fun click03() {
    MyButton.clickMe()
}

fun click04() {
    MyButton.clickMe()
}

fun main(args: Array<String>) {
    MyButton.clickMe()
```

```
    MyButton.clickMe()
    click03()
    click04()
}
```

Trigger the `clickMe` function by using the `MyButton` object function and the `click03`, `click04` functions.

Take a look at the following output:

```
I have been clicked 1 times
I have been clicked 2 times
I have been clicked 3 times
I have been clicked 4 times
```

As mentioned earlier, this class only creates one instance that is accessible globally. First, we call the `clickMe` function from `main` and then we call it indirectly using two other functions, `click03` and `click04`. The `count` property increases on each function call because the same instance of the class is used every time. In the next section, we will see how the `object` class works with inheritance and interfaces.

The object class with inheritance and interfaces

Like normal classes, the `object` class can also make the most of the benefits of inheritance. We can create a normal parent class that can be extended by the `object` class. In the following example, we have a class called `Parent` with one `callMySingleton` function. We also have one `MySingleton` object class, which extends the parent class. The `MySingleton` class overrides the `callMySingleton()` function:

```
open class Parent {
    open fun callMySingleton(){
        println("Parent class is called")
    }
}

object MySingleton : Parent() {
    override fun callMySingleton(){
        super.callMySingleton()
        println("my Singleton class is called")
    }
}
```

In the `main` function, we use a single instance of the `object` class, call the member function, and verify the output. The `object` class calls the function of the parent class with the `super` keyword and then prints its own output on the screen:

```
fun main(args: Array<String>) {
    MySingleton.callMySingleton()
}
```

The output of this is as follows:

```
Parent class is called
my Singleton class is called
```

The object class is also able to implement interfaces. The following example shows the `MyButton` class providing the implementation of a function that is declared in `buttonInterface`:

```
interface buttonInterface {
    fun clickMe()
}

object MyButton : buttonInterface {
    var count = 0
    override fun clickMe() {
        println("I have been clicked ${++count} times")
    }
}

fun main(args: Array<String>) {
    MyButton.clickMe()
    MySingleton.callMySingleton()
}
```

Companion objects

Other programming languages, including Java and C#, allow us to use static variables and static functions. We can declare functions as static when they are utility functions that should be accessible without having to create a `class` object. Kotlin, however, does not provide a static keyword for a variable or a function. Instead, it allows us to add a `companion` object inside the class to declare a static function or variable.

Let's take a look at how to declare a companion object.

Create a normal class called `Parent`. Within the `class` body, declare a `companion` object:

```
class Parent {

    companion object {

        const val count = 10
        fun companionFunction() {
            println("I am your companion")
        }
    }

    fun getCompanions(){
        companionFunction()
    }

    fun memberFunction(){
        println("I am your member function")
    }
}
```

Each function and variable declared within the `companion` object will behave as static. The `companion` object informs its main class that it is the `main` class' companion and that the main class can directly access all the member functions and variables.

`Parent` is a normal class that can access its own functions by creating a class instance. To access the members of the companion object, however, we don't need to create an instance of the `Parent` class. The members of the companion object are accessible directly by using the class name as a reference:

```
fun main(args: Array<String>) {
    Parent.companionFunction()
    println(Parent.count)

    val obj = Parent()
    obj.memberFunction()
    obj.getCompanions()
}
```

CompanionFunction will print the message and Parent.count will display the value in the count variable. The most important point is the getCompanions function, which can call the function from companion object:

```
/Library/Java/JavaVirtualMachines/jdk1.8.0_181.jdk/Contents/Home/bin/java ...
I am your companion
10
I am your member function
I am your companion

Process finished with exit code 0
```

```
Compilation completed successfully with 2 warnings in 7s 98ms (a minute ago)     6:1   LF :  UTF-8 :   Git: dev :
```

As we can see, obj is an instance of the Parent class that can call memberFunction(). All members of the companion objects are directly accessible using the name of the Parent class. We do not need to use the class name as a reference if we are calling the companion class function from inside our class body. The getCompanions() function within the Parent class body calls companionFunction() without using the class name.

We can also assign a name to the companion object. This doesn't make any difference, apart from improving the readability of the code. However, just because Kotlin allows us to assign a name to the companion object doesn't mean that we can declare another companion object in the same class with a different name. Kotlin only allows one companion object per class:

```kotlin
class Parent {
    companion object Static {
        const val count = 10
        fun companionFunction() {
            println("I am your companion")
        }
    }
}
```

Companion functions and interfaces

Interfaces can be implemented by `companion` objects as well as by `normal` and `object` classes. Let's take a look at how this can be done:

1. Create an `Employee` class with two properties, `name` and `id`, and an interface, `EmployeeInterface`, with `add` in the function signature:

```
data class Employee(val name: String, val id: Int)

interface EmployeeInterface{
    fun create(name: String, id: Int) : Employee
}

class EmployeeFactory {

    companion object : EmployeeInterface{

        override fun add(name:String, id: Int): Employee {
            return Employee(name,id)
        }
    }
}
```

This function takes two variables and returns the `Employee` object.

2. Create a class, `EmployeeFactory`, and implement the interface in the `companion` object. Provide the implementation of the `add` function, which is declared in `EmployeeInterface`:

```
fun main(args: Array<String>) {
    val emp1 = EmployeeFactory.add("Abid",1);
    val emp2 = EmployeeFactory.add("Igor",2);

    println(emp1)
    println(emp2)
}
```

We can now call the `add` function from the companion object using the `EmployeeFactory` class and get the `employee` object successfully. Verify this by printing each object on the screen. The output will be as follows:

```
Employee(name= Abid, id=1)
Employee(name= Igor, id=2)
```

Aggregation, composition, and nested classes

When a class inherits another class, we often say that the child class is a kind of parent class. If a car takes the benefits of a vehicle class, for example, we say that a car is a kind of vehicle. In inheritance, classes always have an **is-a** relationship. In this section, we will discuss two more important topics related to object-oriented programming, in which classes have a **has-a** relationship instead. These concepts are aggregation and composition. Let's start by looking at aggregation.

Aggregation

When an object contains another object in its body, the relationship between them is called **aggregation**. This is a loosely-coupled relationship between two objects, in which one object is not completely dependent on the other. Take a look at the following examples:

- A room has a chair
- A garden has a plant
- A dog has a master

This relationship is called a **has-a** relationship because one object has another object. We cannot say that the plant is a garden, but we can say that the garden has a plant. An object can have a relationship with more than one object:

- A garden has many plants
- A company has employees
- A room has chairs

In this relationship, both objects are loosely coupled. This means that if one object is removed from the other object, both objects can maintain their state. Take a look at the following class diagram of aggregation:

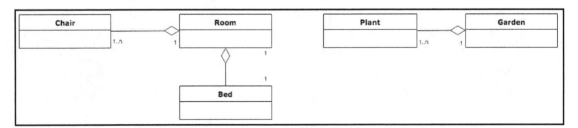

A room contains many objects, including beds and chairs. If we take the chair out of the room and put it in the garden, both the room and the chair will keep their functionalities, or if we remove a plant from the garden and put it in the living room, it would not affect the functionalities of other objects.

Let's consider another example. Nowadays, many people have pets. Some just have one and some have several. The relationship between the pet and the owner is aggregation; both the pet and the owner can live separately as well as together:

```kotlin
class Pet(val petname:String, val breed :String, var owner : Owner?){

    fun displayInfo(){

        println("Pet name is $petname, its breed is $breed")

        if(owner != null) {

            println("and its owner name is ${owner?.name}")

        }
    }
}

class Owner(val name:String, var age: Int)

fun main(args: Array<String>) {

    val bob = Owner("Bob", 35)

    val cat = Pet("Catty", "Ragdoll", bob)
    cat.displayInfo()

    val dog = Pet("Doggy", "Golden retriever", null)
    dog.displayInfo()
}
```

Execute the code and verify the output:

```
/Library/Java/JavaVirtualMachines/jdk1.8.0_181.jdk/Contents/Home/bin/java ...
Pet name is Catty, its breed is Ragdoll
and its owner name is Bob
Pet name is Doggy, its breed is Golden retriever

Process finished with exit code 0
```

Compilation completed successfully wit... (a minute ago)   517 chars, 25 line breaks   3:1   LF ÷ UTF-8 ÷ Git: dev ÷

In this example, we have the `Owner` class, which has a name and age. We also have the `Pet` class, which has three properties: name, breed, and a nullable owner class object. The `cat` object of the `Pet` class contains all information, including its owner, but the `dog` object does not have any owner. The `displayInfo()` function of the `Pet` class verifies whether a pet has an owner. If it does, it will display the details of the owner on the screen. Otherwise, it will skip this information.

Composition

Composition is an advanced form of aggregation, where two objects are highly dependent on each other. In aggression, one object contains the other object, whereas in composition, one object owns the other object. When the object that owns the other is destroyed, the object that is owned is also destroyed. In composition, an object may be composed of small objects. The human body is a good example: a person is composed of a head, arms, legs, and more. Each part of our body is a fully-working object with its own characteristics and behaviors. We can talk, listen, and see using our head, we can walk using our legs, and we can hold different objects using our hands. If a person dies, however, the objects stop working and die as well. A chair is another useful example, as it is made up of different objects including a seat, wooden legs, arms, and a back.

Take a look at the following class diagram of composition:

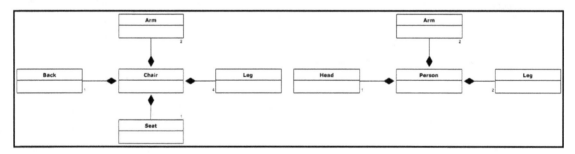

Let's take an example of a `Person` class, where the person is an employee of a company. Create a class called `Job` with the company information, including `department` and `salary`:

```
class Job (val companyName : String, var department : String, var salary :
Long)
```

Create another `Person` class with three properties: name, age, and a `job` object:

```kotlin
class Person(val name: String, var age : Int, val job: Job){

    fun getSalary() : Long {
        return job.salary
    }

    fun getCompanyName() : String {
        return job.companyName
    }

    fun geDepartmentName() : String {
        return job.department
    }

    fun info(){
        println("===================================")
        println("Person name $name , age $age")
        println("Company Name : ${getCompanyName()}")
        println("Department Name : ${geDepartmentName()}")
        println("Salary : ${getSalary()}")
        println("===================================")
    }
}
```

Create an instance of a job with its required parameters and pass this instance to the `Person` class object. Use the `Job` class object in the `person` class and extract the company, department, and salary information from the `job` object:

```kotlin
fun main(args: Array<String>) {
    val job = Job("Microsoft", "Research and Development", 8000)
    val bob = Person("Bob", 35, job)
    bob.info()
}
```

Execute this example and verify the output:

```
/Library/Java/JavaVirtualMachines/jdk1.8.0_181.jdk/Contents/Home/bin/java ...
===================================
Person name Bob , age 35
Company Name : Microsoft
Department Name : Research and Development
Salary : 8000
===================================

Process finished with exit code 0
```

Compilation completed successfully with 9 warnings in 10s 808ms (m.. 154 chars, 8 line breaks   38:1 LF: UTF-8: Git: dev:

Nested classes

If you have worked with C# or Java, you're likely to be already familiar with the declaration of a class inside a class. Kotlin provides a similar feature with more functionalities, which is useful when we need to encapsulate the functionalities of one class. Let's start with normal nested classes. Create a class called Outer with one property, out, and one function, info(). Now, create a nested class called Nested with one property, nest, and one function, info() . Both of the info functions in the Outer and Nested classes display messages on the screen:

```kotlin
class Outer{

    val out = "Outer class"

    fun info() {
        println("I am an outer class function")
    }

    fun getNestedClass() : Nested{
        return Nested()
    }

    class Nested {
        val nest = "Nested class"
        fun info() {
            println("I am a nested class function")
        }
    }
}
```

We can create an instance of the Outer class as we did before. To create an instance of the Nested class, however, we must use the Outer class name as a reference:

```kotlin
fun main(args: Array<String>){

    val outerObj = Outer()
    println(outerObj.out)
    outerObj.info()

    var nestedObj = Outer.Nested()
    println(nestedObj.nest)
    nestedObj.info()

    nestedObj = outerObj.getNestedClass()
    println(nestedObj.nest)
    nestedObj.info()
```

```
}
```

The `main` function contains `outerObj`, which is an instance of the `outer` class that can access its own properties. To create an instance of the `Nested` class, however, we have to use the `Outer` class name as a reference. Once the `class` object is created, we can use it as a `normal` object to utilize class members.

We can get the instance of the `Nested` class from the `Outer` class by creating a function:

```
class Outer{
    ::::::::
    fun getNestedClass() : Nested{
        return Nested()
    }
    class Nested {
        ::::::::
    }
}
fun main(args: Array<String>){

    val outerObj = Outer()
    println(outerObj.out)
    outerObj.info()

    var nestedObj = Outer.Nested()
    println(nestedObj.nest)
    nestedObj.info()

    nestedObj = outerObj.getNestedClass()
    println(nestedObj.nest)
    nestedObj.info()
}
```

The `Nested` class is not accessible if it is declared as private:

```
private class Nested {
    val nest = "Nested class"
    fun info() {
        println("I am a nested class function")
    }
}
```

It is very important to notice that neither the `inner` nor the `outer` class can access the members of the other class. If we want to access the members of the `inner` class, we must define it.

Inner classes

A class that is declared with the `inner` keyword is called an `inner` class in Kotlin. Let's extend the previous example by creating an `Outer` class with one additional property, called `counter`. Add the `inner` keyword with the `Nested` class and create an `incrementCounter()` that increases the counter value. Remember that the counter is not a `Nested` class property but instead an `Outer` class member. The `Nested` class is declared as an `inner` class so the members of the `Outer` class are directly accessible:

```kotlin
class Outer {
    val out = "Outer class"
    var counter = 0
    fun info() {
        println("I am an outer class function")
    }

    inner class Nested {
        val nest = "Nested class"
        fun info() {
            println("I am a nested class function")
        }
        fun incrementCounter(){
            counter++
        }
    }
}
```

Let's create instances of both classes and verify whether the `nested` class increases the value of the `counter` variable from the `outer` class by calling `incrementFunction()` from the `inner` class:

```kotlin
fun main(args: Array<String>) {

    val outerObj = Outer()
    val nestedObj = outerObj.Nested()

    println("Outer class counter before increment = "+ outerObj.counter)
    nestedObj.incrementCounter()
    println("Outer class counter after increment = "+ outerObj.counter)
}
```

Create instances of the `Outer` and `Nested` classes, and display the the output of `counter` by using `outerObj`. Call the `incrementCounter()` function by using `nestedObj` and verify the value of the `counter` property:

```
Outer class counter before increment  = 0
Outer class counter after increment  = 1
```

As we can see, the value of the `outer` variable is increased by the `incrementCounter()` function of the `inner` class. There is one more interesting point to discuss. Declare a new `counter` property inside the `inner` class and execute the program again. This time, `incrementCounter()` will increase the counter from the `Nested` class instead of the `Outer` class, so we can access the `Outer` class member only if the `inner` class contains a member with the same signature:

```
class Outer {

    val out = "Outer class"
    var counter = 0
::::::::::
    inner class Nested {
        val nest = "Nested class"
        var counter = 0
::::::::::::
        fun incrementCounter(){
            this@Outer.counter++
        }
    }
}
```

Use the `this@` keyword to access the `Outer` class and its member. Add the following line to the `incrementCounter()` function and execute the program. You will see the same output as before:

```
class Outer {

    val out = "Outer class"
    var counter = 0

    fun info() {
        println("I am an outer class function")
    }

    inner class Nested {

        val nest = "Nested class"
        var counter = 0
```

```kotlin
        fun info() {
            // this@Outer.info()
            println("I am a nested class function")
        }

        fun incrementCounter(){
            this@Outer.counter++
        }
    }
}
```

`this@Outer.counter++` will access the counter property of the `Outer` class and increment in it.

Class properties

In Kotlin, each class property is considered a first-class citizen, which we discussed in the *Properties – A first class citizen* section of `Chapter 2`, *Introduction to Object-Oriented Programming*. In this section, we will learn more about properties and how to define the `getter` and `setter` functions that are explicitly provided by Kotlin. Let's create a `Person` class with two properties, `name` and `age`:

```kotlin
class Person {
    var name: String = ""
    var age : Int = 0
}
```

Create an instance of the `Person` class. Assign some values to each property and display the values on the screen:

```kotlin
fun main(args: Array<String>) {
    val abid = Person()

    abid.name = "Abid Khan"
    abid.age = 40

    println(abid.name)
    println(abid.age)
}
```

When we assign a value to a class property, such as `abid.name = "Abid Khan"`, or get a value from the property, such as `println(abid.name)`, we are not actually reading or writing the property directly. Instead, Kotlin compiles this code in Java and provides the `getter` and `setter` methods under the hood. When we write `abid.age = 40`, Kotlin calls the `setAge()` function to set or update the value. We can verify this by using decompiled Java code. In the IntelliJ Idea menu, click on **Tools | Kotlin | Show Kotlin Byte code** and press **Decompile**. The following is the Kotlin-generated Java code for the `Person` class. Each property in Kotlin represents its own `getter` and `setter` functions:

```
public final class Person {
    @NotNull
    private String name = "";
    private int age;

    @NotNull
    public final String getName() {
        return this.name;
    }

    public final void setName(@NotNull String var1) {
        Intrinsics.checkParameterIsNotNull(var1, "<set-?>");
        this.name = var1;
    }

    public final int getAge() {
        return this.age;
    }

    public final void setAge(int var1) {
        this.age = var1;
    }
}
```

These are Java methods that are used to access the properties. To override these methods and write our functions, Kotlin provides each function with two fields. All properties of the Kotlin classes contain `get()` and `set()` functions for reading and writing purposes, and they each contain two built-in backing fields as well, which are `value` and `field`. Take a look at the following example:

```
class Person {
    var name: String = ""
    get() = field
    set(value) {
        field = value
    }
```

```
var age : Int = 0
get() = field
set(update) {
    if(update > 0)
        field = update
}
```

To read or access the property, we need to declare the `get` function right after the property declaration and use the implicit backing field that comes with each property and stores the actual data. We can access this backing field using the `field` keyword. Similarly, to set or write class properties, declare the `set` function either right after the property or after the `get` function. The `set` function takes one parameter, `value`, to update the backing field. The parameter value in the `set` function is not a fixed keyword; it can be replaced with something else. In the `set` function, we can verify the value before assigning it to the property as we did previously. We will update the `name` property if the received value is not empty, and update the age if the received value is positive:

```
fun main(args: Array<String>) {
val abid = Person()
abid.name = "Abid Khan"
abid.age = 40

println(abid.name)
println(abid.age)

abid.name = ""
abid.age = 0

println(abid.name)
println(abid.age)
}
```

To verify the `set` function, try to assign `name` and `age` properties with an invalid input; for example, a negative value for the age or an empty string for the name.

Delegate properties

Delegation refers to a situation in which we pass responsibility to someone else. In Kotlin, properties can either be accessed directly, or by using the `get` and `set` functions with the backing field. When properties are not backed by their own class but the responsibility is given to another class instead, these properties are called **delegate properties**. This might look strange at first, but when the class properties are more complex than simply storing values in fields, this feature becomes very convenient. First, let's have a look at how to delegate properties to the helper class. We'll start with a `Person` class with two properties, `name` and `age`:

```
class Person() {
    val name : String by DelegatePersonName()
    var age : Int by DelegatePersonAge()
}
```

There are two things to notice in the `Person` class: the `by` keyword and the class name after the `by` keyword. The `by` keyword shows that the `name` class property delegates its logic to the `DelegatePersonName` class. When we want to delegate the property, we need to implement the class that contains the following member functions:

- `getValue()`
- `setValue()`

For the immutable property, only the `getValue` function is required:

```
class DelegatePersonName {
    var value: String = "Default"

    operator fun getValue(person: Person, property: KProperty<*>): String
{
        println("Property ${property.name}")
        println(person.toString())
        return value
    }
}

class DelegatePersonAge {
    var age : Int = 0
    operator fun getValue(person: Person, property: KProperty<*>): Int {
        return age
    }
    operator fun setValue(person: Person, property: KProperty<*>, i: Int) {
        println("Class name: ${person}")
        println("Property: ${property.name}")
```

```
                age = i
        }
    }
```

Notice that the DelegatePersonAge class contains the getValue and setValue
functions, which are actually operators. The getValue function, as its name suggests,
returns the value when the property is being read, while the setValue function updates
the property when a new value is assigned to the class property. In each class, we need to
declare a backing field. For the DelegatePersonAge class, we have created a property
called age, while for the DelegatePersonName class, we have created a property called
value.

The setValue and getValue functions take two parameters: the first parameter is the type
of class that can use this delegated property, and the second parameter indicates which
value type will be passed to the function. If we pass property.name to the print function,
it will display the name of the property, the name for the DelegatePersonName class, and
the age for the DelegatePersonAge class.

After that, create an instance of the class and perform some read and write tasks:

```
fun main(args: Array<String>) {
    val person = Person()
 println(person.name)
 println(person.age)
 person.age = 40
 println(person.age)
}
```

Notice that the getValue function from the delegated class is triggered when the property
is read. The setValue function is called when the value is assigned to the property.

We can create a generic delegate that can work for any data type:

```
class DelegateGenericClass {
    private var value: Any = "Not initialized"
    operator fun getValue(instance: Any, property: KProperty<*>): Any {

        println("Class name      :   ${instance}")
        println("property name   :   ${property.name}")
        return value
    }

    operator fun setValue(instance: Any, property: KProperty<*>, type:
Any) {
        value = type
    }
```

```
    }
```

Create a class called `DelegateGenericClass` and declare a backing field value of the `Any` type. Declare the `getValue` function with a first parameter of the `Any` class and a return type of `Any` as well. Do the same with the `setValue` function. Now, create two classes, `Person` and `Student`, declare one property in each class (the `address` property in the `Person` class and the `age` property in the `Student` class) and delegate these properties to the generic class:

```
class Person{
    var address: Any by DelegateGenericClass()
}

class Student{
    var age : Any by DelegateGenericClass()
 }
```

Create an instance of the `Person` class and assign a string value to the address. After that, create an instance of the `Student` class and assign an integer value to it:

```
fun main(args: Array<String>) {
    val person = Person()
    person.address = "Stockholm City"
    println("Address "+person.address)

    val student = Student()
    student.age = 40
    println("Age " +student.age)
}
```

Notice that we have assigned a different type of value to each property but the generic delegate class works for both.

Built-in delegates

Aside from user-defined delegates, the Kotlin library also provides some useful built-in delegates that can be used in our applications. One of these delegates is the observable delegate, which triggers when a value is assigned to the property.

The observable takes the following parameters:

- The first parameter is the initial value of the property
- The second parameter is a lambda expression that takes the property type, the old value, the new value, and the body of the lambda expression

The following example shows the observable delegate with the age and name properties of the Person class. This delegate observes the properties and is triggered every time the value of the property changes:

```
class Person {
    var age : Int by Delegates.observable(0) { property, oldValue,
newValue ->
        println("oldValue $oldValue newValue $newValue")
    }

    var name : String by Delegates.observable("Default"){property,
oldValue, newValue -> shock(oldValue,newValue) }

    fun shock(old: String, new: String){
        println("Old name $old and New name $new")
    }
}

fun main(args: Array<String>) {
    val person = Person()
    person.age = 40
    person.name = "Abid"
    person.name = "Khan"
}
```

Notice that the age property is assigned with 0 and the lambda expression holds both the new and the old values:

```
oldValue 0 newValue 40
 Old name Default and New name Abid
Old name Abid and New name Khan
```

In the *Class properties* section, we learned how to protect the properties from an invalid input:

```
var age : Int = 1
    get() = field
    set(update) {
        if(update > 0)
            field = update
    }
```

Before updating the age property, verify whether the provided value is negative. To do this, Kotlin provides the vetoable delegate. Let's see how it works:

```
class Person {
    var name : String by Delegates.vetoable("Default",{property,
oldValue, newValue -> newValue.isNotEmpty()})

    var age : Int by Delegates.vetoable(1 ,{property, oldValue, newValue
-> newValue > 0})
}
```

In the Person class, we implement vetoable for both properties. The vetoable delegate takes the following parameters:

- The first parameter is the initial value of the property
- The second parameter is a lambda expression that takes the property type, the old value, the new value, and the body of the lambda expression

We can apply our logic in the lambda expression. For the name property, we implement logic that ensures we retain the value in the name property if the new property is empty. For the age property, we implement logic that ensures we don't update the age property if the new value is negative:

```
fun main(args: Array<String>) {
    val p = Person()
    p.name = "Bob"
    println(p.name)
    p.name = ""
    println(p.name)

    p.age = 10
    println(p.age)
    p.age = -6
    println(p.age)
}
```

We can verify this code by assigning both valid and invalid values.

Summary

In this chapter, we learned about some of the more advanced concepts of object-oriented programming and why it is better and more convenient than other programming languages. We started by exploring the concept of sealed classes and enumeration. We then moved on to discussing composition, aggregation, and nested classes. After that, we had a detailed discussion about singletons, objects, and companion object classes. We introduced a few more concepts to do with properties and looked at the `get` and `set` functions provided by Kotlin. We ended this chapter by exploring Kotlin's built-in delegates, which can make our lives easier. In the next chapter, we will discuss a very important and completely different topic, called data collection, iteration, and filters.

Questions

1. What is the difference between an object and a companion?
2. What are sealed classes and why do we need them?
3. What is the `Enum` class?
4. What is composition and what is aggregation?
5. What are delegates?

Further reading

- *Learning Object-Oriented Programming* by Gastón C. Hillar, published by Packt: `https://www.packtpub.com/application-development/learning-object-oriented-programming`.
- *Hands-on Design Patterns with Kotlin* by Alexey Soshin Published by Packt: `https://www.packtpub.com/application-development/hands-design-patterns-kotlin`.

5
Data Collection, Iterators, and Filters

This chapter covers the standard Kotlin library of collections. We will learn how Kotlin divides collections into two groups—immutable collections, which are read-only, and mutable collections, which allow us to update them. We will start this chapter by looking at the range collection and its functions. We will then explore arrays, their built-in functions, and arrays with lambda expressions. After that, we will move on to looking at immutable list types and will discuss iterables, collections, and list interfaces. We will then explore mutable lists, including mutable iterables, mutable collections, and mutable list interfaces. We will take a brief look at sets and maps, and finish this chapter by talking about iterators and types of iterators in Kotlin.

The following topics will be discussed in this chapter:

- Range
- Array
- Iterable
- Collection
- List
- Set
- Maps
- Mutable iterable
- Mutable collection
- Mutable list
- Iterators
- Filters

Technical requirements

Other than IntelliJ IDEA, this chapter does not require any specific installations.

The code for this chapter can be downloaded from the following GitHub link: `https://github.com/PacktPublishing/Hands-On-Object-Oriented-Programming-with-Kotlin/tree/master/src/main/kotlin/Chapter05`.

Range

Kotlin provides a collection of elements with a start and end point. This collection is called a range. The quickest way to create a range is as follows:

```
val range = 1..10
```

Kotlin provides a two-dot operator (`..`) to create a range. In the preceding example, we successfully created a range of integers that starts from 1 and ends at 10. Once the range has been created, we can iterate over and access each element using a `for` loop:

```
val range = 1..10
for (value in range){
     println(value)
}
```

We can also check whether a specific value is within a range by using the `in` and `!in` operators:

```
val range = 1..10
if(4 in range){
      println("Yes within Range")
}

if(14 !in range){
 println("Not in Range")
}
```

If range contains specified value, `4 in range` will return true and the `if` block will be executed. Otherwise, it will be skipped.

Types of ranges

Kotlin provides three different types of ranges: integer, long, and character. Each range can be declared with explicit type declaration:

```
val myIntRange  :  IntRange = 1..10
val myLongRange :  LongRange = 1..10L
val myCharRange :  CharRange = 'a'..'z'

for (ch in myCharRange) {
    println(ch)
}
```

Like other variables, a range can also be declared without explicitly declaring the variable type:

```
val IntRange = 1..10
val LongRange = 1..10L
val CharRange = 'a'..'z'
for (ch in myCharRange) {
    println(ch)
}
```

While declaring a range of long type, it is necessary to provide the L character with at least one of the elements to differentiate it from the integer type of range.

Declaring a range

While the two-dot operator (..) is a common way to create a range, there are few more functions that can be used to declare different types of ranges.

The rangeTo function

The rangeTo function is equivalent to the two-dot operator:

```
val myRange1 = 1..10
val myRange2 = 1.rangeTo(10)
println(myRange2)
```

The rangeTo function creates a range of integers up to a specified value.

The until function

If we want to exclude the last element of the range, we can use the until function:

```
val execRange1 = 1.until(10)
println(execRange1)
```

The until function can be declared as follows:

```
val execRange2 = 1 until 10
println(execRange2)
```

When demonstrating a range of character types in Declaring a range section, we created a complete alphabet using two dots. We can also do this using the to operator:

```
val alphabets2 = 'A' to 'Z'
println(alphabets2)
```

Another way to do this is by using ASCII code. 65 is the ASCII code for a capital A, while 90 is the ASCII code for a capital Z:

```
val alphabets3 = 'A'.until(91.toChar())
println(alphabets3)
```

Both ranges will display the same result—a complete alphabet in capital letters.

The downTo function

Neither the two-dots operator nor the rangeTo function can create a range in reverse order. We cannot, for example, write 5.rangeTo1 or 5..1. We can, however, use the downTo function to create a range in reverse order:

```
val range1 = 10.downTo(1)
for(i in range1) {
    println(i)
}

val range2 = 10 downTo 1
for(i in range2) {
    println(i)
}
```

Both range1 and range2 consist of numbers from 10 to 1.

The step function

The `step` function helps us to create a modified range from a range that has already been created:

```
val range1 = 1..10
val newRange = range1.step(2)
for(i in newRange) {
    println(i)
}
```

In this example, `step(2)` will skip every second element of the list. The preceding range, `range1`, will return a range of odd numbers. Similarly, `range2` will return a range of even numbers:

```
val range2 = 10 downTo 1
val evenRange = range2 step 2
for(i in evenRange) {
    println(i)
}
```

The contains function

The `contains` function is used to check whether a range contains a specific element:

```
if(evenRange.contains(2)) {
    println("Found")
}

if(oddRange.contains(3)) {
    println("Found")
}
```

This code checks whether the range of even numbers contains the element 2 and whether the range of odd numbers contains the element 3.

The elementAt function

This function returns an element at a specified index:

```
val myRange = 1..10
println("Element at index 1 =" + myRange.elementAt(1))
```

The `myRange` index starts from 0, so `elementAt(0)` will return 1 and `elementAt(1)` will return 2.

Range properties

Range provides two properties that allow us to access the first element of a range:

```
val myRange = 1..10
println("first " + myRange.first)
println("start " + myRange.start)
```

`first` and `last` properties are pretty much same, behind the scene `start` property calls `first` property.

It also provides two properties that allow us to access the last element of a range:

```
println("last " + myRange.last)
println("endInclusive " + myRange.endInclusive)
```

In these examples, the first block of code will return 1 and the second block of code will return 10.

The coerce functions

Kotlin also provides a useful collection of coerce functions. These are extension functions that take a range and a variable as parameters.

The coerceIn function

The `coerceIn` function verifies whether a given value is within the range. If the value is less than the starting point, the first element of the range will be returned. Similarly, if the value is higher than the ending point, the last element of the range will be returned. If the value is within the range, however, that value itself will be returned:

```
var i = 11.coerceIn(10..20)
println(i)
```

Here, `coerceIn` will return 11, because 11 is within the range. In the following example, `coerceIn` will return 10 because 9 is outside the range and less than the starting point:

```
i = 9.coerceIn(10..20)
println(i)
```

Similarly, in the following example, `coerceIn` will return 20 because 21 is outside the range and is greater than the last element:

```
i = 21.coerceIn(10..20)
println(i)
```

The coerceAtMost(maxValue) function

This function takes one parameter: a maximum value. The function returns the target value if it is less than or equal to `maxValue`, otherwise it returns the `maxValue`. The `coerceAtMost` function makes sure that the returned value is not more than `maxValue`:

```
val i = 2.coerceAtMost(4)
println(i)
```

Here, the answer will be 2, because the target value of 2 is less than `maxValue`, which is 4.

The coerceAtLeast(minValue) function

This function takes one parameter: a minimum value. It returns the target value if it is greater than or equal to `minValue`, otherwise it returns `minValue`. The `coerceAtLeast` function makes sure that the returned value is at least as great as the value that is mentioned in `minValue`:

```
val i = 2.coerceAtLeast(4)
println(i)
```

Here, the answer will be 4, because `minValue` is greater than the target value, 2.

Arrays

A variable that refers to a block of memory that can hold multiple values in a sequence is called an array. The individual value in an array is called an element and each element is assigned a number, which starts from zero.

These numbers are called the indexes of the array:

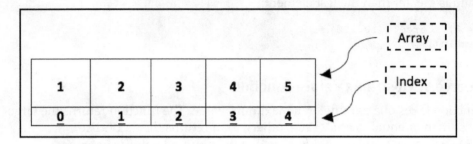

Defining arrays

Kotlin provides different ways of defining an array. The simplest method is by using an `arrayOf` keyword with a list of comma-separated values:

```
val intArr = arrayOf(1,2,3,4,5)
val strArray = arrayOf("ONE","TWO","THREE","FOUR","FIVE")
val charArray = arrayOf('a','b','c','d','e')
```

The `arrayOf` function not only defines the array but also initializes it. The size of the array depends on the number of values that are assigned to it. We can check the size of the array using the `size` property:

```
val size = charArray.size
println("charArray size = " + size)
```

The type of array depends on the values that are assigned to it. for example `intArray`, is an array of integers, while `strArray` is an array of strings.

Arrays of a specific type

Kotlin allows us to define an array with an explicit type. We can create an array of integers, or characters, for example, using the `intArrayOf` and `charArrayOf` keywords:

```
var numbers = intArrayOf(1, 2, 3)
var chars = charArrayOf('a', 'b', 'c')
```

Remember that when we declare an array explicitly, we cannot assign a value other than the specified one. We also can't assign an array of a different type. In the preceding integer type array, we can't add a character value or a double value:

```
var numbers = intArrayOf(1, 2, 3, 4.0, 5.0)
```

In this case, the compiler will throw an expected type error.

Index of the array element

There are a number of ways to access the array elements. One method is to use the subscript operator, `[]`. Take a look at the following example:

```
val intArr = arrayOf(1,2,3,4,5)
var element = intArr[0]
```

An individual element can be referenced using the array name along with the `[index]` brackets, which contain the index. As we know, an index always starts from 0. If we create an array of five elements, we can use `index 0`, `intArr[0]`, to access the first element of array and `index 4`, `intArr[4]`, to access the last element of the array. Create an array of integer type and loop through it using a traditional `while` loop:

```
fun readyArrayByIndex(){
    val intArr     = intArrayOf(1,2,3,4,5)
    val arraySize = intArr.size

    var index = 0
    while(index < arraySize){
        println("At index $index Value ${intArr[index]}")
        index++
    }
}
```

Create a variable called `index` and initialize it with 0. In the `while` loop, assign the index variable to `intArr[index]` and increase the `index` value on each iteration.

The get function

Another way to access elements is by using the `get(index)` function. Pass the index number of the list item to the `get` function and it will return the item from the list. `intArr.get(0)` and `intArr[0]` are the same. See the following example, where the `while` loop increments the `index` value and the `get(index)` function returns the item:

```
index = 0
while(index < arraySize){
    println("At index $index Value ${intArr.get(index)}")
    index++
}
```

Both examples will give the same output.

The array and for loop

The `for` loop is used with all collection types, and arrays are no exception. We can access every element of the array using the `for` loop.

Take a look at the following example:

```
fun arrayAndForloop(){
    val strArray = arrayOf("ONE","TWO","THREE","FOUR","FIVE")
    for (element in strArray){
        println(element)
    }
}
```

On each iteration, the `for` loop fetches a value from `strArray` and assigns it to the element. We can use this value in the body of the loop.

Array declaration and initialization

In all of the examples that we have seen so far, we have declared and initialized different arrays at the same time. It is also possible, however, to declare the array first and initialize it later:

```
val intArray = IntArray(5)
```

Here, an array of integers with 5 elements is declared but is not yet initialized. When the array is declared, Kotlin initializes the array with a value of 0.

Values can be assigned in the same fashion by accessing the element's index:

```
intArray[0] = 1
intArray[1] = 2
```

Kotlin provides the `set` function, which is used to assign a value to an array.

The set function

The `set` function takes two parameters: an index of the array and a value to be assigned at that index:

```
intArray.set(2,3)
intArray[3] = 4
intArray.set(4,5)
```

Take a look at the following example:

```
fun declareAndInitArray(){

    var intArray = IntArray(5)
    intArray[0] = 10
    intArray[1] = 20
    intArray.set(2,30)
    intArray.set(3,40)
     for (element in intArray){
        println(element)
    }

}
```

The `set` function takes the 2 index with a value of 30 and the 3 index with a value of 40 to initialize the array.

Mutable arrays with immutable elements

Let's take a look at how the concepts of mutable and immutable types work in an array. The array size is immutable in any case; once the array has been declared, the size of the array cannot be updated. Sometimes, however, things get confusing when it comes to reassigning the variable. To understand this concept, let's take an example. Just like other variables, arrays can be declared with the `val` and `var` keywords:

```
val immutableArray = arrayOf(1,2,3)
var mutableArray = arrayOf(1,2,3)
```

Both the `immutableArray` and `mutableArray` arrays are fixed in size, but the elements of each array are mutable and can be updated as many times as we want:

```
val immutableArray = arrayOf(1,2,3)
immutableArray.set(0,10)
immutableArray[1] = 20

var mutableArray = arrayOf(1,2,3)
mutableArray.set(0,10)
mutableArray[1] = 20
```

The only difference between these arrays is that `immutableArray` is declared with the `val` keyword. This means that this array cannot be reassigned:

```
fun mutableOrImmutable(){
    val immutableArray = arrayOf(1,2,3)
    immutableArray.set(0,10)
    // immutableArray = arrayOf(5,6,7,8,9,10)

    var mutableArray = arrayOf(1,2,3)
    mutableArray.set(0,10)
    mutableArray = immutableArray
}
```

`mutableArray`, however, can be reassigned as many times as we want.

Arrays with lambda expressions

Kotlin allows us to declare and initialize an array with a lambda expression. The array constructor takes two parameters: the size of the array and a lambda expression. If the array is an `IntArray`, the expression takes an integer and returns an integer as well:

```
public inline constructor(size: Int, init: (Int) -> Int)
```

Take a look at the following example. Here, `intArray` has 5 elements, and each element is initialized with an incrementing value that starts from 1:

```
fun arrayWithLambda(){
    val intArray = IntArray(5) { it }
    for (element in intArray){
        println(element)
    }
}
```

Kotlin not only declares an array of a size of 5, but it also initializes the array with a value passed to the lambda expression. The lambda expression takes one parameter, which means that the expression can be represented using the it keyword:

```
val doubleArray = DoubleArray(5) { it.toDouble() }
for (element in doubleArray){
    println(element)}
}
```

We can also create our own function to pass to the lambda expression. Create a function that takes one integer parameter and returns an integer:

```
fun func(i : Int) : Int{
    return i * i
}
fun arrayWithLambda(){
  val arr = IntArray(5){func(it)}
  for (element in arr){
      println(element)
  }
}
```

The elements will start from 0 and will increase on every iteration. The func function will return the square of each element. An array of size 5 is initialized with the values 0, 1, 4, 9, and 16.

Arrays of different elements

At the beginning of this section, we discussed the following methods of declaring arrays:

```
val intArray = arrayOf(1,2,3)
val charArray = arrayOf('a','b','c')
```

Using these methods, each array can contain values of the same types. Kotlin also allows us to create an array that contains different types of values. The arrayOf function not only takes a list of similar values but also takes a generic type, vararg. This stands for variable arguments, and we can use this type to pass mixed values:

```
fun funcVararg() {
  val array = arrayOf(1,"TWO",'c',4.0)
  for (i in array) {
      println(i)
   }
   println(array.contains(2))
   println(array.contains('c'))
```

```
    }
```

This code prints all the values on the screen and also verifies whether the specific values of 2 and c are in the array.

The arrayOfNulls function

Arrays can also be initialized with null. To do this, call the arrayOfNulls function and mention the type to be stored in it:

```
fun nulls() {
    val nullArray = arrayOfNulls<String>(5)
    nullArray.set(0,"hello")
    nullArray.set(3,"kotlin")

    for (i in nullArray){
        println(i)
    }
}
```

This code assigns string values to the 0 and 3 indexes and prints the null array on the screen.

Copying arrays

When assigning one array to another, Kotlin does not create a new copy in memory. Instead, both instances of the array point to the same location. When the source array is assigned to the target array, both arrays will be impacted if either is updated. To understand this problem, take a look at the following example:

1. Create an integer array, source, and assign it to a target array.
2. Print the target array on the screen.
3. Update the first element of the source array and print the target array. Notice that both arrays affect each other and that both arrays share the same memory location:

```
fun arrayInstance01(){

    val source = intArrayOf(1,2,3)
    val target = source

    // print target
    for (element in target){
```

```
        println(element)
    }

    // update source
    source.set(0,10)

    // print target
    for (element in target){
        println(element)
    }

    if(source === target){
        println("pointing to the same memory location")
    }
}
```

If we want an independent instance of an array, we need to create a new array and copy each element of the source array:

1. Create a `target` array that is the same size as the `source` array and use a `for` loop to copy each element.
2. Update the `source` array and verify that it does not affect the `target` array:

```
fun arrayInstance02(){

    val source = intArrayOf(1,2,3)
    val target = IntArray(source.size)

    for (i in 0 until source.size){
        target[i] = source[i]
    }

    // update source
    source.set(0,10)

    // print target
    for (element in target){
        println(element)
    }

    if(source !== target){
        println("pointing to different memory location")
    }
}
```

Kotlin also provides a `copyOf()` function to create a new instance of an array:

```
fun copyArray(){

    val source = intArrayOf(1,2,3)
    val target = source.copyOf()
    // update source
    source.set(0,10)
    if(source !== target){
        println("pointing to different memory location")
    }

    for (element in target) {
        println(element)
    }
}
```

The `copyOf` function creates an independent array of the same type.

Lists in Kotlin

Lists are widely used data structures that hold a number of items in a sequence. Lists are an advanced form of arrays, in which the items are formed in an order. Kotlin provides two different types of lists:

- Immutable lists
- Mutable lists

Lists that do not allow us to update their contents and provide only read-only functionality are called **immutable lists**. Lists that allow us to add new elements and update existing elements are called **mutable lists**. Kotlin provides a number of interfaces and methods that are made for both mutable and immutable lists.

Immutable lists

In this section, will discuss immutable lists and their interfaces. Before going into details, however, let's have a quick look at list declaration. Kotlin provides different ways to define a list, the simplest one being the `listOf` keyword with comma-separated values:

```
val listOfInteger = listOf(1,2,3,4,5,6)
val listOfDouble = listOf(1.0,2.0,3.0,4.0,5.0,6.0)
val listOfString = listOf("One","Two","Three","Four")
```

The `listOf` keyword not only defines the list but initializes it as well. The type of the list depends on the list elements, and the size of the list depends on the number of elements that are assigned to it. We can create lists of integers and strings and display each element using a `for` loop:

```
fun listInt(){
    val listOfInteger = listOf(1,2,3,4,5)
    for (element in listOfInteger){
        println(element)
    }
}

fun listString(){
    val listOfString = listOf<String>("One","Two","Three","Four","Five")
    for (element in listOfString){
        println(element)
    }
}
```

Notice that the `listOf` function can take a declaration of an explicit type, such as `listOf<String>`, but this is optional. Kotlin also allows us to create a list of different data types. In the following example, we have created a list of mixed variables, called `listOfEverything`, which contains integers, strings, and more:

```
fun listOfVararg(){
    val listOfEverything = listOf(1,"Two",'c',4.0,5)
    for (element in listOfEverything){
        println(element)
    }
}
```

Basically, this list is of the `Any` type, which is a root class in Kotlin; all classes are derived from the Any class. Using polymorphism, Kotlin allows us to add different data types in one list.

The listOfNotNull function

As we know, Kotlin is very strict when it comes to null objects. For this reason, we are provided with a dedicated list that ignores null objects if they are added. Create a list with the `listOfNotNull` function and add different variables, including nulls:

```
fun listOfNonNullObjects(){
    val notNulls = listOfNotNull(1,null,"Two",null,'c',4.0,5)
    println("Size = ${notNulls.size}")
```

```
    for (element in notNulls){
        println(element)
    }
}
```

If we take a look at the following output:

1, Two, c, 4.0, 5

we can notice that, although we have added seven objects in this list but we got five elements as an output because listOfNotNull does not insert null objects.

List access

There are a number of ways to access list elements, most of which are similar to the ways in which we access arrays. We can access each element of the list by using either the [ ] subscript operator or the get function:

```
val listOfString = listOf<String>("One", "Two", "Three", "Four", "Three",
"Five")
var element = listOfString[0]
element = listOfString.get(1)
```

listOfString[0] returns One and listOfString.get(1) returns Two.

We can get the index of a specific value in the list using the indexOf function. The following function, for example, will return 2:

```
var index = listOfString.indexOf("Three")
```

If the list contains more elements of the same type, the indexOf function will return the index of the first element. The lastIndexOf function, however, can return the index of the last occurrence of a specific element:

```
fun readListByIndex(){

    val listOfString =
listOf<String>("One","Two","Three","Four","Five","Three")

    var element = listOfString[0]
    println(element)

    element = listOfString.get(1)
    println(element)

    var index = listOfString.indexOf("Three")
```

```
    println(index)

    index = listOfString.lastIndexOf("Three")
    println(index)

    println("With subscript [] operator")
    for (i in 0 until listOfString.size) {
        println("At index $i Value ${listOfString[i]}")
    }

    for (element in listOfString){
        println("Value $element at index
${listOfString.indexOf(element)}")
    }
}
```

The `get` function returns the element at a specific index, while the `indexOf` function returns the index number of a specific element.

Immutable lists and interfaces

In the previous section, we learned about list declaration, its implementation, and different ways to access list elements. This, however, is just the tip of the iceberg. Kotlin provides a rich library of list interfaces for both mutable and immutable lists. In this section, we will focus on immutable lists and their interfaces.

Iterable interfaces

This is a parent interface in the interface hierarchy. Any data structure that contains a sequence of elements inherits from this interface. The `Iterable` interface provides an iterator, which is used to iterate over the elements.

The `Iterable` interface contains only one function, which returns the iterator:

```
public interface Iterable<out T> {
    public operator fun iterator(): Iterator<T>
}
```

To expose the interface to the list, it is necessary to define it in the declaration of the list:

```
val iterableValues : Iterable <Int> = listOf(1,2,3,4,5)
```

Now, the `iterableValues` variable can access the iterator to iterate over the list:

```
val iterator = iterableValues.iterator()
```

The `Iterator` interface provides two functions:

- `hasNext()`: This functions returns `true` if the iterator finds the element in the list. Otherwise, it returns `false`.
- `next()`: This function returns the element of the list.

Consider the following diagram. The list iterator provides the `hasNext` and `next` functions. If the `hasNext` function finds an element in the list, it returns `true` as a result, and the `next` function takes the element and moves the iterator to the next element:

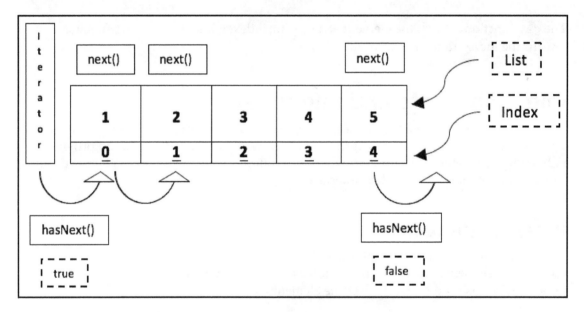

The following code is an exact representation of the preceding diagram:

```
fun iterableWithListOfInt(){
    val listOfInteger : Iterable<Int> = listOf(1,2,3,4,5)
    val iterator = listOfInteger.iterator()
     while (iterator.hasNext()) {
        print(iterator.next())
    }
}
```

The iterator iterates over the list and returns `true` if the `hasNext` function finds the element in the list. The `next` function returns the element and moves the iterator forward.

Collection interfaces

The `collection` interface is the main interface that represents a collection of items. The `collection` interface is a member of the immutable type of list and therefore provides read-only functionalities. The `collection` interface inherits the `Iterable` interface and provides its own functions:

```
fun collectionInterface(){
    val collectionValues : Collection <Int>     = listOf(1,2,3,4,5)
    val collectionIterator = collectionValues.iterator()
    while (collectionIterator.hasNext()) {
        print(collectionIterator.next())
    }
}
```

Take a look at the following diagram, which shows the properties and functions that are provided by the `collection` interface:

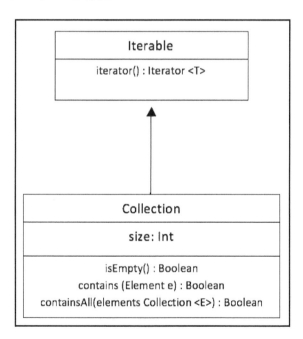

The following is a list of the properties and functions of the collection interface:

- `size`: This property return the size of the collection.
- `isEmpty()`: This function returns `true` if the collection is empty. Otherwise, it returns `false`.
- `contains()`: This function returns `true` if the specified element is in the list. Otherwise, it returns `false`.
- `containsAll()`: This function returns `true` if a list is a subset of a collection. Otherwise, it returns `false`.

Take a look at the following example:

```
fun collectionFunctions(){
    val collectionValues : Collection <Int> = listOf(1,2,3,4,5)
    println("Size ${collectionValues.size}")
    println("is collection empty: ${collectionValues.isEmpty()}")
    println("collection contains element 3:
${collectionValues.contains(3)}")

    var mini = listOf(2,3,4)
    var answer = collectionValues.containsAll(mini)

    println("Does collection contain mini collection: $answer")
}
```

The output of the preceding code is as follows:

```
Size 5
is collection empty: false
contains contains element 3: true
Collection contains mini collection true
```

List interfaces

The `list` interface is the last interface in the hierarchy related to the immutable collection. This is probably the most used collection in Kotlin.

The `list` interface inherits all functions from its parents interfaces and provides its own functions as well:

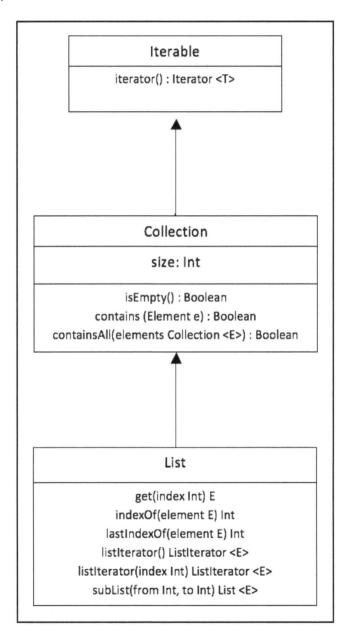

The list interface is an ordered collection, so we can access its elements using its index. Let's have a look at the functions it provides:

- get(index): This function returns an element at a specific index
- indexOf(element): This function returns the index of a specific element
- lastIndexOf(): This function returns the last value of the list
- subList(from, to): This function returns a subset from the list

At the beginning of this section, we created different types of lists using the listOf function:

```
val listOfInteger = listOf(1,2,3,4,5)
```

All of these lists are basically exposed by the List interface. The complete syntax of the list interface is as follows:

```
val listOfInteger:List<Int> = listOf(1,2,3,4,5)

fun listInterfaceFunctions(){

    val listOfInteger:List<Int> = listOf(1,2,3,4,5)
    var index = 0
    println("At index $index element ${listOfInteger.get(index)}")

    var element = 1
    println("List contains $element at index
${listOfInteger.indexOf(element)}")
    println("List contains $element at last index
${listOfInteger.lastIndexOf(element)}")

    println("Subset of list")

     val subsetOfList = listOfInteger.subList(0,3)
     for (value in subsetOfList){
         println(value)
      }
}
```

We have already discussed most of these functions in previous sections. The only new function is the `subList` function, which returns the subset of a list between specified indexes. This function takes two integer parameters. The first parameter represents the starting index and the second parameter represents the last index that is not included:

```
val subsetOfList = listOfInteger.subList(0,3)
```

The `subList()` function will return the first three elements of the list. The `List` interface provides two special types of iterators, which will be discussed in the *Iterators* section.

Mutable lists

In this section, we will discuss mutable lists in Kotlin. These lists are not write-protected, which means that we can add new elements, update existing ones, and remove any element from the list. Just like immutable lists, Kotlin provides dedicated interfaces and iterators for mutable lists, which contain useful sets of functions. Let's see how we can create a mutable list:

```
val list = mutableListOf(1,2,3,4,5)
```

The `mutableListOf` keyword is used to declare and initialize a list. The size of the list depends on the number of values, and the type of the list depends on the type of the value. Let's explore the interfaces of the mutable list and discuss all of the functions and iterators step by step.

The MutableIterable interface

This MutableIterable interface inherits the Iterable interface and contains its own mutable iterator. The mutable iterator provides a remove function, which removes the underlying element in the list. Take a look at the following diagram of the MutableIterable interface, which inherits the Iterable interface:

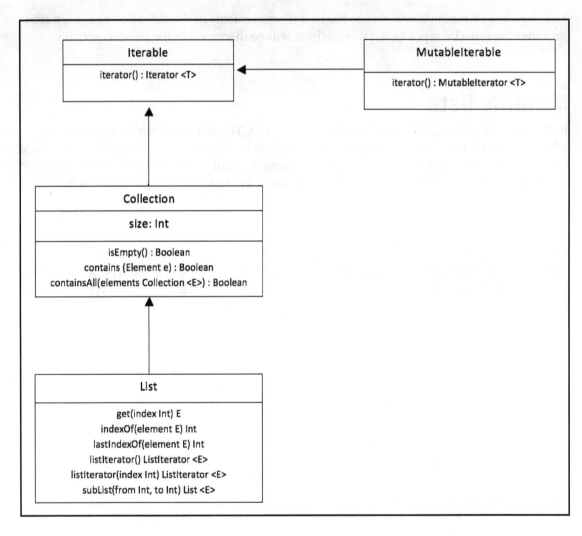

Create a mutable list and expose it with the `mutableIterable` interface.
Get `mutableIterator` from the list and use the `remove` function to remove the underlying
element of the list:

```
fun iterableIterface(){

    val mutableList : MutableIterable<Int> =
mutableListOf(1,2,3,4,5,6,7,8,9)
    val mutableIter : MutableIterator <Int> = mutableList.iterator()

    val element = 7
    while (mutableIter.hasNext()) {
        if(mutableIter.next() >= element) {
            mutableIter.remove()
        }
    }

    println(mutableList)
}
```

The mutable iterator extends the iterator interface so that we can use the `hasNext()` and
`next()` functions, along with `remove()`. This example removes all elements in the list that
are greater than or equal to seven.

Mutable collection interfaces

The `mutableCollection` interface extends two rich interfaces—the `mutable` iterable
interface and the `collection` interface. It provides its own functions to add or remove
elements. First, create a list of a mutable collection using the `mutableCollection`
interface. Take a look at the following example:

```
val mutableCollectionList : MutableCollection <Int> =
mutableListOf(1,2,3,4,5)
```

Take a look at the following diagram of the `MutableCollection` interface, which inherits both the `MutableIterator` interface and the `Collection` interface:

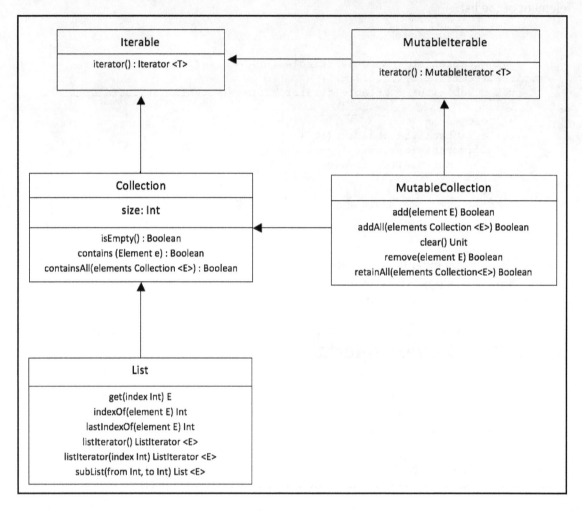

The `MutableCollection` interface provides the following functions:

- `Add()`: This function inserts an element at the end of list. It returns `true` if the operation is successful, otherwise it returns `false`:

```
var item = 6
var result = mutableCollectionList.add(item)
println("Item $item is added in collection = $result")
```

- Remove(): This function removes the first occurrence of the specified element. It returns true if the operation is successful, otherwise it returns false:

```
item = 7
mutableCollectionList.remove(item)
```

- retainAll(): This function takes a list as a parameter. It removes all elements from the main list, except the elements in the list parameter. It returns true if the operation is successful, otherwise it returns false:

```
val retain = listOf(2,4,6,8)
mutableCollectionList.retainAll(retain)
```

- addAll(): This function inserts another list at the end of main list. It returns true if the operation is successful, otherwise it returns false. Create a list called miniCollection and insert it in the main list as follows:

```
var miniCollection = listOf(9,8,7)
result = mutableCollectionList.addAll(miniCollection)
println("Mini collection is added in collection = $result")
```

- clear(): This function removes all elements from the list:

```
mutableCollectionList.clear()
if (mutableCollectionList.size == 0 ) {
    println("List is clear, add mini collection")
    mutableCollectionList.addAll(miniCollection)
}
println(mutableCollectionList)
```

Mutable list interfaces

This is the most powerful collection among all the lists in this hierarchy because it inherits all the functions from both sides – from the MutableCollection interface as well as the List interface, and it contains its own functions too. We can declare a mutable list interface by using the MutableList keyword.

Take a look at the following example:

```
val mutableListValues : MutableList<Int> = mutableListOf(1,2,3,4,5)
```

Take a look at the following diagram, which shows the `MutableList` interface:

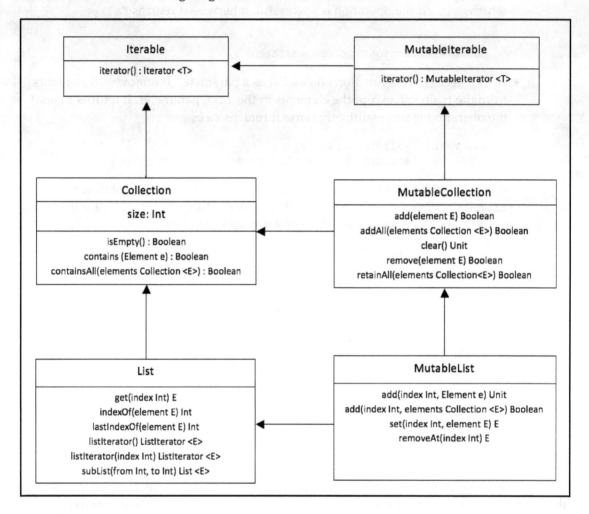

Mutable list interfaces provide the following functions:

- `add(index, item)`: As we have seen, the `MutableCollection` interface provides the `add` function, which inserts the element at the end of the list. The `MutableList` interface, however, provides an `add` function that inserts a value at a specific location.

For example, the following function will insert element 0 at the beginning of the list:

```
mutableListValues.add(0,0)
```

The first parameter represents the list index and the second parameter is an element to insert at the specified index. For example, we can add item 9 at index 3 as follows:

```
mutableListValues.add(3,9)
```

Add item 6 at the end of the list, as follows:

```
mutableListValues.add(6)
mutableListValues.add(mutableListValues.size,6)
```

When inserting an item in a list, make sure that the index is within the correct range. Kotlin will throw an out-of-bounds exception if, for example, the list contains 5 elements and the item is inserted at index 9.

- addAll (index, list): The addAll function allows us to insert a new list at a specified location. It takes an index and a list. It returns true if the operation is successful, otherwise it returns false:

```
fun mutableLisFunctionAddAll(){
    val mutableListValues : MutableList<Int> =
mutableListOf(1,2,3,4,5)
    println(mutableListValues)

    var miniCollection = listOf(9,9,9)
    if (mutableListValues.size > 1) {
        var result = mutableListValues.addAll(1,miniCollection)
        println("Mini list is added = $result")
    }
    println(mutableListValues)
}
```

Here, a list is initialized with the values (1, 2, 3, 4, 5). Then, we create another list. Before inserting the new list into the main list, we first verify whether the list size is more than one. This is because we want to insert it at location 1. Once the list is inserted successfully, we get the following result:

```
Mini list is added = true
[1, 9, 9, 9, 2, 3, 4, 5]
```

- `set(index, item)`: The `set` function replaces the old value with a new one at the specific index. The `set` function takes two parameters—the index and the new value to replace. It returns the old value at the specified index. The following example will replace element 1 with 5 at index 0:

```
fun mutableLisFunctionSetRemove(){
    val mutableListValues : MutableList<Int> =
mutableListOf(1,2,3,4,5)
    println(mutableListValues)

    val replaceWith = 5
    val index = 0
    val replaced = mutableListValues.set(index, replaceWith)

    println("Element $replaced is replaced with element
$replaceWith at index $index")
    println(mutableListValues)
}
```

An alternative way to update the list element is as follows:

```
mutableListValues[0] = 5
```

- `removeAt(index)`: The `removedAt` function removes the element from the specified index. This function takes an index as a parameter and returns the removed value:

```
var index = 0
var removed = mutableListValues.removeAt(index)
println("Element $removed is removed at index $index")
println(mutableListValues)
```

Sets in Kotlin

This is a special type of collection that does not support duplication. It contains lists of unique values. Just like lists, there are two types of sets in Kotlin:

- Immutable sets
- Mutable sets

In this section, we will start by looking at the immutable set.

Immutable sets

We can create an immutable set using the `setOf` keyword. The `set` element is inherited from the `collection` interface, which means that it is the immutable type collection that provides read-only functionality. Create a set and add some duplicate values in it:

```
val setItems = setOf(1,1,2,3,3,4,5,5)
```

Now, check the size of this collection. As mentioned earlier, sets don't support duplicate elements, so the size of the collection will be 5 instead of 8:

```
println("Set size ${setItems.size}")
```

Sets don't contain their own functions, but they do override all functions from the `collection` interface. We can check the presence of any element by using the `contains` function:

```
var element = 5
var result = setItems.contains(element)
println("Set $setItems contains $element")
```

We can also use the `containsAll` function to check whether a list contains another list. When it comes to finding a list, the `containsAll` function takes care of duplicates values:

```
val setItems = setOf(1,1,2,3,3,4,5,5)
var miniCollection = listOf(1,1,2,3,3)

result = setItems.containsAll(miniCollection)
println("setItems contains $miniCollection =  $result")

miniCollection = listOf(1,2,3,4)
result = setItems.containsAll(miniCollection)
println("setItems contains $miniCollection =  $result")
```

The `containsAll` function returns `true` for both single and duplicate values.

Mutable sets

A **mutable set** is an extension of a set that supports adding and removing elements. Like a set, a mutable set does not provide its own function, but it does extend two interfaces: set and `mutableCollection`. Mutable sets also override all functions from their parent interfaces. This means that we can use all functions, including `size`, `isEmpty`, add, `contains`, and `retainAll`:

```
fun mutableSetFunction() {

    val mutableSetItems : MutableSet<Int>    =
mutableSetOf(1,1,2,3,3,4,5,5)
    var mutableSetIterator =  mutableSetItems.iterator()

    while (mutableSetIterator.hasNext()) {
        print(mutableSetIterator.next())
    }

    println("")
    println("Set size ${mutableSetItems.size}")

    var item = 5
    var result = mutableSetItems.contains(item)
    println("Mutable item contains $item = $result")

    result = mutableSetItems.remove(item)
    println("Mutable item removed $item = $result")

    item = 6
    println("$item is added")
    mutableSetItems.add(item)
    println(mutableSetItems)

    // Keep only mentioned items in list
    mutableSetItems.retainAll(listOf(2,4,6,8))

    // Clear all items
    mutableSetItems.clear()

    var miniCollection = listOf(1,1,2,3,3)
    if (mutableSetItems.size == 0 ) {
        println("List is clear, add mini collection")
        mutableSetItems.addAll(miniCollection)
        println(mutableSetItems)
    }
}
```

Implement this example and check each function of the mutable set one by one.

Map

A list contains a collection of single objects. Maps, on the other hand, are data structures that hold collections of key value pairs. In Kotlin, there are three different types of pairs:

- Pairs of strings: `<String,String>`
- Pairs of ints: `<Int,Int>`
- Pairs of an init and a string: `<Int,String>`

The following is an example of a pair:

```
var p1 = Pair(1,"One")
var p2 = 2 to "Two"
```

Just like other Kotlin collections, there are two types of maps:

- Immutable maps
- Mutable maps

In this section, we will start by looking at immutable maps.

Immutable maps

Create an immutable map using the `mapOf` function and insert different pairs that contain `init` as a key and a string as a value:

```
val map: Map<Int,String> = mapOf( Pair(1,"One"), Pair(2,"Two"),
,Pair(3,"Three"), 4 to "Four", 5 to "Five")
```

Take a look at the following diagram of the `Map` interface:

Map
size: Int
keys: Set<K>
values: Collection<V>
entries: Set<Map.Entry<K, V>>
isEmpty(): Boolean
containsKey(key: K): Boolean
containsValue(value: V): Boolean
get(key: K): V
getOrDefault(key: K, defaultValue: V): V

We can access each pair using a `for` loop. Pairs provide two properties: `key` and `value`. Take a look at the following example, which uses a `for` loop to print each pair:

```
for(pair in map) {
    println("${pair.key} ${pair.value}")
}
```

Like sets, maps do not support duplicate values. We can check this by adding more than one pair of the same type and printing the map on the screen:

```
val map: Map<Int,String> = mapOf( Pair(1,"One"), Pair(1,"One"),
Pair(2,"Two"), Pair(3,"Three"), 4 to "Four", 5 to "Five")
```

Here, the map will only contain one `Pair` of the `(1, "One")` value.

Maps provide a number of useful functions and properties:

- **Size**: This property returns the size of a map.
- **isNotEmpty()**: This returns `true` if the map is empty. Otherwise, it returns `false`:

```
if( map.isNotEmpty()) {
    println("Map size is  ${map.size}" )
}
```

- **Keys and values**: These properties return the set of keys and the set of values:

```
val setofkeys = map.keys
println("Keys $setofkeys")

val setofvalues = map.values
println("Values $setofvalues")
```

- **Entries**: This property returns a set of pairs:

```
val setOfPairs = map.entries
for ((key, value) in setOfPairs) {
    println("$key $value")
}
```

- **get(key)**: The `get` function takes a key as a parameter and fetches the value from the list. It returns null if the key does not exist.
- **containsKey(key)**: The `containsKey` function takes `key` as a parameter. It returns `true` if the key exists, otherwise it returns `false`:

```
var key = 1
if(map.containsKey(key)) {
    val value = map.get(key)
    println("key: $key value: $value")
}
```

As we know, the `get` function will return null if `map` does not contain the key, so it is necessary to provide a nullable data type. Create a function that takes an integer as a parameter and returns a string. The `daysOfWeek` map contains an `init` and string pair, and the `get` function returns a value against `key`, which is the number of the day. If the `get` function cannot find a key, it will return null. To make this function compilable, we must declare the result and the function return type to be nullable (`?`):

```
fun mapDaysOfWeek(day: Int): String? {
    var result : String?
    val daysOfWeek: Map<Int, String> = mapOf(1 to "Monday", 2 to
"Tuesday", 3 to "Wednesday", 4    to "Thrusday", 5 to "Firday", 6
to "Saturday", 7 to "Sunday")

    result = daysOfWeek.get(day)
    return result
}
```

- **getOrDefault()**: To avoid the confusion of the nullable variable, we can use `getOrDefault`. While the `get` function returns null if the key does not exist, this function returns a default value instead:

```
fun mapDaysOfWeek(day: Int): String {

    var result : String
    val daysOfWeek: Map<Int, String> = mapOf(1 to "Monday", 2 to
"Tuesday", 3 to "Wednesday", 4 to "Thrusday", 5 to "Firday", 6 to
"Saturday", 7 to "Sunday")
    result = daysOfWeek.getOrDefault(day, "Invalid input")
    return result
}

fun main(args: Array<String>) {
    var result = mapDaysOfWeek(1)
    println(result)
    result = mapDaysOfWeek(9)
    println(result)
}
```

Here, the first function call will return `Monday` and the second function call will return `Invalid input`.

Mutable maps

The mutable map supports adding and removing pairs, and provides a number of functions to update the existing collections. We can create a mutable map by using the `mutableMapOf` function:

```
val map : MutableMap<Int,String> = mutableMapOf ( Pair(1,"One"),
Pair(1,"One"), Pair(2,"Two"), Pair(3,"Three"))
```

Take a look at the following diagram of the `MutableMap` interface:

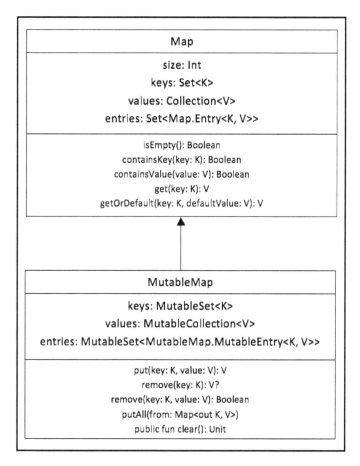

The mutable map provides the following functions:

- `put(Pair)`: This function inserts a pair at the end of the map:

```
val result = map.put(4 ,"Four")
```

It returns null if the new pair is successfully inserted. Maps can't contain duplicate keys, so if the key already exists, the put function will replace the value with the existing one and return the value of the existing key:

```
var result = map.put(4 ,"Four")
result = map.put(4 ,"FOUR")
println(map)
println(result)
```

- `remove(key)`: This function is used to remove a pair from a map using a key. It returns null if the pair is successfully removed, otherwise it returns null.
- `remove(key,value)`: While the `remove(key)` function removes the pair from the map, the `remove(key,value)` function goes one step further and asks for both the key and the value to make sure that the desired pair is removed. It returns `true` if it is successful, otherwise it returns `false`:

```
fun mutableMapRemove() {

    val map : MutableMap<Int,String> = mutableMapOf (
    Pair(1,"One"),Pair(2,"Two"), Pair(3,"Three"), Pair(4,"Four"))
        println(map)

        var result = map.remove(4)
        println("Remove " + result)

        var success = map.remove(2,"Two")
        println("Remove " + success)

        println(map)
}
```

- `clear()`: The `clear` function removes all pairs from the map. Although it removes all the elements, it doesn't remove the map itself.
- `putAll()`: The `putAll` function is used to add an independent map in an existing one:

```
fun clearAndPutAll() {

    val map : MutableMap<Int,String> = mutableMapOf (
    Pair(1,"One"), Pair(2,"Two"),   Pair(3,"Three"))
        println(map)

        val miniMap = mapOf(Pair(4,"Four"),Pair(5,"Five"))
        map.putAll(miniMap)
        println(map)

        map.clear()
        println(map)

        map.putAll(miniMap)
        println(map)
}
```

First, create a map and display it on the screen. Then, create another map and add it in the existing one using the `putAll` function. After that, verify the main map by printing it on the screen. Once you have finished, clear the map using the `clear` function and add `miniMap` using the `putAll` function.

Iterators in Kotlin

In the previous section, we looked at different examples of iterable collections and lists. Each of these contains an iterator, which is used to iterate on the list. Kotlin provides different iterators for different types of collections. In this section, we will discuss each iterator in detail.

Iterators

This is the parent or base interface in the iterator hierarchy. This iterator can be accessed by any list using `list.iterator()`. This is why iterators can work with lists, collections, and mutable lists:

Iterator
next() : T
hasNext(): Boolean

The iterator contains two functions that help to access elements:

- `hasNext()`: This returns `true` if the iterator finds an item to iterate on. Otherwise, it returns `false`.
- `next()`: This returns an element of the list and moves the cursor forward:

```kotlin
fun iteratorFunction() {
    val list = listOf(1,2,3,4,5)
    var listIterator = list.iterator()

    while (listIterator.hasNext()) {
        println(listIterator.next())
    }
}
```

Use the `hasNext` function to verify whether an item is in the list. You can get an element using the `next()` function.

List iterators

The `list` iterator extends from the iterator interface and also has some additional functions. While the iterator interface can only move in one direction, the `list` iterator can move in both directions. It can check the next element with the `hasNext()` function, and it can also check the previous function with the `hasPrevious()` function. Take a look at the following diagram of `ListIterator`, which inherits from the Iterator interface:

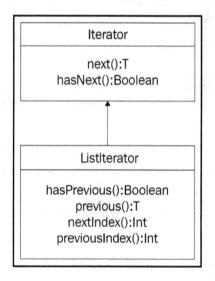

Let's have a quick look at all of the provided functions:

- `hasPrevious()`: This function returns `true` if the iterator finds an element at its previous location from its current location. Otherwise, it returns `false`.
- `previous()`: This function returns the previous element from its current location and moves the cursor backward.
- `nextIndex()`: `Int`: This function returns the next index from the current position.
- `previousIndex()`: `Int`: This function returns the previous index from the current position:

Take a look at the following example, where `ListIterator` is used to iterate over the list, moving forward and backward using the `next` and `previous` functions:

```
fun listIterator() {

    val list: List<Int> = listOf(10, 20, 30)
    var iteraror: ListIterator<Int> = list.listIterator()

    println("has next and next function")
    while (iteraror.hasNext()) {
        println(iteraror.next())
    }
    println("has previous and previous function")
    while (iteraror.hasPrevious()) {
        println(iteraror.previous())
    }

    println("nextIndex ${iteraror.nextIndex()}")
    println("next ${iteraror.next()}")

    println("nextIndex ${iteraror.nextIndex()}")
    println("next ${iteraror.next()}")

    println("previousIndex ${iteraror.previousIndex()}")
    println("previous ${iteraror.previous()}")
}
```

Verify each function of the iterator by looking at the result.

Mutable iterators

The `mutable` iterator extends from the iterator interface as well. As indicated by its name, this iterator works with mutable lists and can help to remove the underlying item in the list.

Take a look the following diagram of the `MutableIterator` interface, which inherits the `Iterator` interface:

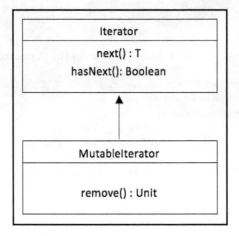

This interface provides only one function, which is `remove()`. This function removes the current element of the list.

The following example removes all items that are equal to 3:

```
fun mutableIterator(){

    val mutableListValues : MutableList<Int> = mutableListOf(1,2,3,4,5)
    val mutableIterator : MutableIterator<Int> =
mutableListValues.listIterator()

    while(mutableIterator.hasNext()) {
        if(mutableIterator.next() == 3) {
            mutableIterator.remove()
        }
    }
}
```

The `next()` and `hasNext()` functions are from the `iterator` interface and the `remove()` function is from the `mutableIterator` interface. The iterator removes the element from the list if the underlying element is 3.

If the `iterator.hasNext()` function returns `true`, it is necessary to move the iterator onto the target element using the `next()` function.

Execute the following example:

```
while(mutableIterator.hasNext()) {
    mutableIterator.remove()
}
```

If the `remove()` function is called before calling the `next()` function, Kotlin will throw `IllegalStateException`.

Mutable list iterators

This is the most powerful iterator. The mutable list iterator extends both the list iterator and the `MutableListIterator` interface, and has its own functions. In the following diagram, we can see how `MutableListIterator` inherits both `MutableIterator` and `ListIterator`:

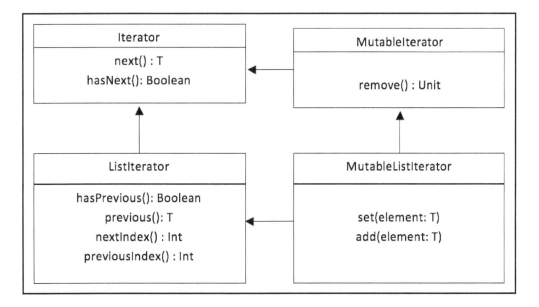

Let's take a look at the functions provided:

- `add(element)`: The `add` function inserts the element in the list. The element will either be inserted before the element that is returned by the `next()` function or after the element that is returned by the `previous()` function:

```
fun mutableListIteratorFunctionAdd() {

    val mutableListValues: MutableList<Int> = mutableListOf(2, 3, 6)
    var mutableListIterator: MutableListIterator<Int> =
mutableListValues.listIterator()

    while (mutableListIterator.hasNext()) {
        if (mutableListIterator.next() == 3)
            mutableListIterator.add((4))
    }

    println(mutableListValues)
    while (mutableListIterator.hasPrevious()) {
        if (mutableListIterator.previous() == 6)
            mutableListIterator.add((5))
    }
    println(mutableListValues)
}
```

- `set(element)`: The `set()` function updates the element that is called by `next()` or `previous()`:

```
fun mutableListIteratorFunction() {
    val mutableListValues: MutableList<Int> = mutableListOf(2, 3, 6)
    var mutableListIterator: MutableListIterator<Int> =
mutableListValues.listIterator()

    println(mutableListValues)

    while (mutableListIterator.hasNext()) {
        if (mutableListIterator.next() == 3) {
            mutableListIterator.set(4)
        }
    }
    println(mutableListValues)
}
```

Here, the `set` function has replaced element 3 with element 4.

Filters and collection functions

Kotlin provides a rich library of filters and collection functions. In this section, we will start by looking at filters, which help to filter out the desired results from the collection, allowing us to ignore unwanted elements. We will then move on to looking at collection functions, which are functions that are specially designed for collections.

The filter function

This is the most commonly used function in Kotlin. The `filter` function takes one lambda expression, which takes one variable as an input and returns the same variable as a result. The `filter` function applies the lambda expression and returns a list as a result. Let's create a list of integers and apply some filters:

```
var numbers = listOf<Int>(1,2,3,4,5,6,7,8,9,10)
```

We can filter out all elements that are greater than five as follows:

```
var newList = numbers.filter{ i -> i > 5 }
println("Filter out greater than 5")
println(newList)
```

`i` represents the element in the list and `i > 5` is a condition that filters the results. The lambda expression filters the elements and the `filter` function returns a new list.

We can filter out all elements that are smaller than or equal to five as follows:

```
newList = numbers.filter { i -> i <= 5 }
```

The it keyword

The `filter` function takes a lambda expression that takes one variable type as an input and returns a result. If the lambda expression deals with a single variable, it can be represented with the it keyword. We can write a filter that can filter out all the even numbers, as follows:

```
newList = numbers.filter { it % 2 == 0 }
println("Filter out Even numbers")
println(newList)
```

Instead of writing `i-> i % 2 == 0`, we can directly write it as `% 2 == 0`, which can handle everything by itself.

The filterNot function

filterNot is the opposite of the filter function. It takes a lambda expression and returns a new list. We can write a filter that can filter out odd numbers as follows:

```
newList = numbers.filterNot { it % 2 == 0 }
println("Filter out Odd numbers")
println(newList)
```

The filterNotNull function

The filterNotNull function ignores all null values and returns a new list without null elements. Let's create a list of different data types, including null values, and then apply the filterNotNull() function:

```
val list = listOf("One", 2, 3, null, "Four", null)
var newList = list.filterNotNull()
println(newList)
```

The output of the list is as follows:

```
[One, 2, 3, Four]
```

The filterNotNull function can be used instead of the listOfNotNull function, which is used to create a list of non-null elements:

```
var notNullList =  listOfNotNull(1,2,null,"Three","Four")
println("Not null $notNullList")
```

Here, any null value that is inserted is ignored.

The filterIsInstance<dataType> function

This function allows us to filter out elements of specific types. We can create a list of different elements and call the filterIsInstance<type> function by explicitly defining a data type that we want to filter out. Take a look at the following example:

```
val list = listOf("One", 2.0, 3, null, "Four", 5)

val stringList = list.filterIsInstance<String>()
println("Filter string elements")
println(stringList)

val intList = list.filterIsInstance<Int>()
```

```
println("Filter int elements")
println(intList)
```

The `filterIsInstance<String>` function will return a list of String elements, while `filterIsInstance<Int>` will return a list of Int elements.

The slice function

The `slice` function takes a list or range as an argument and returns a list of elements at specified list indexes.
Take a look at the following example:

```
var numbers = listOf<Int>(1,2,3,4,5,6,7,8,9,10)

var newList = numbers.slice(0..4)
println("Slice of first four elements")
println(newList)

newList = numbers.slice(listOf(1,4,8))
println("Slice of selected elements")
println(newList)
```

The `numbers.slice(0..4)` function takes a range from zero to four and returns a list of elements from index 0 to index 4 from the numbers list.

The `numbers.slice(listOf(1,4,8))` slice function can pick elements from different locations. In this example, the slice function picks elements 2, 5, and 9 from indexes 1, 4, and 8. Verify the output of the slice function by providing different values:

```
[1, 2, 3, 4, 5]
[2, 5, 9]
```

The take function

This is a very straightforward function. It accepts an argument to take a number of elements from a list:

```
var numbers = listOf<Int>(1,2,3,4,5,4,3,8,9,10)
var newList = numbers.take(5)
println("Take first 5 elements")
println(newList)
```

The `number.take(5)` function will return a list of the first five elements. The `take` function also has a number of variants.

takeLast

This function takes an argument to return the last elements of a list:

```
newList = numbers.takeLast(5)
println("Take last 5 elements")
println(newList)
```

The `number.takeLast(5)` function will return a list of the last five elements.

takeWhile

The `takeWhile` function accepts a lambda expression. This function keeps fetching elements until the condition is not satisfied:

```
var numbers = listOf<Int>(1,2,3,4,5,4,3,8,9,10)
newList = numbers.takeWhile { it < 5 }
println("Take all elements from the beginning of the list, until the
element is 5 or more").
println(newList)
```

Here, the output is [1, 2, 3, 4]. Notice that the numbers list contains a total of six elements that are less than five, but the `takeWhile` function immediately stops executing when the condition becomes `false`.

takeLastWhile

The `takeLastWhile` function also accepts a lambda expression. This function takes elements from the end of a list until the condition is not satisfied:

```
newList = numbers.takeLastWhile { it > 5 }
println("Take all elements from end of the list, which are greater than 5")
println(newList)
```

Here, the output is [8, 9, 10]. The `takeLastWhile` function starts executing from the end of the list and stops executing when the given condition becomes `false`.

The drop function

This is another very straightforward function. The `drop` function accepts an argument, ignores a number of elements from the main list, and returns a new list as a result. Take a look at the following example:

```
var numbers = listOf<Int>(1,2,3,4,5,4,3,8,9,10)
var newList = numbers.drop(5)
println("Drop first 5 elements")
println(newList)
```

The `drop` function drops the first five elements from the list and returns `[4, 3, 8, 9, 10]` as a result. The `drop` function has a number of other variants.

dropLast

The `dropLast` function ignores the last number of elements in the list:

```
newList = numbers.dropLast(5)
println("Drop last 5 elements")
println(newList)
```

dropWhile

The `dropWhile` function accepts a lambda expression. This function keeps ignoring the elements until the condition is satisfied and returns a new list as a result:

```
newList = numbers.dropWhile { it < 5 }
println("Drop from beginning : while element is less than 5")
println(newList)
```

dropWhileLast

The `dropLastWhile` function accepts a lambda expression. This function keeps ignoring the elements from the end of the list until the condition is satisfied:

```
newList = numbers.dropLastWhile { it > 5 }
println("Drop from end : while element is greater than 5")
println(newList)
```

The fold function

This function performs arithmetic operations on all the elements of a list and returns a result. To understand the concept of the `fold` function, we'll use addition as the operation. Let's add all the elements of the list and return a result. The `fold` function takes an integer parameter and a lambda expression. The first parameter indicates the initial value, and the second parameter takes a lambda expression for adding two values:

```
var numbers = listOf<Int>(1,2,3,4,5)

var result = numbers.fold(0){i,j -> i + j}
println("From beginning : add all elements of the list, Initial value is 0:
" + result)
```

The `fold` function takes 0 as an initializer, adds all elements, and returns a result. To understand how things works under the hood, create a function that matches the signature of the lambda expression that takes two parameters of the integer type and returns a result:

```
fun foldHelper(i : Int, j : Int) : Int{
    println("$i , $j")
    return i + j
}
```

We can print the the value of i and j, and return the value by adding them together. Pass `foldHelper` to the `fold` function, as shown here, and execute the program:

```
var numbers = listOf<Int>(1,2,3,4,5)
var result = numbers.fold(0, ::foldHelper)
println("Answer = " + result)
```

The output of this function will be as follows:

```
0 , 1
1 , 2
3 , 3
6 , 4
10 , 5
Answer = 15
```

On each iteration, the `fold` function takes an element from the list, assigns it to i, and stores it in j after the arithmetic operation. There are two variants of the `fold` function.

foldRight

To understand the concept of the `foldRight` function, we'll use addition as an operation. The `foldRight` function adds all the elements of the list and returns the result. Just like the `fold` function, it takes an integer parameter and lambda expression. The difference is that the `foldRight` function starts executing at the end of the list:

```
result = numbers.foldRight(0){i,j -> i + j}
println("From End : add all elements of the list " + result)
```

The reduce function

To understand the concept of the `reduce` function, we'll use addition as an operation. The `reduce` function adds all elements in the list and returns a result. The difference between the `fold` and `reduce` function is that the `fold` function provides an initial value, `fold(0){i,j -> i + j}`, but the reduce function does not, `reduce { acc, i -> i + acc}`.

The `reduce` function takes a lambda expression that takes two variables and returns a result, as follows:

```
var numbers = listOf<Int>(1,2,3,4,5)
var result = numbers.reduce { acc, i ->  i + acc}
println("From beginning : add all elements of the list $result")
```

The `reduce` function has two different variants.

reduceRight

The `reduceRight` function takes a lambda expression that takes two variables and returns a result. The difference between reduce and `reduceRight` is that the `reduce` function starts iterating from index 0 and `reduceRight` starts from the end of the list:

```
result = numbers.reduceRight { i, acc -> i + acc}
println("From end : add all elements of the list $result")
```

reduceRightIndexed

This function works exactly the same as the reduceRight function, except for the lambda expression, which takes three variables and returns a result:

```
result = numbers.reduceRightIndexed { index , i, acc -> i + acc }
println("From end : add all elements of the list $result")
```

Some important functions

Kotlin provides a huge amount of useful functions, but not all of them can be covered in this book. We highly recommend that you explore the Kotlin SDK and implement all of the functions to learn more about them. In this section, we will discuss some important functions that can be used in our everyday programming life.

foreach

The forEach function evaluates each element of the list:

```
var numbers = listOf<Int>(1,2,3,4,5,6,7,8,9,10)
println("Print all elements of list")
numbers.forEach{ println(it) }
```

forEachIndexed

The forEachIndex function evaluates each element of the list and provides the element's index:

```
println("Print elements with index")
numbers.forEachIndexed { index, element -> println("Element $element at
index $index") }
```

onEach

The onEach function evaluates each element of the list and returns the original list afterward:

```
println("Get original list back and print square of each element")
var newNumbers = numbers.onEach{ println(it * it) }
```

max and maxBy

The `max` function returns the largest value of the list. The `maxBy` function takes a lambda expression with one value. We can pass a negative value to the lambda expression to get the smallest value in the list, as follows:

```
println("Get max value ${numbers.max()}")
println("Get min value ${numbers.maxBy { -it }}")
```

min and minBy

The `min` function returns the smallest value of the list. The `minBy` function takes a lambda expression with one value. We can pass a negative value to the lambda expression to get the largest value in the list, as follows:

```
println("Get min value ${numbers.min()}")
println("Get max value ${numbers.minBy { -it }}")
```

Summary

In this chapter, we learned about the different types of collections, lists, and iterators, and how these can work together. We started this chapter by discussing the simplest forms of collection, ranges, and arrays. We then moved on to looking at immutable and mutable types of collections and their built-in functions. After that, we discussed different interfaces and the inheritance of these interfaces. We then talked about sets and maps and how these are different from arrays and lists. Later, we explored mutable and immutable iterators, and ended by discussing collection filters and collection functions in detail.

Questions

1. What is a range and what is an array?
2. What are immutable and mutable collections?
3. What is an iterator in a collection?
4. What are iterable collections and lists?
5. What are sets and maps, and why they are unique?
6. What are mutable iterators, mutable collections, and mutable lists?

Further reading

Learning Object-Oriented Programming by Gastón C. Hillar published by Packt: `https://www.packtpub.com/application-development/learning-object-oriented-programming`.

6
Object-Oriented Patterns in Kotlin

A pattern is a concept that relates to software architecture. By architecture, we mean a high-level structure of programming code that includes elements and relationships. It's important to make the right decision when it comes to a pattern that will be used to solve everyday problems. This is because choosing and implementing a pattern is a one-time procedure that is expensive to change.

Before we begin, let's review the topics we will be looking at in this chapter:

- What design patterns are and how they help
- Types of design patterns
- Creational patterns
- Structural patterns
- Behavioral patterns

Technical requirements

To run the code from this chapter, we just need IntelliJ IDEA as well as Git installed. This chapter doesn't require any additional installations.

You can find examples from this chapter on GitHub at the following link: `https://github.com/PacktPublishing/Hands-On-Object-Oriented-Programming-with-Kotlin/tree/master/src/main/kotlin/Chapter06`.

What design patterns are and how they help

The process of software development involves creating new classes and interfaces, building an inheritance hierarchy, and establishing communication between objects. Object-oriented programming helps us to build an abstraction of entities and processes using extremely powerful concepts such as encapsulations, composition, inheritance, polymorphism, and so on and so forth.

We should understand that a developer writes code to solve one or more sets of problems. Software designing is a process of describing how to apply the concepts of object-oriented programming together to implement a solution.

An implementation of a commonly occurring solution is a software design pattern if it can be reused in many different situations. The most common reasons to use a design template are as follows:

- Acceleration of the development process
- Increasing the quality of code
- Decreasing communication time between developers

Reusing patterns helps us to prevent common issues, which is why we can increase the quality of code. It also improves readability and understanding for developers who are familiar with a pattern that decreases the time for communication and code review. As a result, we can speed up the development process.

Software design patterns in object-oriented programming show relationships and communications between classes and objects. That's why using a **Unified Modeling Language** (**UML**) is a common practice for describing a structure and how to apply a template to your software design. The following diagram represents the **Strategy** pattern:

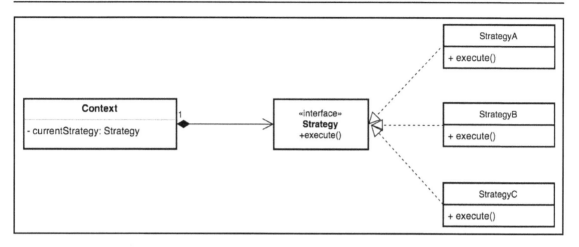

This diagram shows a relationships between classes and interface according to the Strategy pattern. We will go over this template further, but first let's look at types of patterns.

Types of design patterns

Software design patterns provide solutions to problems such as creating objects that require complex initialization or need to establish communication between objects. In addition, patterns define approaches to composing objects or building an inheritance hierarchy to obtain new functionality.

There are three types of design patterns:

- Creational
- Behavioral
- Structural

The following diagram shows the most common patterns, divided by groups:

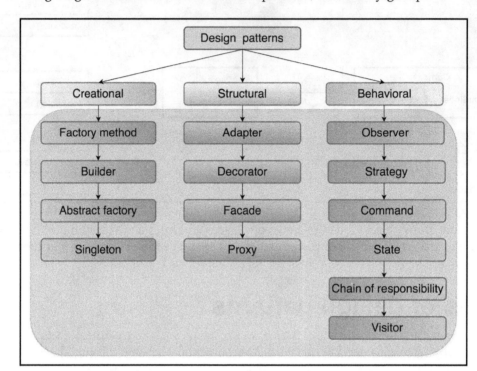

Creational patterns

It can be difficult to control the creation of objects that need complex initialization. In addition, sometimes, we need to decide which object in a class should be created at runtime. This can depend on a state or external values that became known just before a certain moment at runtime, for instance, values that are retrieved from a server or a file. The most common patterns that belong to the creational group are listed here:

- Factory method
- Builder
- Abstract factory
- Singleton

Structural patterns

This group of patterns helps us to organize the inheritance of hierarchy in such way that it allows our types to obtain new functionality or a simplified interface. We can also wrap an object with another one that restricts access to an interface of underlying instance. The following list contains the most common structural patterns:

- Adapter
- Decorator
- Facade
- Proxy

Behavioral patterns

If we need to dynamically change the behavior of an object, we should consider using behavioral patterns. This group is responsible for communication between objects, and it also contains the following patterns:

- Observer
- Strategy
- Command
- State
- Chain of responsibility
- Visitor

We will now dive deeper into each one of these design patterns.

Creational patterns

When we want to make the process of object creation more abstract or determine a certain type of object dynamically, we should consider using creational patterns. In addition, you can specify the order of field initialization or make the process of object creation more flexible. It's worth mentioning that since Kotlin has many more modern features in comparison with Java, the implementation of certain patterns may differ significantly. It's better to demonstrate this through the use of an example.

This section covers the following patterns:

- Builder
- Factory method
- Abstract factory
- Singleton

Builder

The Builder pattern is useful when we need to initialize many fields during new object creation. According to this pattern, instead of using a constructor with a lot of parameters, we can create a nested class that collects all passed arguments and constructs a new object. Let's look at the typical implementation of this pattern in a classic Java way. Let's imagine that we need to cook a burger. For this, we need to define classes of ingredients:

```kotlin
class Meat
class Cheese
class Ketchup
class Bun
```

We also need to define the `Burger` class, which encapsulates all ingredients:

```kotlin
class Burger {
    private val meat: Meat
    private val cheese: Cheese
    private val ketchup: Ketchup
    private val topBun: Bun
    private val bottomBun: Bun

    private constructor(meat: Meat, cheese: Cheese, ketchup: Ketchup,
topBun: Bun, bottomBun: Bun) {
        this.meat = meat
        this.cheese = cheese
        this.ketchup = ketchup
        this.topBun = topBun
        this.bottomBun = bottomBun
    }
}
```

The `Builder` pattern assumes that we use the nested `Builder` class that obtains all arguments and creates a new instance. This class can be written as follows:

```
class Builder {
    private var meat: Meat = Meat()
    private var cheese: Cheese = Cheese()
    private var ketchup: Ketchup = Ketchup()
    private var topBun: Bun = Bun()
    private var bottomBun: Bun = Bun()

    fun setMeat(meat: Meat): Builder {
        this.meat = meat
        return this
    }

    ///.............

    fun setBottomBun(bottomBun: Bun): Builder {
        this.bottomBun = bottomBun
        return this
    }

    fun build(): Burger {
        return Burger(meat, cheese, ketchup, topBun, bottomBun)
    }
}
```

We can use this implementation as follows:

```
fun main(args: Array<String>) {
    val burger: Burger = Burger.Builder()
            .setMeat(Meat())
            .setKetchup(Ketchup())
            .build()
}
```

You don't have to use all setters of the `Builder` class because fields have already been initialized by default values.

As you can see, a classic implementation of this pattern requires a lot of boilerplate code, but in Kotlin we can use named and default argument features, for instance. Let's create the `Kotlinger` class:

```
class Kotlinger(private val meat: Meat = Meat(),
                private val cheese: Cheese = Cheese(),
                private val ketchup: Ketchup = Ketchup(),
                private val topBun: Bun = Bun(),
                private val bottomBun: Bun = Bun())
```

You can use this as follows:

```
val kotlinger: Kotlinger = Kotlinger(
        meat = Meat(),
        ketchup = Ketchup()
)
```

Using the named and default argument features, we have the same benefits as when we use classical implementation.

For more complex cases, we can use Type-Safe Builders. This concept is based on the function with the receiver object feature of Kotlin and brings the power of **domain-specific languages (DSLs)** to the Builder pattern. Let's consider the following simplified example of user interface creation:

```
class Window(init: Window.() -> Unit) {
    private var header: TextView? = null
    private var footer: TextView? = null

    init {
        init()
    }

    fun header(init: TextView.() -> Unit) {
        this.header = TextView().apply { init() }
    }

    fun footer(init: TextView.() -> Unit) {
        this.footer = TextView().apply { init() }
    }
}
```

The `Window` class uses the `TextView` class, which looks as follows:

```
class TextView {
    var text: String = ""
    var color: String = "#000000"
}
```

To make creating a new object of the `Window` class more understandable, we can create the following `window` function:

```
fun window(init: Window.() -> Unit): Window {
    return Window(init)
}
```

Finally, we can create a new instance of the `Window` class with complex initialization, like this:

```
window {
    header {
        text = "Header"
        color = "#00FF00"
    }
    footer {
        text = "Footer"
    }
}
```

Factory method

The factory method pattern is used to make the process of object creation more abstract by using the regular method of a special class instead of a constructor. This approach allows us to instantiate an object of a certain subtype at runtime. The following UML diagram shows the organization of classes and interfaces according to this pattern:

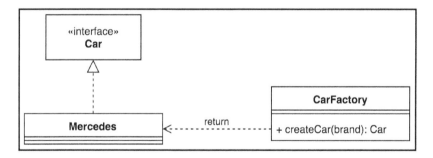

The preceding diagram contains the `Mercedes` class, which implements the `Car` interface. The `CarFactory` class is responsible for creating new instances of the `Car` type.

The implementation may look as follows:

```kotlin
class CarFactory {
    fun createCar(brand: Brand): Car {
        return when(brand) {
            Brand.BMW -> BMW()
            Brand.MERCEDES -> Mercedes()
            Brand.HONDA -> Honda()
            Brand.MAZDA -> Mazda()
        }
    }
}
```

The `CarFactory` class contains the `createCar` function, which returns an instance of the `Car` type:

```kotlin
interface Car
class Mercedes: Car
class BMW: Car
class Honda: Car
class Mazda: Car
```

The `createCar` method also takes an instance of `Brand`:

```kotlin
enum class Brand {
    BMW,
    MERCEDES,
    HONDA,
    MAZDA
}
```

We can use this implementation as follows:

```kotlin
fun main(args: Array<String>) {
    val mercedes = CarFactory().createCar(Brand.MERCEDES)
}
```

Abstract factory

The abstract factory pattern works in a similar way to the factory method, but it's used for complex cases. According to this pattern, we have a factory that generates other factories. The following diagram illustrates types of hierarchy:

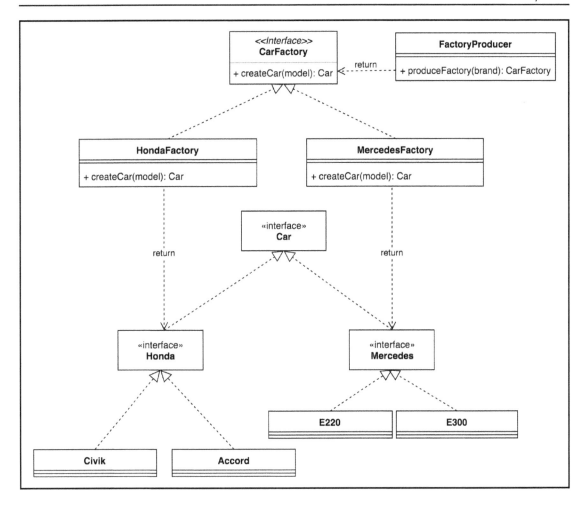

This diagram contains the **MercedesFactory** and **HondaFactory** classes, which implement the **CarFactory** interface. The **FactoryProducer** class contains the **produceFactory** method, which returns a new instance of the **CarFactory** type. The **CarFactory** interface, in turn, contains the **createCar** method, which returns an instance of the **Car** type. The **Car** interface is extended by the **Mercedes** and **Honda** interfaces, which are then implemented by certain classes such as **Civic**, **Accord**, **E220**, and **E300**.

The hierarchy of classes and interfaces displayed in the preceding diagram can be implemented as follows:

```
class FactoryProducer {
    fun produceFactory(brand: Brand): Factory = when (brand) {
        Brand.MERCEDES -> MercedesFactory()
        Brand.HONDA -> HondaFactory()
        Brand.MAZDA -> TODO()
        Brand.BMW -> TODO()
    }
}
```

The Factory interface looks like this:

```
interface Factory {
    fun createCar(model: Model): Car
}
```

The classes that implement the Factory interface may look as follows:

```
class MercedesFactory : Factory {
    override fun createCar(model: Model): Car = when (model) {
        MercedesModel.E220 -> E220()
        MercedesModel.E300 -> E300()
        else -> TODO()
    }
}

class HondaFactory : Factory {
    override fun createCar(model: Model): Car = when (model) {
        HondaModel.ACCORD -> Accord()
        HondaModel.CIVIC -> Civic()
        else -> TODO()
    }
}
```

The Model interface looks like this:

```
interface Model
```

This can be implemented as follows:

```
enum class MercedesModel : Model {
    E220,
    E300
}

enum class HondaModel : Model {
    ACCORD,
    CIVIC
}
```

We can use this implementation of the abstract factory pattern, which may look like this:

```
fun main(args: Array<String>) {
    val e220 =
FactoryProducer().produceFactory(Brand.MERCEDES).createCar(MercedesModel.E2
20)
}
```

Singleton

The singleton pattern is used when we want to be sure that only one instance of a certain class is ever created. According to this pattern, a class is responsible for providing a reference to the same underlying instance. The following example shows the easiest way to implement the singleton pattern in Java:

```
public class Singleton {

    private Singleton() {}
    private static final Singleton INSTANCE = new Singleton();

    public static Singleton getInstance() {
        return INSTANCE;
    }
}
```

However, Kotlin supports the concept of object declaration. For instance, we need to create an object that represents a user who is currently logged in:

```
object User {
    var firstName: String? = null
    var lastName: String? = null
}
```

The version of this code that is decompiled to Java looks like this:

```java
public final class User {
    @JvmField
    @Nullable
    public static String firstName;
    @JvmField
    @Nullable
    public static String lastName;
    public static final User INSTANCE;

    static {
        User var0 = new User();
        INSTANCE = var0;
    }
}
```

As you can see, object declaration looks like the easiest version in Java under the hood. However, this approach can be inefficient because it immediately creates an instance of the class when the application starts, even if it is not needed. To solve this problem, we can use the *lazy-loading singleton,* which may look like this:

```java
public class Singleton {
    private Singleton() {}
    private static JavaSingleton INSTANCE;

    public static JavaSingleton getInstance() throws Throwable {
        if (INSTANCE == null) {
            INSTANCE = new JavaSingleton();
        }
        return INSTANCE;
    }
}
```

Since we can declare variables as first-class citizens in Kotlin, we can use the following implementation:

```kotlin
class User private constructor(
        var firstName: String? = null,
        var lastName: String? = null
) {
    companion object {
        private val user by lazy(LazyThreadSafetyMode.NONE) {User()}
        fun getInstance(): User = user
    }
}

fun main(args: Array<String>) {
```

```
        with(User.getInstance()) {
            firstName = "Ihor"
            lastName = "Kucherenko"
        }
    }
```

In the preceding example, we use the `lazy` delegate , which takes an instance of the `LazyThreadSafetyMode` enum and a lambda that invokes only once when we refer to the `user` variable for the first time.

However, in a multithreaded environment, the `getInstance()` function can return more than one instance of the singleton because this function is not protected by synchronization. To deal with this scenario, we can use the *double-checked locking synchronization* approach:

```
public class Singleton {
    private Singleton() {}
    private static JavaSingleton INSTANCE ;
    public static JavaSingleton getInstance() {
        if (INSTANCE == null){
            synchronized(JavaSingleton.class){
                if(INSTANCE == null){
                    INSTANCE = new JavaSingleton;
                }
            }
            return INSTANCE ;
        }
    }
}
```

In Kotlin, we can use the following declaration:

```
private val user by lazy {User()}
```

In this case, an instance of the `SynchronizedLazyImpl` class has the double-checked locking technique under the hood:

```
public actual fun <T> lazy(initializer: () -> T): Lazy<T> =
SynchronizedLazyImpl(initializer)
```

We know that singleton is an anti-pattern. These are global variables that can be changed at any time, which is why they are enemies of encapsulation; it's difficult to define the state and behavior of an instance that depends on a singleton. In addition, the singleton pattern breaks the single responsibility principle because one class is responsible for creating this class and keeping only one instance at the same time.

Structural patterns

Structural patterns can be used when we need to use an instance with an interface that doesn't match our requirements, or we can improve our code base by building a class hierarchy that assumes each sub-type makes it possible to extend or alter the functionality of objects at runtime. We can also restrict access to an object by using the Proxy pattern.

This section covers the following patterns:

- Adapter
- Decorator
- Facade
- Proxy

Adapter

The Adapter pattern allows us to use a pre-existing interface without modifying the source. Let's imagine that we want to teach a cat how to bark. The following diagram shows how we can implement this:

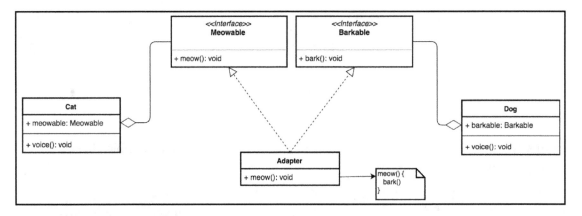

The preceding diagram contains the **Meowable** and **Barkable** interfaces. The **Cat** class implements the **Meowable** interface and the **Dog** class implements the **Barkable** interface. To teach a cat how to bark, we should pass an instance of the **Barkable** type to an instance of the **Cat** class. For this, we can create the **Adapter** class, which has implemented both interfaces, and invoke the **bark** method from **meow**.

The `Meowable` and `Barkable` interfaces look like this:

```
interface Barkable {
    fun bark() {
        println("bark")
    }
}

interface Meowable {
    fun meow() {
        println("meow")
    }
}
```

The `Cat` and `Dog` classes takes instances of the `Barkable` and `Meowable` types as parameters:

```
class Cat(private val meowable: Meowable) {
    fun voice() {
        meowable.meow()
    }
}

class Dog(private val barkable: Barkable) {
    fun voice() {
        barkable.bark()
    }
}
```

The `Adapter` class may look like this:

```
class Adapter: Barkable, Meowable {
    override fun meow() {
        bark()
    }
}
```

Let's run the program:

```
fun main(args: Array<String>) {
    Cat(Adapter()).voice()
}
```

The following is the output:

```
bark
```

Decorator

The decorator pattern allows us to add behavior to the individual object dynamically, without affecting the behavior of other objects from the same class. We can achieve this by wrapping the object into another instance. The following diagram shows a case like this:

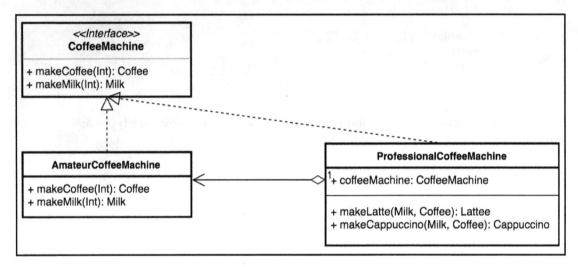

The diagram contains the **AmateurCoffeeMachine** and **ProfessionalCoffeeMachine** classes, which implement the **CoffeeMachine** interface.

The following example shows how this pattern works:

```kotlin
interface CoffeeMachine {
    val leftCoffeeMilliliters: Int
    val leftMilkMilliliters: Int
    fun makeCoffee(milliliters: Int): Coffee {
        leftCoffeeMilliliters - milliliters
        return Coffee(milliliters)
    }
    fun makeMilk(milliliters: Int): Milk {
        leftMilkMilliliters - milliliters
        return Milk(milliliters)
    }
}
```

`CoffeeMachine` is an interface that defines the base functionality for coffee machines. Furthermore, the `Coffee` and `Milk` classes look like this:

```kotlin
class Milk(milliliters: Int)
class Coffee(milliliters: Int)
```

AmateurCoffeeMachine **implements the** CoffeeMachine **interface and looks as follows:**

```
class AmateurCoffeeMachine(
        override val leftCoffeeMilliliters: Int,
        override val leftMilkMilliliters: Int
) : CoffeeMachine
```

The ProfessionalCoffeeMachine **class implements** CoffeeMachine **and uses an instance of the** AmateurCoffeeMachine **class as a delegate:**

```
class ProfessionalCoffeeMachine(coffeeMachine: CoffeeMachine):
CoffeeMachine by coffeeMachine {
    fun makeLatte() = Latte(makeMilk(150), makeCoffee(50))
    fun makeCappuccino() = Cappuccino(makeMilk(100), makeCoffee(70))
}
```

The following snippet demonstrates how to create an instance of the AmateurCoffeeMachine **class and extend its functionality at runtime:**

```
fun main(args: Array<String>) {
    val coffeeMachine = AmateurCoffeeMachine(1000, 1000)
    //.........
    val professionalCoffeeMachine =
ProfessionalCoffeeMachine(coffeeMachine)
}
```

Facade

If a class has a complex interface, we can use the facade pattern. According to this pattern, we should create a new class that contains an instance of a class that we want to use. The following diagram demonstrates when we want to use the Preferences API (https://docs. oracle.com/javase/8/docs/technotes/guides/preferences/overview.html) to persist the state of the User class:

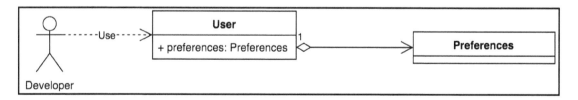

The preceding diagram contains the `User` class, which is responsible for simplifying a public interface of the `Preference` class. The end user works with an instance of the `User` class instead of `Preference`.

The `User` class may look like this:

```kotlin
data class User(
        private val preferences: Preferences =
Preferences.userRoot().node(User::class.java.simpleName),
        val id: Int = preferences.getInt(User::id.name, 0),
        val firstName: String = preferences.get(User::firstName.name, ""),
        val lastName: String = preferences.get(User::lastName.name, "")
) {
    init {
        with(preferences) {
            putInt(User::id.name, id)
            put(User::firstName.name, firstName)
            put(User::lastName.name, lastName)
        }
    }
}
```

In the preceding snippet, we use the `User` class as a facade to simplify work with the Preferences API. We also use it as follows:

```kotlin
fun main(args: Array<String>) {
    User(id = 1, firstName = "Igor", lastName = "Kucherenko").apply {
        println(this)
    }
    println(User())
}
```

The output looks like this:

```
User(preferences=User Preference Node: /User, id=1, firstName=Igor,
lastName=Kucherenko)
 User(preferences=User Preference Node: /User, id=1, firstName=Igor,
lastName=Kucherenko)
```

We can use the `User` class to persist information about a currently logged in user in our system.

Proxy

The proxy pattern is useful when we want to restrict or improve a mechanism for accessing an expensive resource. Let's suppose that we want to access a media file. This is an expensive resource and it's better to cache it to avoid multiple loadings. The following diagram shows how this case can be implemented:

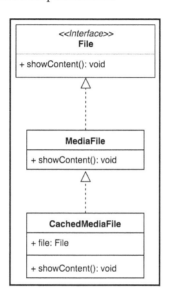

The preceding diagram contains the CachedMediaFile class that extends the MediaFile class which, in turn, implements the File interface. Using CachedMediaFile is preferable to MediaFile because it can save memory resources.

The following snippet shows how this pattern works:

```
interface File {
    fun showContent()
}

class MediaFile: File {
    override fun showContent() = println("showContent")
}

class CachedMediaFile: File {
    private val file by lazy { MediaFile() }

    override fun showContenat() = file.showContent()
}
```

We can use the `CachedMediaFile` class instead of `MediaFile` to save our resources.

Behavioral patterns

Behavioral patterns are useful when we need to change an algorithm followed by objects dynamically, or to implement a special type of communication between instances. Using this type of template, we can observe state changes or send special commands to a certain object.

This section covers the following patterns:

- Observer
- Strategy
- Command
- State
- Chain of responsibility
- Visitor

Observer

The Observer pattern allows an object to determine the state change of another object. An instance that is interested can subscribe and immediately be notified when the value of a certain field is changed. The following diagram shows this case:

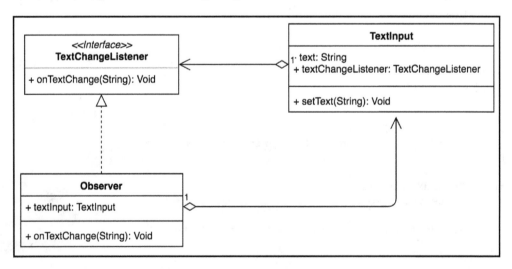

The preceding diagram contains the `TextChangeListener` interface, which is implemented by the `Observer` class. The `TextInput` class contains a reference of the `TextChangeListener` type. Whenever the text property of an instance of the `TextInput` class is changed, the `onTextChange` method is invoked.

The following snippet demonstrates how this pattern can be implemented:

```
typealias TextChangeListener = (text: String?) -> Unit

class TextInput {
    var text: String? = null
    set(value) {
        field = value
        textChangeListener?.invoke(value)
    }
    var textChangeListener: TextChangeListener? = null
}
```

We can observe changes in the `text` property in the following way:

```
fun main(args: Array<String>) {
    val textInput = TextInput().apply {
        this.textChangeListener = {println(it)}
    }
    textInput.text = "Typing"
}
```

The output of this is as follows:

```
Typing
```

It's worth mentioning that we can also use a delegate from the Kotlin standard library:

```
class TextInput {
    var text by Delegates.observable<String?>(null) { _, _, newValue ->
        textChangeListener?.invoke(newValue)
    }
    var textChangeListener: TextChangeListener? = null
}
```

Strategy

The Strategy pattern is used to dynamically change an algorithm. According to this pattern, we should define a common interface and a class that encapsulates a certain implementation for each algorithm. The following diagram shows how class hierarchy can be built in this case:

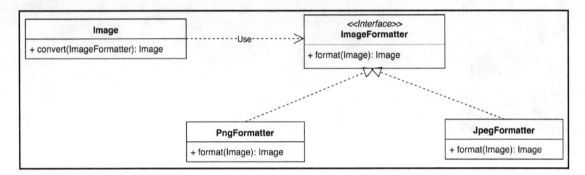

This diagram contains the **ImageFormatter** interface, which is implemented by the **PngFormatter** and **JpegFormatter** classes. The **Image** class contains the convert method that takes an instance of the **ImageFormatter** type. Consequently, we can pass any implementation of **ImageFormatter** and therefore change a converting algorithm at runtime.

The common interface for strategies may look like this:

```
interface ImageFormatter {
    fun format(image: Image): Image
}
```

Implementations of algorithms may look as follows:

```
class PngFormatter: ImageFormatter {
    override fun format(image: Image) = Image()
}

class JpegFormatter: ImageFormatter {
    override fun format(image: Image) = Image()
}
```

Furthermore, the `Image` class contains the `convert` method:

```
class Image {
    fun convert(formatter: ImageFormatter): Image = formatter.format(this)
}
```

The following snippet shows that we can apply different algorithms to the same object:

```
fun main() {
    val image = Image()
    val pngImage = image.convert(PngFormatter())
    val jpegImage = image.convert(JpegFormatter())
}
```

Command

The command pattern is used to encapsulate required information in order to perform an action or start a process. The data is therefore put into an object that is passed to an executor. It's worth mentioning that execution of commands can also be delayed if this is necessary. The following diagram shows how this pattern can be implemented:

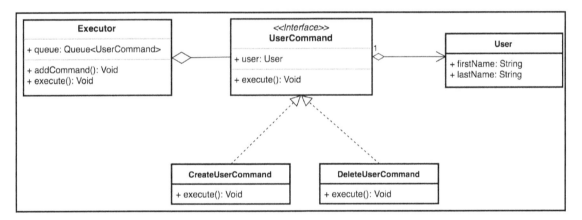

The preceding diagram contains the **UserCommand** interface, which is implemented by the **CreateUserCommand** and **DeleteUserCommand** classes. A constructor of **UserCommand** takes an instance of the **User** class and a certain implementation of the **UserCommand** interface, then encapsulates an operation with a user.

The following example performs operations using the `User` class:

```kotlin
data class User(val firstName: String, val lastName: String)
```

`UserCommand` is a base interface for commands related to a user:

```kotlin
interface UserCommand {
    val user: User
    fun execute()
}
```

This interface obliges classes that implement it to initialize the `user` property and override the `execute` method. Classes that perform certain commands may look something like this:

```kotlin
class CreateUserCommand(override val user: User) : UserCommand {
    override fun execute() {
        println("Creating...")
    }
}

class DeleteUserCommand(override val user: User) : UserCommand {
    override fun execute() {
        println("Deleting...")
    }
}
```

The `Executor` class encapsulates a queue with commands and contains the `addCommand` and `execute` methods, as follows:

```kotlin
class Executor {
    private val queue = LinkedList<UserCommand>()

    fun addCommand(command: UserCommand) {
        queue.add(command)
    }

    fun execute() {
        queue.forEach { it.execute() }
    }
}
```

Use of the Executor pattern might look as follows:

```kotlin
fun main(args: Array<String>) {
    val executor = Executor()
    val user = User("Igor", "Kucherenko")
    //..........
    executor.addCommand(CreateUserCommand(user))
```

```
//..........
executor.addCommand(DeleteUserCommand(user))

executor.execute()
}
```

State

According to the state pattern, we should implement each state of a system as a derived object. We should also declare a class that contains a property that represents the current state and methods that invoke transitions between states. It's worth mentioning that we can consider the state pattern as an extension of the Strategy pattern because methods can change their behavior depending on the state. The following diagram shows what an implementation of this pattern may look like:

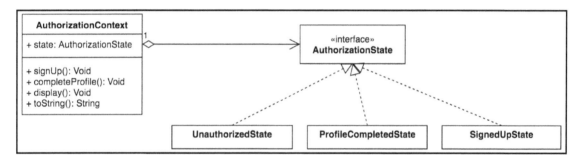

The diagram contains classes such as **UnauthorizedState**, **ProfileCompletedState**, and **SignedUpState**, which all represent a certain state of a program. These classes implement the **AuthorizationState** interface that's encapsulated by the **AuthorizationContext** class.

AuthorizationState is a sealed class that restricts the hierarchy of states:

```
sealed class AuthorizationState
```

The following classes represent states:

```
class SignedUpState: AuthorizationState()

class ProfileCompletedState: AuthorizationState()

class UnauthorizedState: AuthorizationState()
```

The `AuthorizationContext` class encapsulates the current state and contains methods that perform transitions between states:

```
class AuthorizationContext {
    var state: AuthorizationState = UnauthorizedState()

    fun signUp() {
        state = SignedUpState()
    }

    fun completeProfile() {
        state = ProfileCompletedState()
    }

    fun display() = when (state) {
            is UnauthorizedState -> println("Display sign up screen")
            is SignedUpState -> println("Display complete profile screen")
            is ProfileCompletedState -> println("Display main screen")
        }

    override fun toString(): String {
        return "AuthorizationContext(state=$state)"
    }
}
```

Use of this code may look like this:

```
fun main(args: Array<String>) {
    val context = AuthorizationContext()
    context.display()
    context.signUp()
    println(context)
    context.display()
    context.completeProfile()
    println(context)
}
```

The output is as follows:

```
Display sign up screen
AuthorizationContext(state=chapter6.patterns.behavioral.SignedUpState@2626b
418)
 Display complete profile screen
AuthorizationContext(state=chapter6.patterns.behavioral.ProfileCompletedSta
te@5a07e868)
```

Chain of responsibility

The chain of responsibility pattern is an alternative version of the `if { ... } else if { ... } else if { ... } else` block. According to this pattern, we have a source of request objects and a chain of processing objects. A processing object that can't handle a request passes it to another handler. The following diagram demonstrates this:

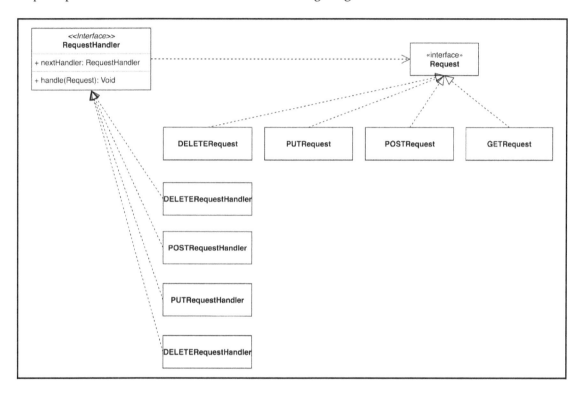

The preceding diagram contains the **Request** interface that is implemented by the **DELETERequest**, **PUTRequest**, **POSTRequest**, and **GETRequest** classes. The **RequestHandler** interface is implemented by the **DELETERequestHandler**, **POSTRequestHandler**, **PUTRequestHandler**, and **DELETERequestHandler** classes. A class that implements the **RequestHandler** interface handles an operation that is encapsulated by an instance of the **Request** type.

The `Request` interface looks like this:

```
interface Request
```

The classes that implement this interface look as follows:

```
class GETRequest: Request

class POSTRequest: Request

class PUTRequest: Request

class DELETERequest: Request
```

The `RequestHandler` interface contains the `nextHandler` property and the `handle` method:

```
interface RequestHandler {
    val nextHandler: RequestHandler?
    fun handle(request: Request)
}
```

The `GETRequestHandler` class overrides the `nextHandler` property and initializes it with an instance of the `POSTRequestHandler` class, as follows:

```
class GETRequestHandler: RequestHandler {

    override val nextHandler = POSTRequestHandler()

    override fun handle(request: Request) {
        if (request is GETRequest) {
            println("Handle GET request...")
        } else {
            nextHandler.handle(request)
        }
    }
}
```

The `handle` method processes an incoming request or passes it to the next `POSTRequestHandler` handler:

```
class POSTRequestHandler: RequestHandler {

    override val nextHandler = PUTRequestHandler()

    override fun handle(request: Request) {
        if (request is POSTRequest) {
            println("Handle POST request...")
        } else {
            nextHandler.handle(request)
        }
    }
```

```
    }
```

The POSTRequestHandler class overrides the nextHandler property and initializes it with an instance of the PUTRequestHandler class:

```
class PUTRequestHandler: RequestHandler {
    override val nextHandler = DELETERequestHandler()

    override fun handle(request: Request) {
        if (request is PUTRequest) {
            println("Handle PUT request...")
        } else {
            nextHandler.handle(request)
        }
    }
}
```

The PUTRequestHandler class overrides the nextHandler property with an instance of the DELETERequestHandler class. DELETERequestHandler is the last link in the chain:

```
class DELETERequestHandler: RequestHandler {
    override val nextHandler: RequestHandler? = null

    override fun handle(request: Request) {
        if (request is DELETERequest) {
            println("Handle DELETE request...")
        }
    }
}
```

We can use this code as follows:

```
fun main(args: Array<String>) {
    GETRequestHandler().apply {
        handle(GETRequest())
        handle(DELETERequest())
    }
}
```

The output is as follows:

```
Handle GET request...
 Handle DELETE request...
```

Visitor

The visitor pattern allows us to add new operations to an existing object without modifying it. This pattern is a way to extend functionality and follow the open/closed principle. It's better to try to understand this pattern using a particular example.

The following diagram represents the example that we will touch upon, as follows:

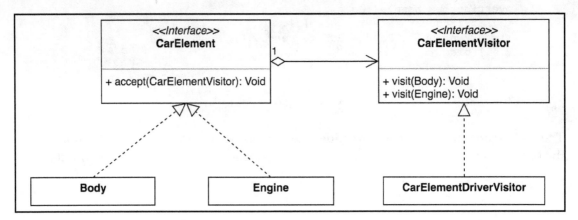

The preceding diagram contains the **CarElement** interface that is implemented by the **Body** and **Engine** classes. The **CarElementDriverVisitor** class implements the **CarElementVisitor** interface, which contains an instance of the **CarElementVisitor** type.

Let's define the `CarElement` interface:

```
interface CarElement {
    fun accept(visitor: CarElementVisitor)
}
```

Now, let's define a visitor for this interface:

```
interface CarElementVisitor {}
```

We'll add methods to this interface and define two classes that implement the `CarElement` interface:

```
class Body : CarElement {
    override fun accept(visitor: CarElementVisitor) = visitor.visit(this)
}

class Engine : CarElement {
    override fun accept(visitor: CarElementVisitor) = visitor.visit(this)
}
```

We should add two overloaded versions of the `visit` method to the `CarElementVisitor` class:

```
interface CarElementVisitor {
    fun visit(body: Body)
    fun visit(engine: Engine)
}
```

We can now create the `Car` class, which uses car elements:

```
class Car : CarElement {
    private val elements = arrayOf(Body(), Engine())
    override fun accept(visitor: CarElementVisitor) {
        elements.forEach { it.accept(visitor) }
    }
}
```

Let's implement the `CarElementVisitor` interface:

```
class CarElementDriverVisitor: CarElementVisitor {
    override fun visit(body: Body) {
        println("Prepare body...")
    }

    override fun visit(engine: Engine) {
        println("Prepare engine...")
    }
}
```

We can use the preceding code as follows:

```
fun main(args: Array<String>) {
    val car = Car()
    car.accept(CarElementDriverVisitor())
}
```

The following is the output:

```
Prepare body...
Prepare engine...
```

Summary

In this chapter, we presented the most common software design patterns in object-oriented programming. It's worth mentioning that Kotlin also supports elements of functional programming that allow for a more concise way of implementing patterns such as strategy or observer. This chapter contains examples and diagrams that show how and in which case we should use patterns.

In the next chapter, we'll introduce coroutines as lightweight threads.

7
Coroutines - a Lightweight Thread?

When we develop an application, we always have to deal with long-running operations such as networks or file input/output. Using a block of code known as a callback to determine when a task is completed is a traditional approach. However, code with callbacks doesn't look natural and it's clearer to read code that is written in a sequential manner. Kotlin brings coroutines to the world of Java virtual machines, which provide an alternative to threads.

In this chapter, we will cover the following topics:

- What are coroutines?
- Coroutines and threads
- Coroutine examples

Technical requirements

To run the examples from this chapter, you should install the `kotlinx-coroutines-core` library. If you use the Gradle build tool, you will have to add the following line to the dependency section of the `build.gradle` file:

```
implementation 'org.jetbrains.kotlinx:kotlinx-coroutines-core:0.23.0'
```

You can find the examples from this chapter on GitHub at the following link: `https://github.com/PacktPublishing/Hands-On-Object-Oriented-Programming-with-Kotlin/tree/master/src/main/kotlin/Chapter07`.

What are coroutines?

Coroutines are components of a computer program that can be considered lightweight threads. Coroutines allow us to suspend the invocation of a function without blocking a thread. Let's imagine a case in which you need to perform a request on the server and display a progress bar until your app receives the response. A request is a long-term operation that should be performed asynchronously because a user interface should stay responsive. This is a common approach to running a new thread that uses a callback so that you're notified when the app receives a response. However, using code with callbacks looks unnatural, complex, and can lead to bugs.

Coroutines can be considered as a library that wraps a particular part of code with the creation of new threads and callbacks. This approach allows you to write asynchronous code in a way that looks as if it were sequentially executed.

The following example demonstrates this:

```
fun main(args: Array<String>) {
    launch {
        delay(500L)
        println(Thread.currentThread().name)
    }
    println(Thread.currentThread().name)
    Thread.currentThread().join()
}
```

The output is as follows:

```
main
ForkJoinPool.commonPool-worker-1
```

launch is a special function that creates and runs a new coroutine. This function isn't contained in the Kotlin Standard Library, and you need to include the kotlinx-coroutines-core library to use it. If you use the Gradle build tool, you should add the following line:

```
implementation 'org.jetbrains.kotlinx:kotlinx-coroutines-core:0.23.0'
```

This should be added to the dependencies section of your build.gradle file. We will look at the launch function in more detail a little bit later.

To support coroutines, Kotlin only contains the `suspend` keyword, which can be applied to a function or a lambda. The Kotlin Standard Library also contains base classes, and interfaces describe a coroutine in programming code, such as `Continuation` and `CoroutineContext`. The `Continuation` interface looks as follows:

```
public interface Continuation<in T> {
    public val context: CoroutineContext
    public fun resume(value: T)
    public fun resumeWithException(exception: Throwable)
}
```

This interface represents a continuation after a suspension point. It contains the `resume` and `resumeWithException` functions, which are used to return the result value or an exception to the outer scope.

At the time of writing this book, the actual version of Kotlin is 1.2.60. However, in version 1.3.0, the `Continuation` interface is simplified and contains only one `resumeWith(result: SuccessOrFailure<T>)` function. `resume` and `resumeWithException` are extracted to extension functions and can still be used.

Each coroutine runs in a context that is represented by the `CoroutineContext` interface. A simplified version may look like this:

```
public interface CoroutineContext {
    public operator fun <E : Element> get(key: Key<E>): E?

    public fun <R> fold(initial: R, operation: (R, Element) -> R): R

    public operator fun plus(context: CoroutineContext): CoroutineContext =
            ///......
        }

    public fun minusKey(key: Key<*>): CoroutineContext

    public interface Key<E : Element>
}
```

The `Element` interface looks as follows:

```
public interface Element : CoroutineContext {
        public val key: Key<*>

        @Suppress("UNCHECKED_CAST")
        public override operator fun <E : Element> get(key: Key<E>): E? =
            if (this.key === key) this as E else null
```

```
        public override fun <R> fold(initial: R, operation: (R, Element) ->
    R): R =
            operation(initial, this)

        public override fun minusKey(key: Key<*>): CoroutineContext =
            if (this.key === key) EmptyCoroutineContext else this
    }
```

The main elements are the instances of the `Job` and `CoroutineDispatcher` classes. Under the hood, coroutines use the usual threads, and `CoroutineDispatcher` decides which thread or threads are used by a coroutine. The `launch` function returns an instance of the `Job` class that implements the `Element` interface and can be used to cancel the execution of a coroutine. To demonstrate this, you can rewrite the preceding example as follows:

```
fun main(args: Array<String>) {
    val job = launch {
        delay(500L)
        println(Thread.currentThread().name)
    }
    println(Thread.currentThread().name)
    job.cancel()
    Thread.currentThread().join()
}
```

The following is the output:

```
main
ForkJoinPool.commonPool-worker-1
```

The `Job` class also contains the `join` function, which can be invoked from another suspended function or a coroutine that suspends a callee function. We can use the `join` function to make the main thread wait until the job is complete. We should rewrite our example as follows:

```
fun main(args: Array<String>) = runBlocking {
    val job = launch {
        delay(500L)
        println("Coroutine!")
    }
    println("Hello,")
    job.join()
}
```

The output is as follows:

```
Hello,
Coroutine!
```

We can set up a breakpoint on the line, as shown in the following screenshot:

```kotlin
fun main(args: Array<String>) = runBlocking {
    val job = launch { this: CoroutineScope
        delay( time: 1000L)
        println("World!")
    }
    println("Hello,")
    job.join()
}
```

In the debug window, we can see that the main thread waits while a coroutine is running:

```
 Frames →"     Threads →"

∨  Thread Group "system"@337

 ∨  Thread Group "main"@601

    >  "ForkJoinPool.commonPool-worker-1"@600 in group "main": RUNNING

    >  "kotlinx.coroutines.DefaultExecutor"@697 in group "main": WAIT

    >  "main"@1 in group "main": WAIT
```

Coroutines and threads

An instance of the `Thread` class represents a native thread in the corresponding operating system when a program is running. This means that each instance of the `Thread` consumes memory for its stack and needs time to be initialized. If you are familiar with multithreaded programming, you know that switching between the contexts of threads is a pretty expensive operation, which is why it makes no sense to invoke short-term tasks in a separate thread.

In Kotlin, a coroutine is a pure language abstraction. Coroutines refer to objects in the memory heap and switching between coroutines doesn't involve operating system kernel operations. You can use a coroutine in the same way as a thread. This means that a coroutine contains a call stack function and stores local variables.

The amount of threads that can be executed in parallel depends on how many logical cores are currently available. How many coroutines can be executed in parallel depends on how many available, running threads are used by coroutine contexts. Let's look at the following example:

```
fun main(args: Array<String>) = runBlocking<Unit> {
 val parentJob = Job()
 (0..10_000)
 .forEach { launch(parent = parentJob) { println("Thread name:
${Thread.currentThread().name}") } }
 parentJob.joinChildren()
}
```

The output looks like this:

```
Thread name: ForkJoinPool.commonPool-worker-4
Thread name: ForkJoinPool.commonPool-worker-2
Thread name: ForkJoinPool.commonPool-worker-4
Thread name: ForkJoinPool.commonPool-worker-7
Thread name: ForkJoinPool.commonPool-worker-1
Thread name: ForkJoinPool.commonPool-worker-5
Thread name: ForkJoinPool.commonPool-worker-3
Thread name: ForkJoinPool.commonPool-worker-6
Thread name: ForkJoinPool.commonPool-worker-3
Thread name: ForkJoinPool.commonPool-worker-5
```

The following diagram shows how threads may share the available CPU time:

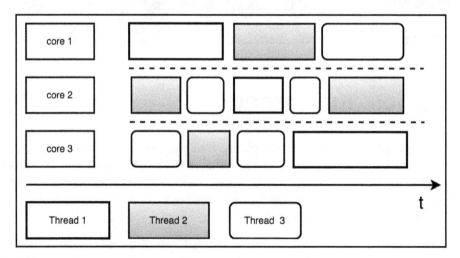

In turn, coroutines share the available thread time:

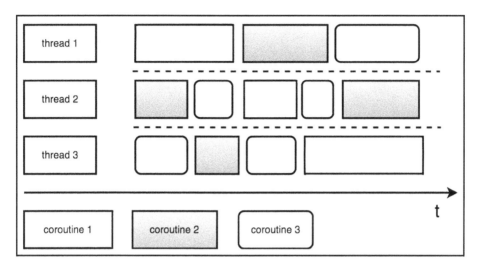

When we start a new coroutine, it doesn't matter that we create a new thread because a new coroutine can use a pre-existing thread from a pool. The `launch` function uses `CommonPool` as a default argument for coroutine context, with a thread pool that calculates the amount of threads using the following method:

```
private val parallelism = run<Int> {
    val property = Try {
System.getProperty(DEFAULT_PARALLELISM_PROPERTY_NAME) }
    if (property == null) {
        (Runtime.getRuntime().availableProcessors() - 1).coerceAtLeast(1)
    } else {
        val parallelism = property.toIntOrNull()
        if (parallelism == null || parallelism < 1) {
            error("Expected positive number in
$DEFAULT_PARALLELISM_PROPERTY_NAME, but has $property")
        }
        parallelism
}
}
```

For my computer, this value is seven. However, this doesn't mean that seven coroutines are running in parallel. Let's set up a breakpoint:

```kotlin
fun main(args: Array<String>) = runBlocking<Unit> { this: CoroutineScope
    CommonPool
    val parentJob = Job()
    (0..10_000)
            .map { async(parent = parentJob) { println(Thread.currentThread().name) } }
            .forEach { it.await() }
    parentJob.joinChildren()
}
```

The debugger window looks as follows:

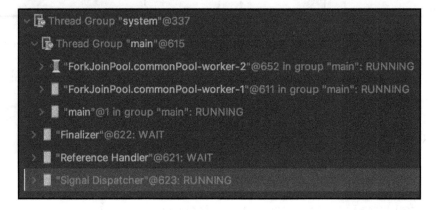

As you can see, we have a pool with seven threads, but several of them have the **WAIT** status because the cores are busy with other threads.

Functions such as `runBlocking` or `launch` are called coroutine builders, and these take the `parent: Job?` parameter. In the preceding example, we passed the `parentJob` variable to invoke the `joinChildren` method. As a result, the main thread waits until all coroutines are complete.

Coroutine examples

This section covers the most common examples of coroutines usage. Here, we will look at how to handle exceptions, close resources, work with channels, and so on. It's important to know how to use coroutines in practice.

This section covers the following topics:

- Exception handling
- Recourse releasing
- Parallel executing
- Lazy executing
- Channels

Exception handling

Coroutines allow us to write asynchronous code in a sequential manner. This includes exception handling, and we can use the usual `try {...}` `catch {...}` block to catch exceptions.

The following example shows how to use it in practice:

```
fun main(args: Array<String>) = runBlocking<Unit> {
    launch {
        val result = try {
            calculateValue()
        } catch (exception: Exception) {
            defaultValue
        }
        println(result)
    }
}

val defaultValue = 1

suspend fun calculateValue(): Int = withContext(DefaultDispatcher) { throw
Exception() }
```

Resource releasing

Resource leaking can significantly impact the performance of an application, which is why it's important to release resources after using them. When we work with coroutines, we can just use the `try {...} finally {...}` block, even with long-term input/output operations.

The following example shows how we can use this block:

```
fun main(args: Array<String>) {
    launch {
        val fileReader = FileReader("path")
        try {
            delay(10000)
            fileReader.read()
        } finally {
            fileReader.close()
        }
    }
}
```

Non-cancelable block

The `launch` function returns an instance of the `Job` class, which means that a coroutine can be cancelled at any time. In this case, if we have a long-term operation in the `finally` block, `JobCancellationException` will be thrown.

The following example shows a case like this:

```
fun main(args: Array<String>) = runBlocking<Unit> {
    val job = launch {
        try {
            delay(1000000)
        } finally {
            try {
                println("start")
                delay(1000)
                println("end")
            } catch (exception: Exception) {
                exception.printStackTrace()
            }
        }
    }
    delay(500)
    job.cancel()
```

```
        job.join()
    }
```

The following is the output:

```
kotlinx.coroutines.experimental.JobCancellationException: Job was cancelled
normally; job=StandaloneCoroutine{Cancelling}@7f77b211
 start
```

As you can see, the `finally` block can't be executed in a canceled coroutine and we can't release resources. We can deal with this using the `withContext` function:

```
withContext(NonCancellable) {
    try {
        println("start")
        delay(1000)
        println("end")
    } catch (exception: Exception) {
        exception.printStackTrace()
    }
}
```

The output now looks as follows:

```
start
end
```

The `withContext` function invokes the passed suspended block with a given coroutine context.

Parallel execution

We considered the synchronous execution of coroutines in the previous sections of this chapter. Synchronous means that tasks are executed sequentially, one after another. However, let's suggest that we need to download and display two pictures. We can run these two tasks in parallel to speed up the process of displaying these images.

Let's define the `Image` class and the `downloadImage` function as follows:

```
class Image

suspend fun downloadImage(): Image {
    delay(Random().nextInt(10) * 1000)
    return Image()
}
```

The `displayImage` function will look as follows:

```
fun displayImages(image1: Image, image2: Image) {
    println("$image1 ${LocalDateTime.now()}")
    println("$image2 ${LocalDateTime.now()}")
}
```

The `displayImage` function prints objects and the current time to the console.

We can use the preceding code as follows:

```
fun main(args: Array<String>) = runBlocking<Unit> {
    Job().also { parentJob->
        val deferred1 = async(parentJob) { downloadImage() }.apply {
            invokeOnCompletion { println("Image 1 downloaded
${LocalDateTime.now()}") }
        }
        val deferred2 = async(parentJob) { downloadImage() }.apply {
            invokeOnCompletion { println("Image 2 downloaded
${LocalDateTime.now()}") }
        }
        displayImages(deferred1.await(), deferred2.await())
    }.joinChildren()
}
```

In the preceding snippet, we used the `async` function. This is a coroutine builder that returns an instance of a `Deferred` class. The `Deferred` class extends the `Job` class and can hold a value that will be computed in the future. The most common use of an instance of this class is invoking the `await` method, which suspends execution until it returns the result.

There are other languages that use the *async-await* approach, including JavaScript:

```
async function asyncFunction() {

    let result = await new Promise((resolve, reject) => {
        setTimeout(() => resolve("done!"), 1000)
    });

    alert(result); // "done!"
}
```

In JavaScript, *async-await* is a language-level construction. However, in Kotlin, it's simply a library function. Kotlin supports coroutines in an extremely flexible way by making it possible to create your own coroutine builders with custom thread pools and contexts.

The output of the preceding example looks as follows:

```
Image 1 downloaded 2018-08-16T11:11:05.296
Image 2 downloaded 2018-08-16T11:11:11.225
chapter8.Image@4b9af9a9 2018-08-16T11:11:11.226
chapter8.Image@5387f9e0 2018-08-16T11:11:11.226
```

As you can see, the second image was downloaded six seconds after the first one. After this, the `displayImages` function was immediately invoked.

We can now set up a breakpoint, as shown in the following screenshot:

The debug window looks like this:

As you can see from the preceding screenshot, there are two threads from a pool running at the same time.

Lazy execution

Lazy execution or call-by-need is a common approach in software development. This strategy allows us to delay the evaluation of an expression until we need it. in Kotlin, coroutines also allow us to use this approach. Coroutine builders such as `launch`, `withContext`, and `async` contain a `start:` `CoroutineStart` parameter with the following default argument—`CoroutineStart.DEFAULT`.

The following example shows how to start a coroutine lazily using this parameter:

```
fun main(args: Array<String>) = runBlocking<Unit> {
    Job().also { parentJob->
        val job = launch(parent = parentJob, start = CoroutineStart.LAZY) {
downloadImage() }
        //........
        job.start()
    }.joinChildren()
}
```

The job will only be started when we invoke the `start` method.

Channels

The `Deferred` class, which was touched upon in the *Parallel executing* section, can be used to compute a single value. If we need to deal with a sequence of values, we can use channels. The `Channel` class contains the `send` and `receive` methods, which can be used in the following way:

```
fun main(args: Array<String>) = runBlocking<Unit> {
    val channel = Channel<Int>()
    launch {
        for (x in 1..50) channel.send(x * x)
    }
    repeat(50) {
        delay(500)
        println(channel.receive())
    }
    println("Done!")
}
```

Channels also allow us to transfer values from one coroutine to another safely in a multithreaded environment.

Summary

In this chapter, we looked at coroutines and how they work under the hood, and presented the most common examples of usage. In Kotlin, coroutines are implemented in a very flexible way, so we can create our own coroutine builders and contexts. We also looked at the differences between threads and coroutines, and found out why we should consider using coroutines.

In the next chapter, we'll explore the interoperability of Kotlin and Java code.

8
Interoperability

In this chapter, we will focus on the interoperability of Java and Kotlin. Interoperability refers to the ability to use both the Java and Kotlin languages in a single project. We can call Kotlin functions in Java as well as Java methods and variables in Kotlin code. This gives us the advantage of code reusability. For example, if we have an existing Java project with classes and functions, then we do not need to rewrite everything in Kotlin from scratch. Instead, we can use each and every line of Java code in Kotlin and start writing new functionalities here. Similarly, we can call Kotlin code in Java.

The following topics will be covered in this chapter:

- Calling the Java static variable in Kotlin
- Calling the Java static function in Kotlin
- Calling the Java collection in Kotlin
- Calling the Java class in Kotlin
- Handling Kotlin reserve keywords
- Calling the Kotlin class in Java
- Calling the Kotlin function in Java
- Calling the Kotlin extension function in Java
- Using JVM annotations in Kotlin

Technical requirements

Other than IntelliJ IDEA, this chapter does not require any specific installations.

The code for this chapter can be downloaded from the GitHub repository: `https://github.com/PacktPublishing/Hands-On-Object-Oriented-Programming-with-Kotlin/tree/master/src/main/kotlin/Chapter08`.

Calling Java code in Kotlin

In this section, we will learn how to use Java code in a Kotlin file. For the sake of simplicity, begin by creating a package and adding both Java and Kotlin files in one place, as we know that Kotlin makes it possible to keep both Java and Kotlin files in one project. So, we have two Java classes, called `CallJava` and `Shape`, and in the same folder we have one Kotlin file, called `FromKotlin`:

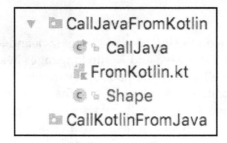

Let's start with the Java static variable and function.

Calling static variables and functions

Open the `CallJava` file and add one static variable message:

```
public static String message = "Hello from Java";
```

As well as this, include one static method, `add`, which adds two variables and displays a message on the screen:

```
public static void add(int i, int j){
    System.out.println(i + " + " + j + "=" + (i + j));
}
```

Calling a static function or variable from Java to Kotlin is very simple. To do this, use the Java filename as a reference and call the required function or variable.

Look at the following Kotlin example to call the Java static variable:

```
fun callStaticFromJava() {
    var message = CallJava.message
    println("Java Message : ${message}")
    CallJava.add(4,5)
}
```

To call the static variable, use the Java class name as a reference along with the `CallJava.message` variable name. This value can be assigned to a local variable and used like a normal Kotlin variable. Similarly, we can call the Java static function by using the class name as a reference along with the function name. Call the `add` method from Java by using `CallJava.add(4,5)` and pass two integer variables as parameters.

Calling the Java collection in Kotlin

Create a method in Java that returns an `arrayList` of integers:

```
public static ArrayList<Integer> getIntList(){

    ArrayList<Integer> integers = new ArrayList<>();
    integers.add(1);integers.add(2);integers.add(3);

    return integers;
}
```

`getIntList` returns an array that contains three elements. Call this function in Kotlin to access the list and add more elements in it:

```
var list = CallJava.getIntList()
//var list: ArrayList<Int> = CallJava.getIntList()

list.add(4)
for (element in list) {
   println("Element $element")
}
```

`CallJava.getIntList()` returns `ArrayList`, which can be assigned to a list type of variables. We explicitly declare the type of the list by using the `ArrayList<Int>` name:

```
var list: ArrayList<Int> = CallJava.getIntList()
```

Alternatively, we can directly assign a list to the variable and Kotlin will figure out the list type by itself:

```
var list = CallJava.getIntList()
```

We can treat this as a normal immutable list and we can add or remove elements.

Reserve words in Kotlin

There are a number of keywords that are used by Kotlin for its internal purposes and these cannot be used as variable names and function declarations. Some of the reserve words are as follows:

```
in, is, as, object, val, var, for, fun, interface, when
```

There are reserve words that Kotlin has reserved for itself, but when it comes to Java, most of Kotlin's reserved keywords are normal variables for Java. See the following example:

```
public static void is(){
    System.out.println("is is a reserved keyword in Kotlin :-) ");
}

public static void var(){
    System.out.println("var is a reserved keyword in Kotlin :-) ");
}
```

var and is are normal keywords for Java but not for Kotlin. If we need to call a function with Kotlin's reserved words, we need to use a backtick operator. See the following Kotlin example:

```
CallJava.`is`()
CallJava.`var`()
```

Use the backtick (` `) operator to call Java functions whose names are reserved keyword words for Kotlin. Let's look at more examples and see how to use Java functions whose names contain Kotlin's reserved keywords.

Write a function in Kotlin that takes input from the user and displays a message on the screen. Kotlin uses a Java-provided Scanner class to take input from the keyboard, as follows:

```
fun inputFromKeyboard() {
    println("Enter Your name .... ")
    val scanner = Scanner(System.`in`)
    println("My name is ${scanner.nextLine()}")
}
```

The Scanner class takes System.in as an input stream in order to scan input. As we can see, in is a reserved keyword but we can use this by using backticks operators. Similarly, we can use all reserved keywords as a function or variable name in this way:

```
fun `in`(){
    println("I am in function")
}

fun `as`(){
    println("I am as function")
}

fun `object`(){
    println("I am object function")
}

var `var` = "Reserved keyword var"
var `object` = "Reserved keyword object"
```

Java classes in Kotlin

Let's explore how to create a Java class object in Kotlin. To do this, create a Shape.java file with three properties: height, width, and name with getters and setters:

```
public class Shape {

    private int width;
    private int height;
    public static final double PI = 3.1415;
    private final String name;

    public Shape(int width, int height, String name) {
        this.width = width;
        this.height = height;
        this.name = name;
    }
    public final int getHeight() {
        return this.height;
    }

    public final void setHeight(int value) {
        this.height = value;
    }

    public final String getName() {
        return this.name;
```

```
    }
    public final void shapeMessage() {
        System.out.println("Hi i am " + this.name + ", how are you doing");
    }
}
```

Creating an instance of the Java class in Kotlin is similar to creating an instance of the Kotlin class. See the following example:

```
val shape = Shape(5,10,"Square")
```

shape is an instance of the Shape class, which can access functions and update the class properties:

```
shape.shapeMessage()
shape.height = 10
println("name ${shape.name} height = ${shape.height}")
```

Calling Kotlin code in Java

Calling Kotlin code in Java is similar to calling Java code in Kotlin, except for a few things that must be considered before beginning. Let's start with a function call. To do this, create a new folder and add both Java and Kotlin files in one place:

```
▶  📁 CallJavaFromKotlin
▼  📁 CallKotlinFromJava
       🟦 CallKotlin.kt
  ▶  © CallKotlinClass.java
       🟦 CallKotlinUtil.kt
     © ▫ FromJava
```

Calling the Kotlin function

Now create two functions in Kotlin, add and addAndReturn. The add function takes two integer variables, adds them, and prints them on the screen, while addAndReturn adds two values and returns the result:

```
fun add(a : Int, b : Int) {
    println("Result of $a + $b is ${a+b}")
}
```

```
fun addAndReturn(i: Int, j: Int): Int {
    return i + j
}
```

We can call each Kotlin function by using the filename as a reference. `CallKotlin.kt` is a file that contains a Kotlin function. When calling a Kotlin function in the Java file, it is important to remember that we must add the `kt` keyword with the Kotlin filename to call our desired function. For example, we can call the `add` function by using `CallKotlinKt.add`. See the following example of the Java file:

```
public static void main(String args[]) {

    CallKotlinKt.add(5,5);

    int result = CallKotlinKt.addAndReturn(5,5);
    System.out.print("From Kotlin: result = " + result);

}
```

Execute this code and it will display the following output:

```
Result of 5 + 5 is 10
From Kotlin: result = 10
```

Extension functions

It is also possible to call Kotlin's extension function in Java. In Kotlin, create an extension function that takes one parameter, multiplies the value by 2, and returns the result. See the following Kotlin extension function:

```
fun Int.doubleTheValue() = this * 2
```

Create this extension function in the Kotlin class and call this function into Java's `main` function by using the `CallKotlinKt.doubleTheValue` function. See the following example:

```
public static void main(String args[]) {
    int i = 5;
    int result = CallKotlinKt.doubleTheValue(i);
    System.out.print("Kotlin's Extension function, Multiply "+ i +" with 2
= "+ result);
}
```

As a result, the output will be as expected:

```
Kotlin's Extension function, Multiply 5 with 2 = 10
```

Functions with mutable collections

Create a mutable list in the getMutableList function and return the list, as follows:

```
fun getMutableList() : MutableList<Int> {
    val list = mutableListOf(1,2,3,4,5)
    return list
}
```

Create a listFromKotlin variable in Java and assign a list to this variable by using the CallKotlinKt.getMutableList function from Kotlin.

See the following example:

```
public static void main(String args[]) {

    System.out.print("Kotlin mutable list");
    //List<int> listFromKotlin = KotlinToJavaKt.mutableList();

    List<Integer> listFromKotlin = CallKotlinKt.getMutableList();
    listFromKotlin.add(6);
    for (int i = 0; i < listFromKotlin.size(); i++) {
        System.out.println("Element " +  listFromKotlin.get(i));
    }
}
```

Notice that Kotlin is not familiar with primitive data types. As a result, we must provide a list of Integer classes:

```
//List<int> listFromKotlin = KotlinToJavaKt.mutableList(); // list of int
List<Integer> listFromKotlin = CallKotlinKt.getMutableList(); // List of
Integers
```

Functions with immutable collections

Let's see how to get an immutable list from the Kotlin function to Java. Create an immutable list in the getImmutableList function and return the list:

```
fun getImmutableList() : List<Int> {
    val list = listOf(1,2,3,4,5)
    return list
```

```
}
```

Get a Kotlin list by calling the `getImmutableList` function and displaying list elements. See the following example:

```
public static void main(String args[]) {
    System.out.println("Kotlin immutable list");

    List<Integer> listFromKotlin = CallKotlinKt.getImmutableList();

    for (int i = 0; i < listFromKotlin.size(); i++) {
        System.out.println("Element " +  listFromKotlin.get(i));
    }
}
```

Since we know that the immutable list cannot be updated, we can read the list but cannot add or update elements. Once the immutable list is called in Java, it is the programmer's responsibility to verify the type of list before updating it because the Java compiler could not catch the error at compile time. If we try to add an element in the immutable list of Kotlin, we will get the following result:

```
List<Integer> listFromKotlin = KotlinToJavaKt.getImmutableList();
listFromKotlin.add(6);
```

This shows that Java will throw the `java.lang.UnsupportedOperationException` exception at runtime and the application will crash.

Functions with the JVM annotation

We can call the Kotlin function in Java by using the filename as a reference. We also need to add the `kt` keyword with the filename; for example, `KotlinToJavakt`. However, Kotlin makes it possible to assign different names to our file and function names. Create a new class named `CallKotlinUtil.kt` and add the following code:

```
@file:JvmName("KotlinUtil")
package Chapter08.CallKotlinFromJava

fun addition (a: Int, b : Int){

    println("Result of $a + $b is ${a+b}")

}
```

Use the `@file:JvmName("KotlinUtil")` annotation at the beginning of the file. Now we can call the `addition` function by using `KotlinUtil.addition` instead of `CallKotlinUtilkt.addition`. See the following example:

```
public static void main(String args[]) {
    KotlinUtil.addition(4,4);
}
```

This is a much better and cleaner approach. We can now specify the Kotlin filename for the Java class to use as a reference. Kotlin also makes it possible to specify the name of the Kotlin function for Java. Create an `addition` function in the Kotlin file and add the `@JvmName` annotation with a new function name, as follows:

```
@file:JvmName("KotlinUtil")
package CallKotlinFromJavaPackage

@JvmName ("addDouble")
fun addition (a: Double, b : Double){
   println("Result of $a + $b is ${a+b}")
}
```

Now we can call the `addition` function by using `addDouble`. See the following example:

```
public static void main(String args[]) {
    KotlinUtil.addDouble(5.0, 5.0);
}
```

Calling the Kotlin class

In this section, we will see how to call the Kotlin class in Java. Create a `Shape` class in Kotlin with three properties, `height`, `width`, and `area`, and two functions, `shapeMessage` and `draw`:

```
class Shape(var width : Int, var height : Int , val shape: String) {

    var area : Int = 0
    fun shapeMessage(){
        println("Hi i am $shape, how are you doing")
    }
    fun draw() {
        println("$shape is drawn")
    }

    fun calculateArea(): Int {
        area = width * height
```

```
            return area
    }
}
```

We can create an instance of the Kotlin class in the same way as we create an instance of a normal Java class. See the following example:

```
class FromKotlinClass {

    public void callShpaeInstance()
    {
        Shape shape = new Shape(5,5,"Square");

        shape.shapeMessage();
        shape.setHeight(10);
        System.out.println(shape.getShape() + " width " +
shape.getWidth());
        System.out.println(shape.getShape() + " height " +
shape.getHeight());
        System.out.println(shape.getShape() + " area " +
shape.calculateArea());

        shape.draw();
    }
}
```

Create a `shape` instance by adding constructor parameters. We can use the `shape` instance to access all class properties by using getter and setter methods. We can also call the `shapeMessage` or `draw` functions of the `Shape` class using the `shape` instance.

Calling the Kotlin singleton class

We can also call the Kotlin singleton class in Java. Let's create a singleton class in Kotlin by using the `object` keyword:

```
object Singleton {
    fun happy() {
        println("I am Happy")
    }
}
```

Furthermore, we can call the `Singleton` class and the `happy` function in Java by using the `INSTANCE` keyword:

```
public static void main(String args[]) {
    Singleton.INSTANCE.happy();
```

```
    }
```

Notice that we do not need to use a Kotlin filename as a reference, but the `object` class name, `Singleton`, is sufficient. We can skip the `INSTANCE` keyword as well. Add the `@JvmStatic` annotation at the beginning of the function signature:

```
object Singleton {

    fun happy() {
        println("I am Happy")
    }

    @JvmStatic fun excited() {
        println("I am very Excited")
    }
}
```

Once this is done, call the `excited` function directly without using the `INSTANCE` keyword in Java:

```
public static void main(String args[]) {
    Singleton.INSTANCE.happy();
    Singleton.excited();
}
```

Execute the Java program and verify the output, as follows:

```
I am Happy
I am very Excited
```

Summary

In this chapter, we learned about one of the most exciting features of Kotlin: interoperability. Here, we can call Kotlin code in Java and vice versa. We started this chapter by calling Java static variables and functions in Kotlin, then we moved onto the Java collections, and we explored some examples of calling Java classes in Kotlin.

We then discussed how to handle the Kotlin reserve words and utilized Kotlin written code in Java with variables, functions, extension functions, and the Kotlin class. We also discussed the replacement of Kotlin filenames and function names by using a Kotlin-provided JVM annotation. Finally, we had a quick look at how to call Kotlin's `object` class in Java. In next chapter we will discuss about regular expression and serialisation in kotlin.

Questions

1. What is interoperability ?
2. Why do we use JVM annotation?

Further reading

Learning Object-Oriented Programming by Gastón C. Hillar, published by Packt: `https://www.packtpub.com/application-development/learning-object-oriented-programming`.

9
Regular Expression and Serialization in Kotlin

In this chapter, we will be discussing **regular expression**, which is also known as **regex** or **regexp**. It is an approach that's designed to define a pattern that can be used to find a sequence of characters in text. This is an extremely useful technique that is supported by many text editors and integrated development environments.

Another topic that will be covered in this chapter is **serialization**. This is the process of translating an object state into a format that can be stored, such as **JavaScript Object Notation** (**JSON**) or **Extensible Markup Language** (**XML**).

This chapter covers the following topics:

- Introducing regular expression
- Kotlin and regular expression
- Introducing serialization
- Serialization and Kotlin support

Technical requirements

To run the code from this chapter, you need to install the serialization plugin for IntelliJ IDEA. Use this link and the following steps to download the latest version: `https://bintray.com/kotlin/kotlinx/kotlinx.serialization.plugin`:

1. To install this plugin, you should open **Preferences** | **Plugins** | **INSTALL PLUGIN FROM DISK...**:

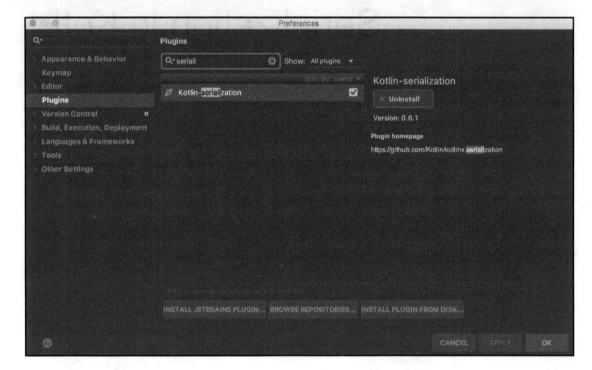

2. Choose the downloaded `.zip` archive and press **Apply**.

   You should also add the following line in the `repositories` section of the `build.gradle` file:

   ```
   maven { url "https://kotlin.bintray.com/kotlinx" }
   ```

In addition, you should add this line to the `dependencies` section:

```
implementation "org.jetbrains.kotlinx:kotlinx-serialization-
runtime:0.6.1"
```

You can find examples from this chapter on GitHub
at: `https://github.com/PacktPublishing/Hands-On-Object-Oriented-Programming-with`
`-Kotlin/tree/master/src/main/kotlin/Chapter09`.

Introducing regular expression

The use of regular expressions is a widespread approach that is used in search engines and text-processing utilities. Many programming languages support regexes out-of-the-box or use libraries. Good examples of such usage include the **Find** and **Find in path actions** in IntelliJ IDEA, which can be used to find code. The **Find in path** window looks as follows:

To find a sequence of characters using regular expressions, we have to provide a pattern that consists of special characters; these are listed as follows:

Subexpression	Matches
^	The search sequence of characters must start from the beginning of the line.
$	The search sequence of characters must be at the end of the line.
.	The search character may be any except the new line. The m option allows you to find the new line character as well.
[...]	The search character may be any one in brackets.
[^...]	The search character may be any one without brackets.
\A	The search sequence of characters must be at the beginning of the entire string.
\z	The search sequence of characters must be at the end of the entire string.
\Z	The search sequence of characters must be at the end of the entire string, if it doesn't contain a final-line terminator.
*	This means that the previous expression may occur any number of times, or not at all.
re+	This means that the previous expression may occur at least once.
re?	This means that the previous expression may occur any number of times, or not at all.
re{ n}	This means that the previous expression may occur n times.
re{ n,}	This means that the previous expression may occur n or more times.
re{ n, m}	This means that the previous expression may occur at least n and at most m times.
a|b	This means that a pattern matches a character, a or b.
(re)	This means that r and e characters group into one expression and remember the matched text.
(?: re)	This means that r and e characters group into one expression without remembering the matched text.
(?> re)	This refers to the independent pattern without using remembering.
\w	This matches a word.
\W	This matches if a piece of text doesn't contain words.
\s	This matches a white space and equals [\t\n\r\f].
\S	This doesn't match a white space.
\d	This matches a digit and equals [0-9].
\D	This doesn't match a digit.
\G	This can be used to define a point where the last match finished.
\n	This refers to a back-reference to capture the group number, n.
\b	This matches the backspace when it is inside brackets.
\B	This doesn't match word boundaries.
\n, \t, and more.	This matches special symbols such as newlines, carriage returns, and tabs.

\Q	This escapes all characters up to \E.
\E	This refers to end escaping.

Using the ^ symbol, we can establish that we can find a sequence of characters from the start of the string, and we can use $ symbol in a similar way but for the end of the string. For instance, the following regular expression means that we want to find The at the beginning of the line:

```
^The
```

We can also find the following example for the end of the line:

```
end$
```

We can combine subexpressions to create a more complex pattern:

```
^The end$
```

In a similar way, the . symbol matches any single character, and \d matches any digit.

Kotlin and regular expression

In Kotlin, regular expressions are represented by the Regex class from the kotlin.text package. Instances of this class are immutable, and we can create a new one by using one of the following constructors:

```
public actual constructor(pattern: String) : this(Pattern.compile(pattern))

public actual constructor(pattern: String, option: RegexOption) :
this(Pattern.compile(pattern, ensureUnicodeCase(option.value)))

public actual constructor(pattern: String, options: Set<RegexOption>) :
this(Pattern.compile(pattern, ensureUnicodeCase(options.toInt())))
```

RegexOption is an enum that we can use to specify any additional options. This defines the following objects:

- IGNORE_CASE: You can use this if you need to ignore a string
- MULTILINE: This is a line terminator or the end of the input sequence, and it must be used just after or just before ^ and $ subexpressions
- LITERAL: This ignores all special symbols and metacharacters
- UNIX_LINES: With this, only the \n means a line terminator

- COMMENTS: This allows you to use white space and comments in the pattern
- DOT_MATCHES_ALL: This allows the . subexpression to match any character
- CANON_EQ: This enables special equivalence by canonical decomposition

We can also use the toRegex() extension function to create a new instance:

```
"^The".toRegex()
```

We can also use the containsMatchIn method that returns true if the regular expression can find at least one match in the specified input.

We can use these functions as follows:

```
fun main(args: Array<String>) {
    println("^The".toRegex().containsMatchIn("The"))
}
```

The output is as follows:

```
true
```

Another useful method is split, which allows you to split an input into a list of substrings. This method can be used as follows:

```
fun main(args: Array<String>) {
    println("""\d""".toRegex().split("abc2abc4abc"))
}
```

The following is the output:

```
[abc, abc, abc]
```

Introducing serialization

When we need to transform the state of an object to a format that can be stored or sent and restored after this, we can use serialization. The most common approach that is used in development is the serialization of objects to JSON format. An object represented in JSON is a collection of key-value pairs, while a key is represented by a string, and a value can have the following types:

- string
- number
- array

- `object`
- `boolean`

The value can also be null. Keys and values are separated by colons, and pairs are separated by commas. In the following example code, JSON contains two pairs that contain values with string types:

```
{
    "first_name": "Igor",
    "last_name": "Kucherenko"
}
```

The following example code contains the `"user"` key in accordance with a value of an object type that, in turn, contains an array of phones:

```
"user": {
            "101": {
                "id": 101,
                "first_name": "Igor",
                "last_name": "Kucherenko",
                "phones": [
                    +3443432343,
                    +4324233423,
                    +6453454353
                ]
            }
        }
```

Serialization and Kotlin support

In this section, we will look at the `kotlinx.serialization` library. This consists of three parts:

- Plugin
- Compiler
- Library

To make a class serializable, we should mark it with the `@Serializable` annotation:

```
@Serializable
data class Person(
        val id: Int = 0,
        val first_name: String,
        val last_name: String,
```

```
        val phones: List<String> = listOf()
)
```

We can serialize an instance of this class to JSON by using the following code:

```
fun main(args: Array<String>) {
    println(JSON.stringify(Person(first_name = "Igor", last_name =
"Kucherenko")))
}
```

The output looks like this:

```
{"id":0,"first_name":"Igor","last_name":"Kucherenko","phones":[]}
```

We can deserialize JSON by using the following code:

```
val jsonPerson =
"""{"id":0,"first_name":"Igor","last_name":"Kucherenko","phones":[]}"""
println(JSON.parse<Person>(jsonPerson))
```

The output looks like this:

```
Person(id=0, first_name=Igor, last_name=Kucherenko, phones=[])
```

The following example code demonstrates that we can work with lists without any problem:

```
fun main(args: Array<String>) {
    val jsonPerson = JSON.stringify(Person(first_name = "Igor", last_name =
"Kucherenko", phones = listOf("+34434344343", "+33434344242")))
    println(jsonPerson)
    println(JSON.parse<Person>(jsonPerson))
}
```

This is the output:

```
{"id":0,"first_name":"Igor","last_name":"Kucherenko","phones":["+3443434434
3","+33434344242"]}
 Person(id=0, first_name=Igor, last_name=Kucherenko, phones=[+34434344343,
+33434344242])
```

If you want to print JSON in a classic pretty-printed multiline style, you can use the following code:

```
val jsonPerson = JSON.indented.stringify(Person(firstName = "Igor",
lastName = "Kucherenko", phones = listOf("+354445545454",
"+433443343443")))
println(jsonPerson)
```

The output looks like this:

```
{
    "id": 0,
    "firstName": "Igor",
    "lastName": "Kucherenko",
    "phones": [
        "+354445545454",
        "+433443343443"
    ]
}
```

You can also use the @SerialName annotation for overriding a property name. The following example code shows a case such as this:

```
@Serializable
data class Person(
        val id: Int = 0,
        @SerialName("first_name") val firstName: String,
        @SerialName("last_name") val lastName: String,
        val phones: List<String> = listOf()
)
```

The firstName and lastName properties will look like first_name and last_name in JSON. To serialize and deserialize this in an instance of this class, we will use the following code:

```
fun main(args: Array<String>) {
    val jsonPerson = JSON.indented.stringify(Person(
            firstName = "Igor",
            lastName = "Kucherenko",
            phones = listOf("+354445545454", "+433443343443")))
    println(jsonPerson)
    println(JSON.parse<Person>(jsonPerson))
}
```

The following is the output:

```
{
    "id": 0,
    "first_name": "Igor",
    "last_name": "Kucherenko",
    "phones": [
        "+354445545454",
        "+433443343443"
    ]
}
Person(id=0, firstName=Igor, lastName=Kucherenko, phones=[+354445545454,
```

```
+433443343443])
......
```

We can also use custom serializers and deserializers. Let's say that we want to serialize an instance of the `Person` class to JSON that contains the `name` property instead of `first_name` and `last_name`. For this, we can create our own saver, which may look as follows:

```
val saver = object : KSerialSaver<Person> {
    override fun save(output: KOutput, obj: Person) {
        @Serializable
        data class JSONPerson(val id: Int, val name: String, val phones:
List<String>)
        output.write(JSONPerson(obj.id, "${obj.firstName} ${obj.lastName}",
obj.phones))
    }
}
```

We can also use this object like this:

```
val jsonPerson = JSON.indented.stringify(saver, Person(
        firstName = "Igor",
        lastName = "Kucherenko",
        phones = listOf("+354445545454", "+433443343443")))
println(jsonPerson)
```

The following is the output:

```
{
    "id": 0,
    "name": "Igor Kucherenko",
    "phones": [
        "+354445545454",
        "+433443343443"
    ]
}
```

Summary

In this chapter, we covered regular expressions and serialization topics. Regex is an extremely powerful text-processing approach that is widely used in development, while serialization allows you to save an object state to formats such as JSON or XML. We learned how to use these techniques by using the most common examples.

In the next chapter, we'll introduce **exception handling**.

10
Exception Handling

When the normal flow of a program is disrupted, an exceptional event occurs. This can be caused by a user, a developer error, or a lack of physical resources. There is a special hierarchy of classes designed to handle different types of exceptional events, and you can also create your own class to handle a case that is unique for your application.

This chapter covers the following topics:

- What is exception handling?
- Checked and unchecked exceptions
- Using the `try` block as an expression
- Writing your own exception

Technical requirements

To run the code from this chapter, we just need IntelliJ IDEA and Git installed. This chapter doesn't require any additional installations.

You can find examples from this chapter on GitHub at the following link: `https://github.com/PacktPublishing/Hands-On-Object-Oriented-Programming-with-Kotlin/tree/master/src/main/kotlin/Chapter10`.

What is exception handling?

If the execution of a function can't be completed, an exception can be thrown. The most common causes of this are listed as follows:

- Invalid incoming data
- A file cannot be found
- Termination of a network connection
- Java Virtual Machine needs more available memory

The `throw` keyword is used to interrupt the execution of a current function and to notify a caller about an exceptional event. Let's look at the constructor of the `FileInputStream` class:

```
public FileInputStream(File file) throws FileNotFoundException {
    String name = (file != null ? file.getPath() : null);
    SecurityManager security = System.getSecurityManager();
    if (security != null) {
        security.checkRead(name);
    }
    if (name == null) {
        throw new NullPointerException();
    }
    if (file.isInvalid()) {
        throw new FileNotFoundException("Invalid file path");
    }
    fd = new FileDescriptor();
    fd.attach(this);
    path = name;
    open(name);
}
```

As you can see, if a path to a file is invalid and the file can't be found, `FileNotFoundException` is thrown. The signature of a constructor is marked with the `throw` keyword as well as exceptions that can be thrown by this function. In Kotlin, the `@Throws` annotation is used instead of the `throw` keyword:

```
@Target(AnnotationTarget.FUNCTION, AnnotationTarget.PROPERTY_GETTER,
AnnotationTarget.PROPERTY_SETTER, AnnotationTarget.CONSTRUCTOR)
@Retention(AnnotationRetention.SOURCE)
public annotation class Throws(vararg val exceptionClasses: KClass<out
Throwable>)
```

In most cases, we should wrap an invoking of a function that can throw an exception in the `try { ... } catch { ... }` block. In other cases, an exception can be thrown, as demonstrated in the following example:

```
@Throws(IOException::class)
fun main(args: Array<String>) {
    FileInputStream("invalid/path")
}
```

The output of this example is as follows:

```
Exception in thread "main" java.io.FileNotFoundException: invalid/path (No
such file or directory)
 at java.io.FileInputStream.open0(Native Method)
 at java.io.FileInputStream.open(FileInputStream.java:195)
 at java.io.FileInputStream.<init>(FileInputStream.java:138)
 at java.io.FileInputStream.<init>(FileInputStream.java:93)
 at chapter10.Example1Kt.main(Example1.kt:6)
```

However, if we want to handle this exception, we should use the `try { ... } catch { ... }` block:

```
fun main(args: Array<String>) {
    try {
        FileInputStream("invalid/path")
    } catch (exception: Exception) {
        println("${exception::class.java.name} was handled!")
    }
}
```

The output looks like this:

```
java.io.FileNotFoundException was handled!
```

If a function throws different types of exceptions, you can define several `catch` blocks:

```
try {
    FileInputStream("invalid/path")
} catch (exception: FileAlreadyExistsException) {
    println("${exception::class.java.name} was handled!")
} catch (exception: IOException) {
    println("${exception::class.java.name} was handled!")
} catch (exception: Exception) {
    println("${exception::class.java.name} was handled!")
}
```

If the `try { ... } catch { ... }` block catches an exception, the execution of a function won't be interrupted. The following example demonstrates this:

```
fun main(args: Array<String>) {
    try {
        FileInputStream("invalid/path")
    } catch (exception: FileAlreadyExistsException) {
        println("${exception::class.java.name} was handled!")
    } catch (exception: IOException) {
        println("${exception::class.java.name} was handled!")
    } catch (exception: Exception) {
        println("${exception::class.java.name} was handled!")
    }
    println("Done!")
}
```

The following is the output:

```
java.io.FileNotFoundException was handled!
 Done!
```

An instance of the `Exception` type contains different information about an error that has occurred. For instance, you can get the following message:

```
fun main(args: Array<String>) {
    try {
        FileInputStream("invalid/path")
    } catch (exception: IOException) {
        println(exception.message)
    }
}
```

The output is as follows:

```
invalid/path (No such file or directory)
```

Alternatively, you can invoke the `printStackTrace()` method:

```
fun main(args: Array<String>) {
    try {
        FileInputStream("invalid/path")
    } catch (exception: IOException) {
        exception.printStackTrace()
    }
}
```

The following is the output:

```
java.io.FileNotFoundException: invalid/path (No such file or directory)
 at java.io.FileInputStream.open0(Native Method)
 at java.io.FileInputStream.open(FileInputStream.java:195)
 at java.io.FileInputStream.<init>(FileInputStream.java:138)
 at java.io.FileInputStream.<init>(FileInputStream.java:93)
 at Chapter10.Example1Kt.main(Example1.kt:9)
```

Checked and unchecked exceptions

An exception is an anomalous condition in a program that requires special processing. There are many different causes of exception throwing, such as resource leaking, logical error in program code, or network connection interruption.

This section covers the following topics:

- Exception hierarchy
- Exceptions in Java
- Exceptions in Kotlin

Exception hierarchy

All exception classes in Kotlin and Java are inherited from the `Throwable` class. The `Throwable` class has two direct inheritors—`Exception` and `Error`. The `Exception` class, in turn, has inheritors for more specific cases, such as the `IOException` and `RuntimeException` classes:

- `IOException` is a general class of exceptional events related to input/output operations
- `RuntimeException` is the superclass for exceptions such as `NullPointerException`, which can be thrown during Java Virtual Machine operation invoking

Subclasses of the `Error` class are used to indicate abnormal conditions that may occur in the application. The widely occurring inheritor of `Error` is the `OutOfMemoryError` class. Instances of this class can be thrown when the Java Virtual Machine cannot allocate memory for a new object.

The following diagram shows class hierarchy:

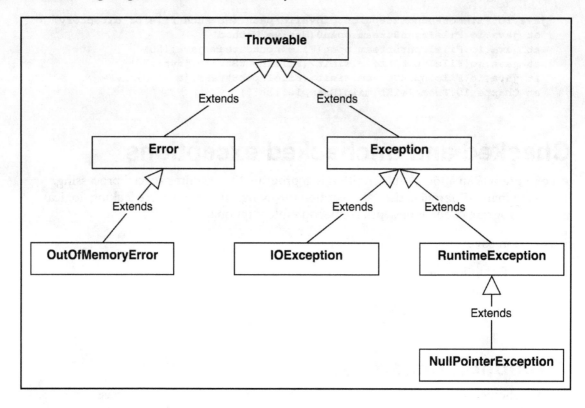

To overview all direct inheritors of the `Exception` class, you can go to the source code of this class and open **Navigate | Type Hierarchy**:

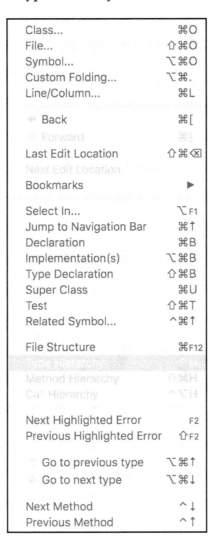

You will then see a window that shows all of the direct subclasses of the `Exception` class:

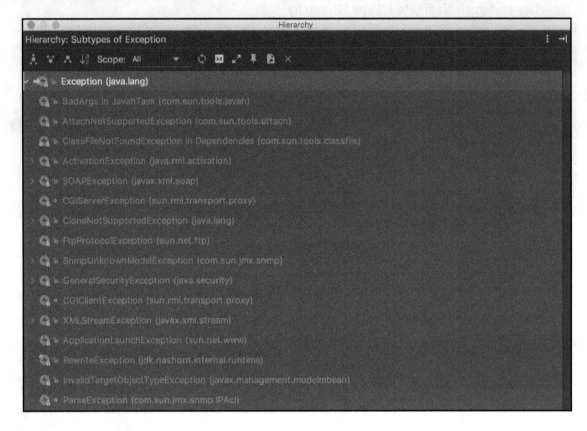

Exceptions in Java

In Java, all exceptions are divided into two groups:

- Checked
- Unchecked

If a class isn't a subtype of `RuntimeException` and it inherits the `Exception` class, then this class belongs to **checked** exceptions. If a function throws checked exceptions, then we have to wrap its invoking into the `try { ... } catch { ... } finally { ... }` block. The `finally` block can be omitted.

The following example contains the `main` function that creates a new instance of the `FileInputStream` class:

```
public class Example2 {
    public static void main(String[] args) {
        new FileInputStream("invalid/path");
    }
}
```

Since a constructor of `FileInputStream` throws `FileNotFoundException`, we can't compile this code. IntelliJ IDEA shows the following tip:

To fix this error, we can surround this code with a `try { ... } catch { ... }` `finally { ... }` block, or add an exception to the method signature. If you use `try {` `... } catch { ... } finally { ... }`, an implementation may look like this:

```
public static void main(String[] args) {
    try {
        new FileInputStream("invalid/path");
    } catch (FileNotFoundException e) {
        e.printStackTrace();
    }
}
```

In the second case, if we use the `throws` keyword, it may look like this:

```
public static void main(String[] args) throws FileNotFoundException {
    new FileInputStream("invalid/path");
}
```

The following code throws `NullPointerException`, because the value reference is null:

```
public static void main(String[] args) {
    Integer value = null;
    value.hashCode();
}
```

However, we don't have to handle this exception because it's **unchecked**.

Exceptions in Kotlin

Checked exceptions force handling, even if we don't need this. This is the root of many problems and that's why Kotlin doesn't have checked exceptions. Let's imagine that we want to implement our own class for logging that implements the `Appendable` interface from the `java.lang` package:

```
class Logger implements Appendable {

    @Override
    public Appendable append(CharSequence csq) throws IOException {
        throw new NotImplementedException();
    }

    @Override
    public Appendable append(CharSequence csq, int start, int end) throws
IOException {
        throw new NotImplementedException();
    }

    @Override
    public Appendable append(char c) throws IOException {
        throw new NotImplementedException();
    }

}
```

We can use this class to print logs as follows:

```
public static void main(String[] args) {
    Logger logger = new Logger();
    logger.append("Start...");
    //....
    logger.append("Done...")
}
```

This code doesn't compile because methods from the `Appendable` interface throw a checked exception. Furthermore, we have to wrap this code into the `try { ... } catch { ... }` block. This can be very annoying if we use the `append` method in lambda:

```
Arrays.asList(0, 1, 3, 4).forEach(integer -> {
    try {
        logger.append(integer.toString());
    } catch (IOException e) {
        e.printStackTrace();
    }
});
```

The preceding snippet demonstrates that a lambda with the `try { ... } catch { ... }` block inside doesn't look concise.

Interoperability

Kotlin is a language that is designed to maintain interoperability with Java code. The following example shows a nuance that we should take into account when we invoke Kotlin code from Java code. Let's create a simple Kotlin function that throws an exception:

```
fun testMethod() {
    throw IOException()
}
```

This function can be called from Java code like this:

```
public class Example5 {
    public static void main(String[] args) {
        Example5Kt.testMethod();
    }
}
```

And this code can be compiled. This behavior can be unexpected for a Java developer who is used to dealing with checked exceptions. See what happens if we write something like this:

```
public static void testMethod() {
    throw new IOException();
}
```

The compiler will show the following error:

Error:(11, 9) java: unreported exception java.io.IOException; must be caught or declared to be thrown

To fix this error, we have to add the `@Throws` annotation, as follows:

```
@Throws(IOException::class)
fun testMethod() {
    throw IOException()
}
```

Now, we have to handle an exception that can be thrown by the `testMethod` function in Java code:

```java
public static void main(String[] args) {
    try {
        Example5Kt.testMethod();
    } catch (IOException e) {
        e.printStackTrace();
    }
}
```

Using the try block as an expression

When we run program code, we deal with **expressions** and **statements** all the time. It's very important to understand the difference between these. Let's look at the following code:

```
1 + 1
```

This code is an expression because it contains variables, operators, and returns a single result. If a standalone element of program code represents an action, it is a statement:

```
println("Hello")
```

In the context of this section, the main point for us is that an expression returns something. In Kotlin, the `try { ... } catch { ... } finally { ... }` block is an expression and we can write something like this:

```kotlin
fun loadValue(): Int = throw Exception()

fun main(args: Array<String>) {
    println(try { loadValue() } catch (exception: Exception) { 4 })
}
```

Under the hood, this code works in the same way as if we were to write it in Java. To check this, you can decompile this code to Java:

```java
public final class Example6Kt {
    public static final int loadValue() {
        throw (Throwable)(new Exception());
    }

    public static final void main(@NotNull String[] args) {
        Intrinsics.checkParameterIsNotNull(args, "args");

        int var1;
```

```
    try {
        var1 = loadValue();
    } catch (Exception var3) {
        var1 = 4;
    }

    System.out.println(var1);
    }
}
```

As you can see, there is no magic here. In contrast with Java, all control flow elements in Kotlin are expressions, which provides a more concise solution for common issues.

Writing your own exception

If the Java standard library doesn't contain an exception that fits with the business requirements of your application, you can implement your own exception. All exceptions that inherit the Error class must be thrown by the Java Virtual Machine, so we shouldn't extend this class. If you decide to implement your own exception, you should prefer to create only checked exceptions because, if you throw an exception with the RuntimeException type, there is no guarantee that it will be caught in Java code. In Kotlin, you can extend any subtype of the Exception class because Kotlin doesn't support a checked exception.

Let's suggest that we want to develop a ToDo list application that contains the ToDoStorage class, which contains the set method and throws ToDoAlreadyExistException. The ToDoStorage class may look as follows:

```
class ToDoStorage {
    private val todos = HashMap<String, ToDo>()

    operator fun get(name: String) = todos[name]

    operator fun set(name: String, todo: ToDo) {
        if (todos.contains(name)) {
            throw ToDoAlreadyExistException()
        }
        todos[name] = todo
    }
}
```

This contains the `todos` property that stores an instance of the `ToDo` class:

```
class ToDo(val name: String, val content: String)
```

The `ToDoStorage` class also contains the `get` and `set` operator methods to access values from the `todos` property. If we try to set a `ToDo` with a name that is already used as a key by the `todos` property, the `ToDoAlreadyExistException` will be thrown:

```
class ToDoAlreadyExistException(
        message: String? = null,
        cause: Throwable? = null,
        enableSuppression: Boolean = true,
        writableStackTrace: Boolean = true
) : Exception(message, cause, enableSuppression, writableStackTrace)
```

We can check this by using the following code:

```
fun main(args: Array<String>) {
    val storage = ToDoStorage()
    val todo = ToDo("name", "content")
    storage[todo.name] = todo
    storage[todo.name] = todo
}
```

The output looks like this:

```
Exception in thread "main" Chapter10.ToDoAlreadyExistException
 at Chapter10.ToDoStorage.set(Example7.kt:20)
 at Chapter10.Example7Kt.main(Example7.kt:30)
```

Summary

In this chapter, we have learned about exceptions and exception handling. We have also looked at examples that show how to create our own exceptions and explored why we need it. The *Checked exception* section showed us the difference between exceptions in Java and Kotlin. In addition to this, we have learned the difference between statements and expressions and looked at an example that shows us how to use the `try { ... } catch { ... }` block as an expression.

In the next chapter, we will learn how to test in object-oriented programming with Kotlin.

Questions

1. What is an exception?
2. What is an expression?
3. What is exception handling?
4. What is a checked exception?

Further reading

Kotlin Programming by Example by Iyanu Adelekan, published by Packt: `https://www.packtpub.com/application-development/kotlin-programming-example`.

11
Testing in Object-Oriented Programming with Kotlin

Before delivering it to the end user, an application should be tested. The process of software testing consists of a program executing with the purpose of finding bugs. By bugs, we mean mistakes that relate to logical errors in code or misunderstanding the application flow. The main reason for testing is to make sure that a product meets the end user's expectations and software requirements.

This chapter covers the following topics:

- Why testing?
- Types of testing
- The Kotlin test library
- Testing examples

Technical requirements

To run the code from this chapter, we just need IntelliJ IDEA and Git installed. We also need to add dependencies on the JUnit test engine, the Spek framework, and the Kotlin test library. You should add the following line to the dependencies section of the buildscript block in your `build.gradle` file:

```
buildscript {
    dependencies {
        classpath 'org.junit.platform:junit-platform-gradle-plugin:1.0.0'
    }
}
```

We should also apply the `junit.gradle` plugin by using the following lines:

```
apply plugin: 'org.junit.platform.gradle.plugin'

junitPlatform {
    filters {
        engines {
            include 'spek'
        }
    }
}
```

To make the Gradle build system able to find the Spek repository, we should add this line:

```
repositories {
    maven { url "http://dl.bintray.com/jetbrains/spek" }
}
```

The following lines should be added to the `dependencies` section:

```
dependencies {
    testCompile 'org.jetbrains.spek:spek-api:1.1.5'
    testRuntime 'org.jetbrains.spek:spek-junit-platform-engine:1.1.5'
    testCompile 'org.junit.platform:junit-platform-runner:1.0.0'
    testCompile 'io.kotlintest:kotlintest-runner-junit5:3.1.7'
}
```

The entire code can be found
at `https://github.com/PacktPublishing/Hands-On-Object-Oriented-Programming-with-Kotlin/blob/master/build.gradle`.

You can find examples from this chapter on GitHub at `https://github.com/PacktPublishing/Hands-On-Object-Oriented-Programming-with-Kotlin/tree/master/src/test/kotlin/Chapter11`.

Why testing?

We need testing because humans make mistakes. The software development life cycle includes several steps such as specifying requirements, design, development, and delivery. If a mistake occurs in one of these steps, it can lead to mistakes in further steps.

The following diagram shows how mistakes in different steps can impact on the whole process:

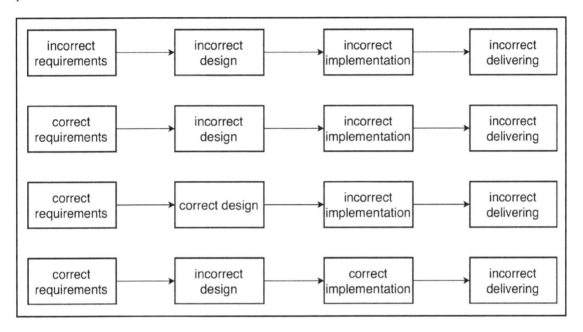

As you can see, it's important to detect a bug as soon as possible. There are many different types of testing that can be applied in different cases to recognize a defect as soon as possible.

Types of testing

There are many different types of testing that can be applied to make sure that an application works as expected. Different approaches provide different results, depending on what exactly we want to test. In general, we can divide these into two groups:

- Manual testing
- Automated testing

Manual testing

Manual testing is performed by someone who interacts with an application by clicking and checking the application programming interface using special tools, such as Charles (`https://www.charlesproxy.com/`). This tool is a proxy that makes it possible to view all HTTP and HTTPS traffic between a client application and a server.

The main window of this tool looks as follows:

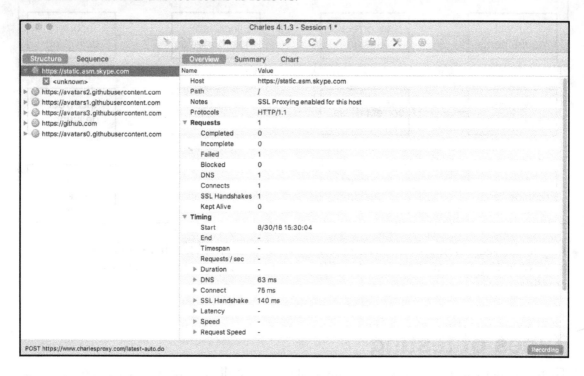

Manual testing is expensive as it requires a qualified person and a configured environment. We should also take into account human errors, since a tester can omit some steps and conditions.

Automated testing

Automated tests consist of test scripts that are performed by a machine. In general, these scripts are written by qualified developers or testers. They can be very different in complexity and require different machine resources.

An example can be a simple method that equals two values, as shown in the following example:

```
class Tests {
    @Test
    fun testMethod() {
        assertEquals(3, 1 + 2)
    }
}
```

The preceding example uses JUnit (`https://junit.org/junit5/`), which is a framework used by Java developers for unit testing.

Unit testing

Unit testing assumes that a program is logically divided into the smallest testable parts (units). The main purpose here is to check that each unit of an application works as it was designed. In object-oriented programming, a unit may be a method that belongs to a public interface of a class.

This approach increases the developer's confidence with regards to the fact that the code works in the right way while the codebase is changing. If unit tests are written correctly and we execute them every time code is changed, we are able to detect a defect. Unit testing also forces us to write reusable code because it can be modular to be tested. Another benefit of this approach is that a tester isn't needed in order to test code.

The following example shows how to test the `additionOfThreeAndTwoShouldReturnFive` method of the `Calculator` class:

```
class Tests {
    @Test
    fun additionOfThreeAndTwoShouldReturnFive() {
        val calculator = Calculator()
        assertEquals(5, calculator.addition(3, 2))
    }
}
```

The Kotlin test libraries

In this section, we will look at the Spek testing framework (`https://spekframework.github.io/spek/docs/latest/#_what_is_spek`) for Kotlin. Spek, contrary to other frameworks, such as JUnit, provides a way to describe requirements along with a test script. The fact that tests have passed successfully, doesn't mean that our code works as expected and meets our requirements.

As you can see in the previous example, we should use class and method names to describe a case that we want to test. Using the Spek framework, we can rewrite this example as follows:

```
object CalculatorSpec: Spek({
    given("a calculator") {
        val calculator = Calculator()
        on("addition") {
            val sum = calculator.addition(3, 2)
            it("adding 3 and 2 should return 5") {
                assertEquals(5, sum)
            }
        }
    }
})
```

Spek is written in Kotlin because this language provides many advantages over Java, such as the ability to use **domain-specific language (DSL)**. A specification should also be written in Kotlin, but you can test your Java code just as Kotlin because this is designed to interoperate with Java. Spek, by specification, refers to a class with tests because it looks like a specification and is written in a declarative manner.

Installation

This section describes how to integrate the Spek framework. These instructions cover the following built-in tool systems:

- Gradle (using the Groovy script)
- Gradle (using the Kotlin script)
- Maven

Gradle with Groovy

You should add the path to `junit-platform-gradle-plugin` to a classpath, and add test dependencies to the appropriate section in the `build.gradle` file. As a result of this, your `build.gradle` file will look as follows:

```
buildscript {
    dependencies {
        classpath 'org.junit.platform:junit-platform-gradle-plugin:1.0.0'
    }
}

apply plugin: 'org.junit.platform.gradle.plugin'

junitPlatform {
    filters {
        engines {
            include 'spek'
        }
    }
}

repositories {
    maven { url "http://dl.bintray.com/jetbrains/spek" }
}

dependencies {
    testCompile 'org.jetbrains.spek:spek-api:1.1.5'
    testRuntime 'org.jetbrains.spek:spek-junit-platform-engine:1.1.5'
}
```

Gradle with the Kotlin script

With the Kotlin script, we should add the same dependencies. Your `build.gradle.kts` file will look as follows:

```
import org.gradle.api.plugins.ExtensionAware

import org.junit.platform.gradle.plugin.FiltersExtension
import org.junit.platform.gradle.plugin.EnginesExtension
import org.junit.platform.gradle.plugin.JUnitPlatformExtension

buildscript {
    dependencies {
        classpath("org.junit.platform:junit-platform-gradle-plugin:1.0.0")
    }
}
```

```
}

apply {
    plugin("org.junit.platform.gradle.plugin")
}

configure {
    filters {
        engines {
            include("spek")
        }
    }
}

dependencies {
    testCompile("org.jetbrains.spek:spek-api:1.1.5")
    testRuntime("org.jetbrains.spek:spek-junit-platform-engine:1.1.5")
}

fun JUnitPlatformExtension.filters(setup: FiltersExtension.() -> Unit) {
    when (this) {
        is ExtensionAware ->
extensions.getByType(FiltersExtension::class.java).setup()
        else -> throw Exception("${this::class} must be an instance of
ExtensionAware")
    }
}
fun FiltersExtension.engines(setup: EnginesExtension.() -> Unit) {
    when (this) {
        is ExtensionAware ->
extensions.getByType(EnginesExtension::class.java).setup()
        else -> throw Exception("${this::class} must be an instance of
ExtensionAware")
    }
}
```

Maven

To integrate `junit-platform`, you need to add the following lines to your `pom.xml` file:

```
<build>
    <plugins>
        ...
        <plugin>
            <artifactId>maven-surefire-plugin</artifactId>
            <version>2.21.0</version>
            <dependencies>
```

```
                <dependency>
                    <groupId>org.junit.platform</groupId>
                    <artifactId>junit-platform-surefire-
provider</artifactId>
                    <version>1.2.0</version>
                </dependency>
            </dependencies>
        </plugin>
    </plugins>
</build>
```

To integrate the Spek framework, you should add the following lines:

```
<dependency>
    <groupId>org.jetbrains.spek</groupId>
    <artifactId>spek-api</artifactId>
    <version>1.1.5</version>
    <type>pom</type>
</dependency>
```

Testing examples

In this section, we will practice writing tests with the Spek framework. We touched on the benefits of this framework and automated testing in the previous sections, and we are ready to test the functionality of the ToDoStorage class from Chapter 10, *Exception Handling*. Let's modify the build.gradle file to integrate the Spek framework and Unit engine, as follows:

```
  buildscript {
      //.......
      dependencies {
+         classpath 'org.junit.platform:junit-platform-gradle-plugin:1.0.0'
      }
  }
 //.........
+ apply plugin: 'org.junit.platform.gradle.plugin'

+ junitPlatform {
+     filters {
+         engines {
+             include 'spek'
+         }
+     }
+ }
```

```
  repositories {
      //.........
+     maven { url "http://dl.bintray.com/jetbrains/spek" }
  }
  dependencies {
      //.........
+     testCompile 'org.jetbrains.spek:spek-api:1.1.5'
+     testRuntime 'org.jetbrains.spek:spek-junit-platform-engine:1.1.5'
+     testCompile 'org.junit.platform:junit-platform-runner:1.0.0'
  }
```

In our project, all of the source code is located in the `main` folder and all test code is located in the `test` folder. Let's create the `ToDoSpek` class in the `chapter11` package to test the `ToDoStorage` class. The following screenshot shows what our new project structure looks like:

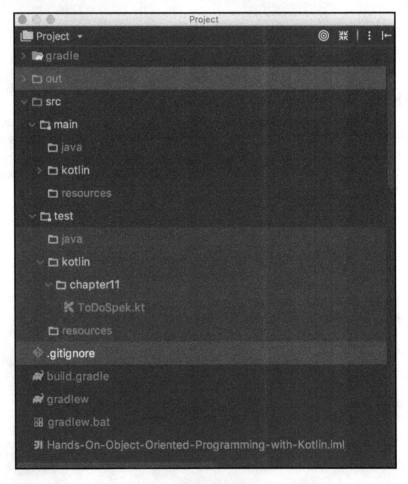

Let's define the `ToDoSpek` class, as follows:

```
import chapter11.ToDoStorage
import org.jetbrains.spek.api.*
import org.junit.platform.runner.JUnitPlatform
import org.junit.runner.RunWith

@RunWith(JUnitPlatform::class)
object ToDoSpek: Spek({
    //.....
})
```

To describe a specification, we should extend the `Spek` class. This class contains a constructor with a receiver and looks as follows:

```
abstract class Spek(val spec: Spec.() -> Unit) {
    companion object {
        fun wrap(spec: Spec.() -> Unit) = object: Spek(spec) {}
    }
}
```

We already explored receivers in object-oriented patterns in Chapter 7, *Coroutines - a Lightweight Thread?* To be able to run our tests, we should mark the `ToDoSpek` class with the `RunWith` annotation and pass a class reference to it.

Class references

The class reference is represented by the instance of the `KClass` class. To obtain the reference to a class, you can use the `::` operator, as follows:

```
JUnitPlatform::class
```

Take into account that an instance of `KClass` isn't the same as an instance of `Class` in Java. To obtain a Java class reference, you can use the `java` property of a `KClass` class property.

Writing specifications

The fact that tests have passed successfully doesn't mean that our application works as expected. A class inherited from the Spek class contains a special DSL block that allows you to write tests along with a specification. The specification describes functional requirements, use cases, and user interactions.

Spek provides two styles of test specifications and these differ according to the functions that are used:

- given, on, it
- describe, it

The given, on, and it blocks

This style assumes the use of the following DSL blocks:

- given: This block defines the context of our test. It can be a class that we want to test.
- on: This block defines the function or action that we want to test.
- it: This block defines an actual test. It can be the input or output of a function.

Let's test the set method of the ToDoStorage class. This test may look as follows:

```
@RunWith(JUnitPlatform::class)
object ToDoSpek : Spek({
    given("A storage") {
        val storage = ToDoStorage()
        on("set a todo with args: name and context") {
            val todo = ToDo("name", "content")
            val result = storage.set("name", todo)
            it("returns true") {
                assert(result)
            }
        }
    }
})
```

Press the **Run** button and you will see the following window:

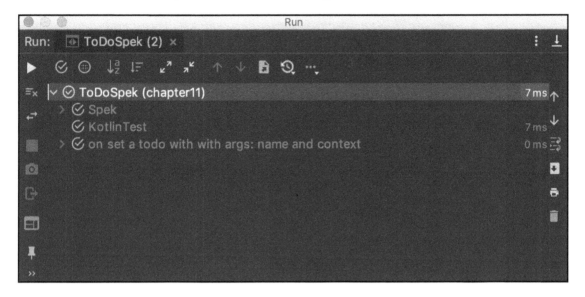

As you can see, the output not only shows that a test has passed successfully, but also contains a description of the test case. We can add one more block to test the `get` method. This test may look as follows:

```
on("""get a todo by "name" key""") {
    val todo = storage["name"]
    it("""returns a todo with "content" """) {
        assertEquals("content", todo?.content)
    }
}
```

The run window looks as follows:

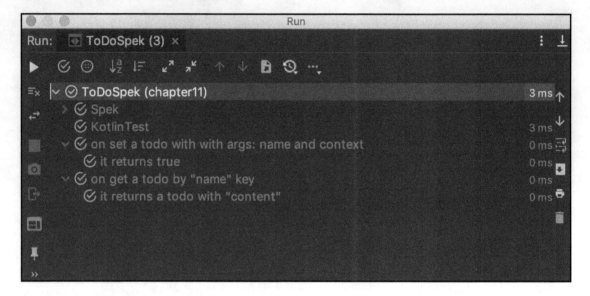

You can add as many on blocks as you want. You can also create different context blocks in the same Spek class.

Testing exceptions

The set method of the ToDoStorage class can throw ToDoAlreadyExistException:

```
operator fun set(name: String, todo: ToDo): Boolean {
    if (todos.contains(name)) {
        throw ToDoAlreadyExistException()
    }
    todos[name] = todo

    return true
}
```

It is also important to make sure that this exception will be thrown when it is needed. For this, we can write one more test that checks whether ToDoAlreadyException is thrown when a user tries to store a todo with a key that already exists.

We need to add a dependency to the `kotlintest` library (https://github.com/kotlintest/kotlintest) to be able to use the `shouldThrow` function. After integrating this library, your `dependencies` section in the `build.gradle` file will look as follows:

```
dependencies {
    implementation "org.jetbrains.kotlin:kotlin-stdlib-jdk8:$kotlin_version"
    implementation 'org.jetbrains.kotlinx:kotlinx-coroutines-core:0.23.0'
    implementation "org.jetbrains.kotlinx:kotlinx-serialization-runtime:0.6.1"
    testCompile 'org.jetbrains.spek:spek-api:1.1.5'
    testRuntime 'org.jetbrains.spek:spek-junit-platform-engine:1.1.5'
    testCompile 'org.junit.platform:junit-platform-runner:1.0.0'
    testCompile 'io.kotlintest:kotlintest-runner-junit5:3.1.7'
}
```

Let's add a test that checks whether `ToDoAlreadyException` is thrown:

```
on("set a todo with a key that already stored") {
    it ("should throw ToDoAlreadyExistException") {
        shouldThrow<ToDoAlreadyExistException> {
            val todo = ToDo("name", "content")
            storage.set("name", todo)
        }
    }
}
```

After running this, you will see the following window:

The describe and it blocks

This style differs from the previous one by using the describe block. The describe block is also used to define a context but we can also nest one describe block into another to provide a more detailed context. Let's create the DescribeStyleToDoSpek object to demonstrate this. Initially, it may look as follows:

```
@RunWith(JUnitPlatform::class)
object DescribeStyleToDoSpek : Spek({
    describe("a storage") {
        val storage = ToDoStorage()
        on("set a todo with with args: name and context") {
            val todo = ToDo("name", "content")
            val result = storage.set("name", todo)
            it("returns true") {
                assert(result)
            }
        }
        on("""get a todo by "name" key""") {
            val todo = storage["name"]
            it("""returns a todo with "content" """) {
                assertEquals("content", todo?.content)
            }
        }
    }
})
```

This object contains a specification with a single context that is defined by the describe block. After running these tests, you will see the following window:

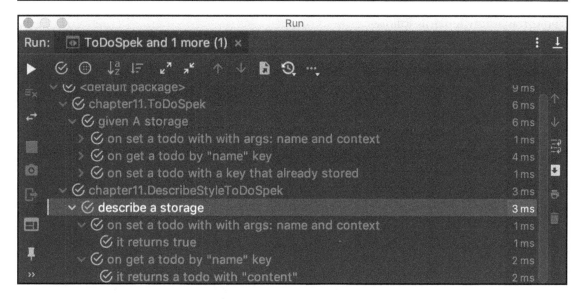

Let's add a new `describe` block to check that a non-empty storage throws `ToDoAlreadyException` if a user tries to set a todo with a preexisting key. This may look as follows:

```
describe("a non-empty storage") {
    on("""set a todo with a key that already stored""") {
        it ("should throw ToDoAlreadyExistException") {
            shouldThrow<ToDoAlreadyExistException> {
                val todo = ToDo("name", "content")
                storage.set("name", todo)
            }
        }
    }
}
```

The run window looks as follows:

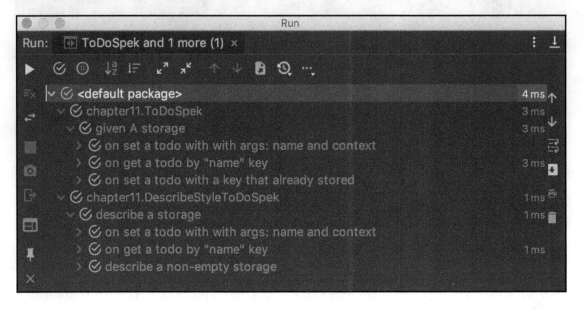

As you can see, a nested `describe` block can be useful if we want to define a more specific context of our test case.

Summary

In this chapter, we learned about testing, the different types of testing, and why we need it. We also learned about Spek, which is an amazing testing framework that allows us to not only check the app's functionality, but also defines a specification of an application. We looked at examples that showed us how to create our own automated tests using the Spek framework.

Thank you for taking the time to read this book and I wish you the best of luck going forward.

Questions

1. What does the process of testing consist of?
2. What is automated testing?
3. What is Spek?
4. Why do we need testing?

Further reading

Learn Java Unit Testing with JUnit 5 in 20 Steps by Ranga Karanam, published by Packt: https://www.packtpub.com/application-development/learn-java-unit-testing-junit-5-20-steps-video.

Assessments

Chapter 1

1. Kotlin's popularity has skyrocketed in recent months due to the fact that it is a simple and concise language that is easy to learn and supports object-oriented and functional programming. Kotlin is a superset of Java that avoids all unwanted Java features, such as verbose, unsafe, and outdated syntax, and includes powerful features from different languages. These features include security, simplicity, and interoperability.

2. Type inference is a mechanism where the Kotlin compiler plays its role in establishing the type of variable. Kotlin will determine the data type by understanding the value assigned. It intelligently infers the type by the value, and then makes the data type variable respectively.

3. Null ability is one of the reasons that most applications crash. Kotlin is very strict when it comes to safety. When it comes to applications, users, especially mobile users, desire a nice, simple, and smooth user experience. In Kotlin, variables are non-nullable by default and you cannot assign null values to them.

4. Kotlin allows specification of the argument's name in a function call. This approach makes the function call more readable and it reduces the chances of passing an incorrect value to the variable, especially when all variables have the same data type.

5. Package-level functions are declared within the Kotlin class and can be accessed directly by using the package name as a reference.

6. Kotlin allows a name to be assigned to the loop so that when loop termination is required, a `break` statement can call the labeled loop to terminate it.

Chapter 2

1. A class is a well-defined idea that explains the existence of an entity. A class is a template that contains lists of two things—attributes and behaviors. The object is an instance of a class, an entity that contains all attributes and behaviors that a class describes.

2. Every class contains a number of attributes and behaviors. Attributes are the characteristics of the class that help to distinguish it from others. Behaviors are the tasks an object should perform.

3. A constructor is a special type of function used to initialize the properties of the class. Kotlin provides three constructors—a default constructor, a primary constructor, and a secondary constructor.

4. Function overloading is a feature where a class can have more than one function with similar names. Each function is uniquely identified by its parameters.

5. Data classes are special types of classes that generate extra functions for programmers. These functions are `tostring()`, `hashCode()`, `equals()`, and `copy()`.

Chapter 3

1. Inheritance is one of the key concepts in object-oriented programming that helps in avoiding code repetition, especially where different classes have common features and all the classes belong to the same type

2. Encapsulation is an object-oriented programming technique that involves binding data and functions into one unit, which is called a class. All properties and functions of the class are tightly coupled and combined in a single place.

3. A visibility modifier helps to set the visibility of functions and properties to achieve encapsulation. A rule of thumb of encapsulation is to restrict those properties accessible to the outside the world and instead implement some functions to access them indirectly. Public, private, protected, and internal are four visibility modifiers provided by Kotlin.

4. Kotlin provides four different types of inheritance:
   - Single inheritance
   - Multi-level inheritance
   - Hierarchical inheritance
   - Hierarchical multi-level inheritance

2. In object-oriented programming, polymorphism is a concept where a function behaves differently, depending on the type of object that calls it. Runtime polymorphism, which is also known as *late or dynamic binding*, is used to determine which method to invoke at runtime.

3. An abstract class is a generic concept and does not belong to a concrete idea. We do not create an instance of an abstract class; its only responsibility is to facilitate the creation of other classes. An abstract class is used to define which behaviors a class should have instead of how it should be implemented

Chapter 4

1. The `object` keyword is used to create a singleton class in Kotlin and a `companion` object is a special type of class that allows its members to behave like static objects.

2. Kotlin provides sealed classes that are restricted to limited classes, and cannot be inherited further. Sealed classes are designed for situations in which a limited set of functionalities are required and no other class is allowed to be part of this set.

3. In Kotlin, enum classes are similar to sealed classes, except that all the values of the enum class are the same type. The enum class is useful when the expected outcome is within a small set, such as a small range of colors, or the days of the week.

4. When an object contains another object in its body, the relationship between them is called **aggregation**. This is a loosely coupled relationship between two objects, in which one object is not completely dependent on the other. Composition is an advanced form of aggregation, where two objects are highly dependent on each other. In aggression, one object contains the other object, whereas in composition, one object owns the other object. When the object that owns the other is destroyed, the object that is owned is also destroyed.

5. **Delegation** refers to a situation in which we pass the responsibility to someone else. In Kotlin, properties can either be accessed directly, or by using the `get` and `set` functions with the backing field. When properties are not backed by their own class, but the responsibility is given to another class instead, these properties are called delegate properties.

Chapter 5

1. Kotlin provides a collection of elements with a start and endpoint. This collection is called a **range**. A range is the quickest way to create a collection of sequences. `1..100` or `'a'` to `'z'` are ranges of the first 100 number or of alphabets.

2. Lists that do not allow us to update their contents, and provide only read-only functionality, are called immutable lists. Lists that allow us to add new elements and update existing elements are called mutable lists. Kotlin provides a number of interfaces and methods that are dedicated for both mutable and immutable lists.

3. An iterator is a special type of data structure that works with collection. The primary responsibility of an iterator is to iterate over the collection and produce the next object from the list if required.

4. Iterable, collection, and list are the names of the interfaces, and all these interfaces belong to the immutable collection.

5. Set is a special type of collection that does not support duplication and contains a list of unique values. Map is a data structure that holds collections of key-value pairs. Similar to `set`, `map` does not support duplicate values.

6. Mutable iterators, mutable collections, and mutable lists are interfaces that belong to the mutable collection. These interfaces allow new items to be added to the list and existing items to be updated as well.

Chapter 6

1. Interoperability refers to the ability to use both the Java and Kotlin languages in a single project. We can call Kotlin functions in Java as well as Java methods and variables in Kotlin code. This gives us the advantage of code reusability.

2. When a Kotlin function is called in Java, it is required use a filename as a reference with `kt` keyword, for example, `KotlinToJavakt.functionName()` However, Kotlin makes it possible to assign different names to file and functions by using JVM annotation. JVM annotation allows the programmer to assign new names to files and functions according to the coding convention.

Chapter 8

1. Interoperability refers to the ability to use both Java and Kotlin languages in a single project. We can call Kotlin functions in Java, as well as Java methods and variables in Kotlin code. This gives us the advantage of code reusability. For example, if we have an existing Java project with classes and functions, then we do not need to rewrite everything in Kotlin from scratch. Instead, we can use each and every line of Java code in Kotlin.

2. JVM annotations are used to make the Kotlin code simple and clean for Java developers. `@file: JvmName` helps us to use another Kotlin filename. `jvmName(functionName)` is used to assign a new name to the existing function, and `@JvmStatic` helps to call static functions from Kotlin.

Chapter 10

1. An exception is an instance of the `Throwable` type that represents a exception event in a program. When an exceptional event happens, the normal flow of a program can't be completed and this case requires special handling.

2. An expression is a combination of variables and operators that returns a new value.

3. Exception handling consists of a special code block that should be executed when an exceptional event occurs.

4. A checked exception is a type of exception in Java that forces a developer to handle an error that has occurred.

Chapter 11

1. The software testing process consists of a program executing with the intention of finding bugs. By bugs, we mean mistakes that relate to logical errors in code or a misunderstanding of the application flow.

2. Automated tests entail test scripts that are performed by a machine. In general, these scripts are written by developers or appropriately qualified testers.

3. Spek is a testing framework that provides a way of describing requirements associated with test scripts.

4. The main reason for testing is to ensure that a product meets end user expectations and complies with software requirements.

Other Books You May Enjoy

If you enjoyed this book, you may be interested in these other books by Packt:

Hands-on Design Patterns with Kotlin

Alexey Soshin

ISBN: 9781788998017

- Get to grips with Kotlin principles, including its strengths and weaknesses
- Understand classical design patterns in Kotlin
- Explore functional programming using built-in features of Kotlin
- Solve real-world problems using reactive and concurrent design patterns
- Use threads and coroutines to simplify concurrent code flow
- Understand antipatterns to write clean Kotlin code, avoiding common pitfalls
- Learn about the design considerations necessary while choosing between architectures

Kotlin Standard Library Cookbook

Samuel Urbanowicz

ISBN: 9781788837668

- Work with ranges, progressions, and sequences in use cases
- Add new functionalities to current classes with Kotlin extensions
- Understand elements such as lambdas, closures, and monads
- Build a REST API consumer with Retrofit and a coroutine adapter
- Discover useful tips and solutions for making your Android projects
- Explore the benefits of standard library features

Leave a review - let other readers know what you think

Please share your thoughts on this book with others by leaving a review on the site that you bought it from. If you purchased the book from Amazon, please leave us an honest review on this book's Amazon page. This is vital so that other potential readers can see and use your unbiased opinion to make purchasing decisions, we can understand what our customers think about our products, and our authors can see your feedback on the title that they have worked with Packt to create. It will only take a few minutes of your time, but is valuable to other potential customers, our authors, and Packt. Thank you!

Index